AMERICAN PROFILES
Norman K. Risjord, Series Editor

Martin Van Buren, ca. 1837–1838, portrait in oil on canvas by Henry Inman. The Metropolitan Museum of Art, Gift of Mrs. Jacob H. Lazarus, 1893, 93.19.2.

DATE DUE

12-12-12			

$1 per day late fee for DVDs, magazines, and ILLs

American Profiles

Martin Van Buren and the Emergence of American Popular Politics

Joel H. Silbey

ROWMAN & LITTLEFIELD PUBLISHERS, INC.
Lanham • Boulder • New York • Oxford

ROWMAN & LITTLEFIELD PUBLISHERS, INC.

Published in the United States of America
by Rowman & Littlefield Publishers, Inc.
A wholly owned subsidiary of The Rowman & Littlefield Publishing Group, Inc.
4501 Forbes Boulevard, Suite 200, Lanham, Maryland 20706
www.rowmanlittlefield.com

PO Box 317; Oxford; OX2 9RU, UK

British Library Cataloguing in Publication Information Available

The hardcover edition was previously catalogued by the Library of Congress as follows:

Silbey, Joel H.
    Martin Van Buren and the emergence of American popular politics / Joel
H. Silbey.
        p. cm. — (American profiles)
Includes bibliographical references (p.) and index.
1. Van Buren, Martin, 1782–1862. 2. Presidents—United
States—Biography. 3. United States—Politics and
government—1837–1841. 4. Political culture—United
States—History—19th century. I. Title. II. American profiles (Lanham,
Md.)
    E387 .S64 2002
    973.5'7'092—dc21   2002005867

ISBN 0-7425-2243-1 (cloth : alk. paper)
ISBN 0-7425-2244-X (pbk. : alk. paper)

Printed in the United States of America

⊖™ The paper used in this publication meets the minimum requirements of American
National Standard for Information Sciences—Permanence of Paper for Printed Library
Materials, ANSI/NISO Z39.48-1992.

To Two Magnificent Teachers:

Madeline Russell Robinton
and
Arthur Charles Cole

Contents

Acknowledgments

ALAN KRAUT ORIGINALLY URGED ME to undertake a new study of Martin Van Buren. I am grateful to him for his suggestion and encouragement. Subsequently, Norman Risjord applied his keen editorial eye to improving what I have written. I very much appreciate his efforts. I am also in debt to Patricia Weir of the Martin Van Buren National Historical Site and Carrie Barratt of the Metropolitan Museum of Art for introducing me to Van Buren's iconography. At Rowman and Littlefield I was fortunate to work closely with a most efficient and committed staff especially Mary Carpenter and Michael Marino. They, too, made important contributions to the final shape of this book.

My understanding of Van Buren has been enriched by my reading of the fine historians who have preceded me in producing biographical studies: Donald Cole, the late John Niven, Major Wilson, James Curtis, the late Joseph Rayback, and Jerome Mushkat, as well as those political historians such as Richard P. McCormick, Robert Remini, Daniel Walker Howe, Michael Holt, Ronald Formisano, William Shade, and Harry Watson, who have wrestled with the age in which Van Buren lived. Lee Benson, as always, deserves special mention. His work on the political world of the Jacksonian era has been an unparalleled stimulant throughout the years that I have been studying nineteenth-century America. I am deeply beholden to him, even as I recognize how much we will probably disagree about the Sly Fox of Kinderhook. Allan G. Bogue, has

ix

been, as always, a font of good sense about American political history and a model scholar always to be emulated.

The Cornell University Library has been the center of my scholarly existence for this book as it has been for others. I owe a great deal to the dedicated staff there, and to those who originally built up its magnificent American history collections. A number of my faculty colleagues have also been quite helpful as I worked on this book. I wish to thank Walter LaFeber, in particular, for his continuing intellectual stimulation and the insight that he provided about the nature of the American experience and the way that Van Buren's enemies read the New Yorker. Michael Kammen, Stuart Blumin, and Glenn Altschuler have also provided wisdom at various moments. I am grateful to each of them for doing so.

The dedication of this book to two exemplary undergraduate teachers only begins to express how much I cherish their efforts on my behalf when I was just beginning to think about history as a subject and as a profession.

Finally, as always, I have received great emotional support from my immediate family, Rosemary, Victoria, and David, as well as from those who have become part of it since I began to work on Van Buren: Mari, Tom, and my grandchildren, Abigail and Thomas. The last two cannot yet read what I have written but I hope that they will someday.

Preface

MARTIN VAN BUREN ENJOYED A LONG CAREER in American politics in the first half of the nineteenth century beginning in the surging socioeconomic and political turmoil that unsettled the nation around the War of 1812, culminating, first, in his election as president of the United States in 1836, and then continuing through his involvement in the first strong impulses of political antislavery at the end of the 1840s. Four times a candidate for the presidency, and twice briefly considered for an appointment to the United States Supreme Court, he held office as a local official, state legislator, state attorney general, United States senator, New York's governor, the nation's secretary of state, minister to Great Britain, and, then, vice president of the United States, the last three posts under Andrew Jackson.

But it is not his office holding or his short-lived presidency that are usually marked as the critical elements in his life. Historians have identified a number of different types of political leaders in America's past, although the categories often overlap. First among these are the leader-statesmen, people such as Andrew Jackson, Abraham Lincoln, and Theodore and Franklin Roosevelt, who stood well above the norm, who represented and articulated major themes of their times, and who set the terms of the business of governing in their particular eras, often during a significant national crisis.

The prophets have been a second type of leader: in Van Buren's lifetime they included the ultra defender of slavery, John C. Calhoun and, on the other side, various antislavery advocates, abolitionists, and reformers, such as John Quincy Adams, Charles Sumner, Elizabeth Cady Stanton and William Lloyd Garrison, each of whom unyieldingly breathed fire on behalf of a single issue, or nonconsensual themes regardless of the difficulties and intense resistance they encountered and, often, the hopelessness of winning a victory for their cause in the political arena.

Third have been the ordinary, run-of-the-mill officeholders, always attentive to their responsibilities but with little flare for public recognition or major accomplishments to their credit. One thinks in the nineteenth century of Van Buren's contemporary, Lewis Cass, the Democratic presidential candidate in 1848, or, later, of the Republican presidents, Benjamin Harrison and Chester Alan Arthur, as examples of this type. They were often hardworking and sometimes useful as they ascended the political ladder but they were rarely memorable for their deep insight or lasting accomplishments.

Finally, there has been a critical fourth group: the organizers/managers of American political life, those who earned their way by their ability to conceptualize, establish, and run the machinery of politics and governing in a contentious, pluralist society. One thinks, in this connection in Van Buren's time, of the great Whig newspaper editor, Thurlow Weed of New York, and his contemporary, the Virginia Democrat, Thomas Ritchie, as well as the young Abraham Lincoln, who, long before his emergence to greatness, first made his name as an effective builder and manager of the Illinois Whig Party in the 1830s.

VAN BUREN IS, OF COURSE, a major example, perhaps the leading one, of this last type. He was a transforming political figure in American history, a persistent and innovative practitioner of a new style of national politics. The America in which he grew to maturity was rooted in a long-dominant conception of civic order and purpose that feared internal societal conflict, was skeptical of too much popular participation in political life, denied the need for organized political parties, and loathed the arts of political management. It was a conception that was increasingly at odds with the disorderly landscape of an emerging mass politics in the tumultous years after the end of the War of 1812.

Van Buren took the lead among his contemporaries in remolding the political order into which he had been born. He was both a reflector and a shaper of the currents loose in his society. His contributions firmly rested on his acceptance of the inevitability of political conflict as a permanent aspect of American life, his cautious recognition of the irreversible evolution of new populist currents in the first half of the nineteenth century—limited, to be sure, almost exclusively to adult white males—and of the political leader's need, in consequence, to find effective means of organizing and working with an expanding and demanding electorate over a complicated, contentious, and often confused political landscape.

The New Yorker's commitment, in consequence, to the national political party as the necessary organizer of the nation's persistent conflict and as the articulator of the people's desires, hopes, and dreams, helped remake America's political culture into one that extolled discipline and collective action with a single partisan voice. By this means Van Buren sought to advance a specific set of policies and promote and protect larger societal values he and his associates held in common, including the need to control social conflict based on ethnic, religious, and economic divisions. They were eminently successful in energizing and advancing their vision until the party system they built became a victim of the overpowering sectional strife that culminated in the Civil War.

VAN BUREN HAS NOT BEEN SHY of biographers. Books about him have appeared from time to time—a few while he was still alive to read them. The total then was never large, and interest in him ebbed as scholars focussed their attention on other political leaders of his generation. After a long period of neglect, however, he enjoyed something of a renaissance in the early 1980s when three major studies about him appeared. Two of them were full-scale biographies, the other an examination of his presidency. Another study, of Van Buren's legal and early political careers, was published as recently as 1997. Why, then, another look at him now?

There are several reasons to do so. There is always room for a fresh overview of a critical career in the history of America's political development, in this case, a concise, synthetic, and pointed profile that distills the essence of Van Buren's important role in the nation's political history. His activities and behavior provide a range of insights into the political world of his time as it evolved and hardened into a modern democracy. It was, as I have argued, the professional politician who gave American popular politics coherence and institutional structure in the nineteenth century in the midst of persistent social and economic turbulence. As one of the most innovative and important of this new breed, Van Buren's thoughts are worth listening to, his activities worth recording, his achievements and failures worth reflecting on as we seek to comprehend both the man himself and the full texture of the complex American political experience.

In addition, in the tradition of interpretive sketches of this kind, I have reflected on some of the contentious contemporary and historiographic disagreements about the man, clarified and reframed emphases where I thought that to be appropriate, suggested virtues where others have denied them, and tried to recast our understanding consonant with the record as I read it. Van Buren can be brought into sharper focus. In so doing, while previous biographies have pointed the way, I have tried to cut out my own distinct perspective. I have often agreed with the findings of earlier scholars. As often I have differed from them in the search for a clear understanding of a particular kind of political actor as he wended his way through, and interacted with, the changing national environment of his day.

Chapter One

─────────────○─────────────

The Tavern
Keeper's Son
The Making of a Politician, 1782–1812

MARTIN VAN BUREN WAS BORN in the small village of Kinderhook in New York's Hudson River valley on December 5, 1782, the third of six children of Abraham and Maria Hoes Van Buren. In similar fashion to his future mentor, Andrew Jackson, and one of his later political antagonists, Abraham Lincoln, he rose to national eminence the hard way. Few prominent American political leaders have started out as so much of an outsider in his society. Born into a predominantly Dutch community in a state increasingly dominated by those of English background, amid all kinds of persistent and often bitter tensions between the different ethnic communities, the son of a tavern keeper with little personal wealth in a society dominated by its economic elites, and never formally educated as the nation's political and social leaders routinely were, he was to travel a very long way by the time he entered the White House in 1837.

AT THE TIME OF VAN BUREN'S BIRTH the Hudson valley was, as it had been throughout the colonial era, a quite traditional, hierarchal society rooted in the values and practices of its past and containing a great many undemocratic elements in its everyday life. Access to political participation, economic achievement, and social status had always been limited by the deeply ingrained notion that to be someone in the community one had to be a substantial property holder. The possession of property was severely restricted, however, by a long-standing pattern in New York of large manorial holdings on

1

which tenants worked the land without owning it and were subject to the rules and dictates of the great manor lords whose property it was.

In this class-ridden society, dominated by the few great families such as the Livingstons and the Van Rensselaers, the Van Buren family was firmly entrenched in the lower middle portion of a rigidly demarcated social scale, a fact that Martin Van Buren never forgot. He described himself, writing late in life, as having risen from his roots "without the aid of powerful family connections." His forebears, who had emigrated in the seventeenth century from the village of Buren in Holland, had originally been people of some substance in the New World, thanks to their landholdings. But by the time Martin came along, their property had largely been dissipated and the family's status had declined sharply. His father was a freehold farmer of modest means who also ran a tavern on his farm site to supplement his income. Thanks to his wife's dowry, the family possessed six slaves when Martin was born.

Van Buren later remembered his father as being "utterly devoid of the spirit of accumulation," so that "his property, originally moderate, was gradually reduced until he could but ill afford to bestow the necessary means upon the education of his children." Whatever his economic limitations, the elder Van Buren had other virtues. He was quite active in local politics as a supporter of the recent Revolution against England (in a region dominated by Loyalists) and, later, as a Jeffersonian Republican (in a Federalist stronghold).

THE POST-REVOLUTIONARY GENERATION

In his early life in "the Dutch counties" Van Buren was remarkably successful in cutting through the boundaries of the static society that encased his family. In his youth his home village was closed, introverted, and clannish, still reflecting the traditional patterns, habits, and caste-ridden culture of the Old World. There was little contact with the larger universe beyond the village's borders. In the crowded family home (which included the three children of his mother's first marriage as well as the six Van Buren siblings) Dutch was ordinarily spoken, as it was among both their neighbors and many of the family tavern's customers.

But this restricted world was on the brink of unsettling changes. The Revolution brought more than national independence. In New York and elsewhere it unleashed a range of liberating forces—economic growth and opportunity, social change and the onset of popular, egalitarian politics. Old values and practices were challenged and many of them were overthrown. Not everyone found their lives altered as a result. But almost everyone was affected to some degree by the processes unleashed by the revolution against Great Britain.

These impulses continued after the winning of American independence in 1783. In the generation following the Revolution a great flood of migrants, largely from New England, settled in and near the state capital at Albany and then pushed up the Mohawk River valley into western New York and beyond. Taking up land abandoned by fleeing supporters of the king or settling on what had been Indian lands west of the Hudson, they first established a subsistence economy, growing crops and raising livestock for their own consumption while remaining largely isolated from larger trade patterns and market forces. But, from the beginning of the post-revolutionary era, commercial agricultural production for distant markets also developed in the Hudson and Mohawk valleys. In the 1780s New York–grown wheat began to move on to the European market. Helped by transportation improvements, from the development of new roads to the building of the Erie Canal (completed in 1825), over the next generation New York State became an important part of the Atlantic commercial world.

The older, socially dominant, families of New York benefited from these changes and expanding opportunities. So did many others on the fringes of the world of the socially prominent. The availability of more land for more people and the growing market opportunities afforded to them made the existing static class differences somewhat more protean and permeable than they had been in the colonial era. Although economic differences and ethnic prejudices between the Dutch and English communities persisted, there were fewer obstacles than there had been to an enterprising individual wishing to break free of his social fetters.

Growing up in this new social order Van Buren found ways to do just that. His childhood was conventional enough in and around his father's farm and tavern. And, at first, the possibility of his advancing beyond the restrictions ordained by his origins appeared to be limited. He spent a few years in the rather undistinguished one-room local school and, briefly, in a more ambitious local academy where he gained a bare smattering of learning (including some Latin). But he was not in any school long enough to master the established range of literary classics and ancient languages, knowledge of which defined the social and political elites of the time.

At the age of fourteen, however, Van Buren's life shifted dramatically. His mother, who apparently was a stronger-willed character than his father, had always encouraged him to reach out beyond the circumstances into which he had been born. He followed her lead, seeking an opening for himself locally. He was lucky. In 1796 he was able to enter the law office of a member of a prominent Kinderhook family, the Sylvesters, as a student and clerk thanks to their willingness to support and encourage a bright, energetic young man of few prospects. Seven years of legal training followed for Van Buren, including a year in New York City in 1802–1803 in the law offices of William Van Ness, a member of another prominent Kinderhook family who had befriended the young Dutchman and paid for his trip to the city. Financially hard pressed throughout his years of study, Van Buren cleaned the Sylvester law office and did other odd jobs in order to pay for his upkeep.

Admitted to the bar in 1803, Van Buren established a law office in Kinderhook with his half brother, James Van Alen, an experienced attorney of some standing. The two of them were busy from the first. "I was not worth a shilling," Van Buren later wrote, "when I commenced my professional career." But over time he built up what he later described as "a successful and lucrative practice," first with Van Alen, and then, moving on after 1808, with new partners in the thriving county seat and commercial center of Hudson on the river south of his home village. His growing practice in these years took him beyond his Columbia County home as he appeared in the courts of Albany and New York City as well as those in Hudson and Kinderhook.

He was successful outside of court as well. He had learned much about the arts of social intercourse as well as mastering the intricacies of the law. Personally attractive and usually quite accommodating to those around him, Van Buren was able to make his way comfortably among the middle class of his home counties, the lawyers, merchants, and farmers who formed an increasingly important element of the emerging civil society of the upper Hudson Valley. He grew to maturity as a slender young man of five feet, six inches height with blue eyes and, at first, curly blond hair. He had learned to dress well and to cultivate his manners carefully as he mingled with his social betters and professional colleagues. But it was never only his appearance, personality, social polish, and deportment that helped him along. Given the chance, he proved to be a first-rate lawyer.

Van Buren's outstanding characteristics as an attorney were his energy, untiring work habits and a well-honed courtroom manner based on thorough preparation of his cases and a sharp wit. His practice was quite varied; he found clients as he could among businessmen and bankers and in divorce and inheritance matters and made a particular name for himself in the contentious disagreements over ancient land claims. A major aspect of the socioeconomic transformation underway in New York State from the 1780s onward was the conflict over Hudson valley land tenure based on often imprecise colonial grants, coupled with strong challenges to the extent of the power claimed by landlords over their tenants. Van Buren took advantage of this, often serving as a lawyer for renters and others who challenged the colonial hangovers of manorial control of the land. (The landlords found their legal counsel among the better-known and more well-established attorneys of the area.)

Despite his heavy workload, Van Buren found time for social life in these years with quite happy results. In February 1807 he married Hannah Hoes, a neighbor and distant cousin from his own Dutch community whom he had known since childhood. Hannah remains an elusive figure. Described as physically small, "doll-like," mild in manner, as well as "amiable and excellent . . . modest and unassuming," dutiful, and undemanding of those around her, there is little record of her and of the nature of the relationship that existed between husband and wife over the next decade. She bore Van Buren five sons during their relatively brief marriage, four of whom grew to maturity. She appears to have spent their time together firmly rooted in the conventional female roles of the day, preoccupied with her family and providing her husband with a stable and secure home environment. Given their common backgrounds in their highly traditional society, his expectations, and her behavior, are unsurprising.

THE AMERICAN POLITICAL NATION BEFORE 1815

Van Buren also found a life beyond his law practice and his family responsibilities. When he entered adulthood the state and national political landscapes were inexorably changing. The civil culture in which he matured was busy, loud, highly combative, and quite volatile, what one historian has characterized as "an unstable hybrid" of traditional practices and notions on the one hand and newer forces emerging out of the state's tumultous Revolutionary experience on the other. Social and political conflict had been endemic in New York before the Revolution, throughout its course, and afterwards as well. There always seemed to be a great deal for people to fight about in the public arena, both new matters and old.

In particular, the Revolution had "clouded the nature of legitimate authority" in New York State and elsewhere. In its wake had come a powerful swelling of populist anger against entrenched privilege and established hierarchies. A defiance of older patterns of deference had been growing since the Revolution. While Van Buren matured in an atmosphere of deference to one's betters and a politics dominated by factional infighting among Columbia County's elite families, the civic culture of the post-Revolutionary Hudson valley increasingly reflected strong democratizing impulses and energies, what one scholar has called "the revolutionary politics of democratic assertion." This went hand in hand with the social transformation that was liberalizing northern society and disrupting the old order that sought stability, calm, and the retention of its members' privileges and the political and social dominance of their neighborhood.

To this populist challenge to the established order was added another political dimension in these years, an explosion in the number of special interests, all jostling with one another for political preferment. Each interest sought government assistance for specific parochial, economic, and other hopes and dreams. Merchants, shippers, land speculators, and small farmers fought one another for policy preferment at the state and national capitals. Looking for government-financed transportation improvements, legislation that expanded credit facilities, and a range of other aid from Albany, anxious entrepreneurs rapidly discovered that they were caught up in a harsh conflict that recognized only winners or losers.

These strong ideological and economic forces were overlaid on top of the existing pattern of the traditional prejudices and long-standing disagreements among New Yorkers of different ethnic and religious backgrounds. New Yorkers remained conscious of their distinct roots and different values, and their inhabiting a land in which both "Yankees," those of English background who had moved into the state largely from Massachusetts, and "Yorkers," the original settlers of Dutch heritage, continued to reside together uneasily even in the post-Revolutionary world of rapid growth, unsettling change, and growing awareness of a larger world beyond the traditional horizons of New York life.

New York's existing ethnic rivalries were intensified by the arrival in the state of large numbers of immigrants from Ireland, both Protestant and Catholic. The long-standing religiously rooted hostilities between these two tribes did not die when they left their homeland. Their persistence in their new land fed on the existing turmoil in New York and added even more intense heat to the state's seething political cauldron.

The result of these contentious impulses, unsurprisingly, was constant conflict over a great many economic and social issues. New York had always churned politically. Rivalry between English and Dutch, between Presbyterians and Anglicans, between merchants and farmers, had led, even before the Revolution, to a vigorous politics of faction in which each fought to attain its specific goals from the government. These factions became better organized once the Constitution had been ratified and the nation's political arena greatly expanded. New Yorkers were now part of a politically vigorous nation and found new allies—and enemies—across state boundaries. In the 1790s the Federalist and Republican Parties appeared and engaged in intense battles over the reach of government power at both the state and national levels. They fought, as well, as over more fundamental questions of the rights and place of individuals, different classes, and specific ethnic and religious groups within American society. It was an exciting and extremely divisive era as a post-Revolutionary nation sought to define and implement its new Constitution and set its future direction.

VAN BUREN ENTERS POLITICS

Van Buren was drawn into this political world at a quite early age. From the first, the intense political excitement of the 1790s was reflected in Kinderhook and its surrounding localities. President Washington's aggressive secretary of the treasury, Alexander Hamilton, sought to enhance national power by appealing to the economic interests of the wealthy while resisting the populist currents present because he considered that they weakened the kind of governmental authority that he believed was crucial for national survival. This Federalist program won the support of many of Hamilton's fellow New Yorkers including large numbers in the upper Hudson valley. Van Buren's home county, Columbia, became one of the strongholds of Federalism in the state.

The Federalist vision of a powerful national government frightened many others in New York and elsewhere who feared that the power that the Hamiltonians sought would inevitably become predatory—as it historically always had—an unacceptable threat to individual liberties and destructive to local interests. The response of those who were calling themselves Republicans was to develop a vision of their own, one that stressed the importance of local interests, the primary power of the states, and the freedom of the individual from government restraint.

When the time came for him to choose sides in this intensifying battle, Van Buren readily followed his father into the Republican Party of Thomas Jefferson. Despite the example set by the elder Van Buren, he showed a certain toughness of character in doing so since he had to resist very strong pressure from his Federalist neighbors, particularly his legal benefactors, who made it clear that they expected him to show his gratitude for the help they had given him by choosing the right side in the battles underway.

There appears to have been no single reason why Van Buren became a Republican, no one event, or clear defining moment, which marked his way. He seems to have been influenced primarily by his father and his father's friends. In the elder Van Buren's tavern, political discussion was constant and sharp. It became a meeting place for the Republicans in Columbia County. The teen-aged Martin listened to the political talk and fully absorbed the Jeffersonian doctrines being championed. As he wrote long afterwards, "from my boyhood I had been a zealous partisan, supporting with all my power the administrations of Jefferson and Madison." He would adhere to that choice, and to his understanding of the Republican vision, all of his life.

His political apprenticeship began when, still in his teens, he participated in a Republican district nominating convention in Troy in 1801. Over the next several years he made himself highly useful in election campaigns and other party work as a speaker and activist. He was increasingly drawn, as a result, into the inner workings of the local organization, participating actively in the discussions that occurred in the party's Kinderhook meeting rooms where campaign strategies were devised, candidates for office were agreed on, and party programs hammered out. It was a heady experience for a young man on the rise.

In these small party gatherings the young lawyer began to develop his political skills, especially learning how to operate effectively in a complex environment. Party leaders were struck by his commitment and willingness to take on jobs and responsibility; they marked him as an energetic, knowledgeable, and enthusiastic soldier in the cause. His law practice furthered his budding political career because many local politicians were also lawyers, and as he traveled on his legal business, he became acquainted with some of the rising political leaders of the state and part of their circle in the taverns and inns that surrounded the courts where they all practiced.

All of this involvement soon paid off. In 1808, still in his mid-twenties, he was appointed by Governor Daniel Tompkins, at the urging of Van Buren's political friends, to the legal post of Surrogate of Columbia County, his first public office—and a post that was also quite congruent with his legal activities as he had often worked in the complex arena of inheritance law. That appointment was only the beginning. Four years later the Republicans of the Middle District—the counties south and southwest of Albany—passed over a number of more prominent candidates to nominate him for the state senate. They did so, apparently, with the support of New York State's powerful Republican leader, DeWitt Clinton.

AS VAN BUREN BECAME MORE AND MORE involved in the political world in the new century, its basic focus was shifting dramatically both nationally and at the state level. The Federalist Party had come on hard times after Thomas Jefferson's election as president in 1800 and went into steep political decline thereafter. Despite the advantage that they gained from their opponents's woes, the Republicans had troubles of their own. They had been beset by simmering personal and policy disagreements among themselves for some time and they splintered badly after Jefferson's retirement from office in 1809. These divisions spread from the nation's capital into state politics. In New York, Republican factions pursued individual, often highly parochial, agendas and attached themselves to the ambitions of different great men of the state: Morgan Lewis, Aaron Burr, Daniel Tompkins, and DeWitt Clinton. Abetted by the Federalists' mischievous meddling, their battles resulted in a confused, nasty, fragmented, and chaotic situation clearly destructive to the Republican cause.

In such an environment it was difficult to maintain friendships and Van Buren was not always able to do so. The number of his political enemies grew despite his practiced geniality toward everyone. His hometown Federalist opponents made clear their strong dislike of him as he climbed the political ladder, a feeling that they demonstrated on every occasion that they could. Nor was he able to satisfy everyone in his own party. During his time in New York City Van Buren had several times met Aaron Burr, then Jefferson's vice president, and some observers considered him to have become part of the latter's faction.

To their disappointment, he avoided any commitment to Burr—or to any other factional leader—keeping his own counsel about where he stood among the Republican leaders. This approach had disadvantages, for it gave birth to the charge that he could not be counted on—that he refused to reveal where he stood on anything until he discovered the most advantageous pathway for himself. His actions, when he finally took them, his foes claimed, stemmed not from any particular policy commitments, or consistent ideology, but, rather, from the personal ambitions of an overaggressive, and too wily, politician.

The charge was overblown and obviously politically motivated. Van Buren's behavior, and the reasons for his reticence and caution, were more complex, and less personally directed, than suggested by his political enemies and disappointed colleagues. To be sure, Van Buren, even this early, did play his cards close—perhaps too close—to the chest. On the other hand, he had reason to be reticent and as unforthcoming as he was. He did not see, then, or later, what gains for the Republican cause and its policies would come from more bold, decisive factional commitment on his part, when the factional infighting of his party was causing it to fumble away opportunities offered by Federalist weakness.

In the immediate term the growing negative perceptions of him erected barriers in his path. In his autobiography, he recalled his first race for office (against one of the Livingston clan) as a particularly fractious and passionate one. His candidacy was challenged, he wrote, by "the entire federal party, the Lewisites, the Burrites, and the supporters of the Bank of America." His enemies were numerous and they seemed to be everywhere, seeking to block his path. Nevertheless, when the time came, and despite the hostility that seem to come from all directions, the neophyte politician proved to be popular enough among the voters. After winning a difficult nominating contest against other Republican challengers for the position, and fighting the "severely contested" campaign against the Federalists that then ensued, Van Buren eked out a very close victory at the polls in April 1812 to win the Middle District's state senate seat.

THE NEW STATE SENATOR had come a very long way from his father's Kinderhook tavern. His world had expanded in many ways. He was comfortably ensconced financially, socially, and politically, in the middle-rank local elites of his home state. Always faultlessly dressed, he had developed a reputation, one that he was never to lose, as a man who enjoyed life's finer comforts and opportunities despite the traditionalism of his background and the simplicity of his home life with Hannah. Moving from court to court on the regular circuit that the state's lawyers routinely followed, practicing in New York City and Albany, as well as in his own rural and small-town neighborhood, his intellectual and social horizons had greatly widened. He had picked up a great deal of information about the political world, information that served as the basis of his growing insight into that environment, its problems, and its needs. His commitment to Jeffersonian Republicanism had hardened, as well, into an unflinching devotion to its basic localist, limited government, tenets, a devotion that he was always quick to express as required, both openly and in private.

Capping a decade of both public and behind the scenes participation in the intricate world of local and state politics, Van Buren had become an increasingly important political player both in his native region and in the larger state arena. By 1812, he was recognized as a promising newcomer by such state Republican leaders as Daniel Tompkins and Governor Clinton, a recognition that was to prove immensely important to his career.

Equally important, he had begun to develop out of his initial experiences an intellectual map of the social and political reality in which he lived. This framework included a strong feel for the many differences that existed in American society, and a sense of the inevitability of constant political conflict as a result of those differences. He had come to understand that policy consensus and political calm were not normal elements in his world.

This led to the realization that his personal goal must center on finding an effective institutional means of managing this persistently fractious political world so as to promote the Republican cause, and firmly implant its vision of localism, government restraint, and democratic strivings on the American landscape. That quest for order in an adversarial society occupied most of the next twenty years of Van Buren's life, first in Albany and, then, after 1821, at the nation's political center, in Washington, D.C.

Chapter Two

─────────────────○─────────────────

"The Partisan Leader" I
Master of the State, 1812–1821

IN THE SIXTEEN YEARS AFTER HIS ELECTION to the New York senate in 1812 Van Buren's political horizons greatly expanded as his public career continued its upward spiral. Leaving his home county and going to Albany to attend the annual sessions of the state legislature, he moved from being a local politician of some promise into someone who became both a force in his own state and, within a relatively brief time, a major player in the national political arena as well. His growing prominence stemmed, originally, from the major role that he played, from the War of 1812 on, in building the American political party system as the prime organizer, articulator, and manager of the nation's political conflict. He began in his own state as the head of first, the "Bucktails," and then, the "Albany Regency," both key organizational elements in a revived and refocused state Jeffersonian Republican Party. From there he became the critical force in the emergence of the Jacksonian Democratic Party at the national level in the 1820s and 1830s. Van Buren's efforts contributed to the fundamental recasting of American political life, a recasting that defined the nation's political structure for more than a century thereafter. At the same time, his dedication to the Jeffersonian tenets of states' rights, and securing the proper (limited) role of government in economic development and social life became more focused than ever, demarcating what he wanted to accomplish through his political involvement.

VAN BUREN SERVED IN THE STATE SENATE until 1821, moving his family from Hudson to a new permanent home in Albany, at the center of the New York's political (and legal) life, in 1816. As a state senator he was automatically a member of the Council of Revision, a body that under the state constitution of 1777 had important legislative functions. As his prominence grew he also became influential on the Council of Appointment, a constitutional body that was responsible for many appointments to office at the state level.

While he was still a state senator the Council of Appointment simultaneously named him, in February 1815, to be New York's attorney general, the state's senior law officer. It was a post that he held until he was removed four years later by a subsequent council, one that had fallen into the hands of his political opponents. Finally, the Republican-controlled state legislature elected him to the United States Senate in 1821 and then reelected him in 1827 for a second six-year term. A year later Senator Van Buren was elected governor of New York State at the same moment that Andrew Jackson won the presidency.

THE PROBLEM OF DEWITT CLINTON

None of this advancement occurred without a great deal of effort. As early as his initial appearance in the state senate, Van Buren was fully engaged at all levels of political activity, busily working in party meetings, as well as on the floor of the legislature, and in large public gatherings, on behalf of the Republican cause. As more and more people recognized his skills as an organizer and promoter of Jeffersonian Republican values, he became an important behind-the-scenes player in his new home. He took the lead in negotiations between the senate, controlled by his party brethren, and New York's other legislative chamber, the Federalist-controlled assembly. He was also energetic on the senate floor during the War of 1812 as a major Republican spokesman and as a legislator of some originality. Among his achievements was a personnel classification bill designed to bring some order to the previously uncoordinated, and often chaotic, enlistment of New Yorkers into the army.

Despite his early successes, and the growing recognition that he enjoyed, Van Buren continued to be dismayed by the dizzying profusion and intensity of the factional divisions that beset the New York political scene. From Martling Men and Tammany Hall in New York City, to the groups organized behind DeWitt Clinton and Daniel Tompkins, to the "High-Minded" Federalists throughout the state, and back, the state's politics during this time were characterized by one observer as "a field of exploration as intricate as the everglades of Florida or the jungles of the Philippines" [sic]. The apparent clarity, and the sharply etched political polarization, of the Federalist-Republican wars of the 1790s had largely disappeared. In their place, as Van Buren had long noted and continued to regret, an array of local leaders battled one another all over the landscape, each of them changing allies, and shifting direction, as their particular needs dictated at some moment, then shifting again to achieve short-term electoral advantage.

Van Buren was particularly concerned about the condition of the Republican Party in this fragmented world. At the presidential level the incumbent, James Madison, the third member of the Virginia Dynasty to lead the nation, was the acknowledged Republican candidate for reelection. But Clinton, New York City's formidable mayor (and, simultaneously, the state's lieutenant governor), who was rapidly emerging as the outstanding political figure in his home state, had other ideas. He offered himself as a Republican candidate for president against Madison, arguing that the Virginia dynasty had held that office long enough. It was now New York's turn to rule. The Empire State, he pointed out, had always accepted second place in national politics behind the Old Dominion but it no longer needed to do so—and it should not.

Van Buren, claiming that he was influenced primarily by the obligation to be loyal to his state, supported his fellow New Yorker for the nomination in the party's state caucus. His commitment led in later years to his opponents charging that he not only opposed Madison's candidacy, but, also, the vigorous prosecution of the war against England. The charges were nonsense. Van Buren, who had been a loyal supporter of Jefferson and Madison's policies that had led to the war, remained staunchly behind the administration once the conflict broke out. He was, in fact, deeply pained by Clinton's action because he believed that it gave heart to the war's Federalist opponents. (The latter did not put forward a presidential candidate of their own in 1812, supporting Clinton instead.) Nevertheless, Van Buren supported his fellow New Yorker as a mark of his solidarity with his state's Republicans and, undoubtedly, because, to do otherwise, would seriously affect his standing (and future prospects) among New York's Republican leaders.

This episode was the forerunner of much that was still to come. The role played by the often mercurial, but very skillful, Clinton in state political activities was usually quite difficult for the senator from Hudson—although when he first arrived in Albany, Van Buren and Clinton were outwardly amicable and found ways to work together. But that cooperative spirit did not last. Despite Van Buren's original support for Clinton's presidential ambitions, the two were at each other's throats politically most of the time from 1812 onward.

Part of the differences between them were ideological. Clinton, with his vision of the Empire State's expanding commercial leadership of the American economy, had an important following among both growth-oriented Republicans and some Federalists. He was extremely popular outside the local and Jeffersonian elites where Van Buren showed so well. His popularity was much enhanced among those who wished to used the government to promote economic development by his successful championing of the state-funded building of the Erie Canal. But Clinton's promarket, economic expansionary, ideas clashed with Van Buren's quite different vision of Republicanism, which stressed commitment to those who were less commercially minded: small landholders, village artisans, and urban workers, who did not need, nor benefit from, the expansionary government projects that an aggressive market orientation demanded. Van Buren's definition of core Republican values included a role for markets to be sure, but he believed that Clinton's activities were too extravagant in cost, and of little use to a majority of New York Republicans.

Further, whatever his alleged principles were, Clinton was not loyal to the larger Republican movement. He moved too readily and adroitly, for Van Buren's taste, among the various factions on the scene, often siding with the Jeffersonians' Federalist enemies in order to advance his own aims and ensure the dominance of his own group at whatever disruptive cost to the Republican Party and the things that it stood for. He still clung, in Van Buren's eyes, to the older idea that it was the specific leadership qualities of individuals, free of external fetters (such as party "dictation") on them, that was what primarily counted in public affairs, not commitment to a particular set of principles, nor to a vision of the political scene that stressed, as Van Buren did in these years, the importance of Republicans organizing together to resist the unwavering Federalist threat to them.

The lack of clarity and direction in New York politics, its world of personal factions and volatile alliances as revealed in Clinton's ongoing activities, sorely tested the ability of the Republican Party to maintain its dominance in the state or the nation. Madison lost New York to Clinton in 1812—but won reelection anyway. The factional infighting that had accompanied the contest had made victory difficult and remained deeply threatening, thereafter, providing, in Van Buren's eyes, too great an opportunity for the unacceptable resurgence of Federalism and its iniquitous policies.

The Bucktails

Of course, at the outset of his career Van Buren played New York's factional wars extremely well. He was widely viewed, in these early days, not as the enemy of Republican factionalism, but, rather, as part of it, as the leader of one of the major party blocs with its own interests to be won by whatever means necessary. When he first went to Albany, he had become associated with a group of like-minded individuals, some of them lawyers, others bankers and small-scale entrepreneurs, most of them, at the outset, members of the state senate. Van Buren drew great political sustenance from these colleagues, together they formed the powerful element known, at first, as the "Bucktails," which rapidly became prominent enough in the state capital to play the fragmented politics of the time with great authority.

Van Buren was the acknowledged leader of this unusual group of politicians. His Bucktail colleagues included seasoned political activists such as William L. Marcy of Troy, later governor of the state, and then prominent in national Democratic administrations in the 1840s and 1850s. Among them, as well, were a number of bright, vigorous, younger men just coming on to the scene, such as Benjamin F. Butler, from the same Hudson valley milieu as Van Buren, and Silas Wright, from the far northern reaches of the state, both of whom were to rise to great heights in American national politics and who became the closest allies and friends that Van Buren ever had.

Butler, born in 1795, started out as a student and clerk in Van Buren's Albany law office. He soon became the older man's law partner, lived in the Van Buren home for a time, and remained always one of his mentor's principal agents, particularly after Van Buren went to Washington in 1821. Wright, also born in 1795, came from a farm family in Canton on the Canadian border, attended Dartmouth College and was elected to the state senate in 1824. He was to become, over the years, Van Buren's most trusted confidant, whose counsel was always heeded, second in command of their organization as it developed, and the designated successor to Van Buren in higher offices on the national scene.

The Bucktails had among themselves different regional and other interests, came together for different reasons, and could be fractious, often disagreeing about specific policies and problems. But, whatever their disagreements, they also had much in common. They always shared a commitment to sustaining the Jeffersonian political outlook in the state against its always present Federalist enemies, and, as well, against what they saw as the quixotic political maneuverings of DeWitt Clinton. From the outset, Bucktails argued for party loyalty, unity on behalf of Republican principles and candidates, instead of only to individuals or parochial interests, a dedication to a larger whole that was their distinguishing characteristic from other factions. Once decisions had been reached among them, they stuck together on the campaign trail, and in the legislature, on behalf of the cause, whatever their individual inclinations.

Van Buren always embraced the argument that his group was different from the other factions since, unlike them, the Bucktails were

never willing to desert their Republican commitments for any immediate personal advantage. The constant factional maneuvering that he
and his friends practiced, was, therefore, acceptable as a temporary
expedient to keep the enemies of Republicanism at bay. His group was
the Republican Party so far as he was concerned, their Clintonian opponents a cabal of irregulars outside the Republican circle who had to
be opposed for the good of the cause. Van Buren's "mania to defeat
Clinton," two scholars have written, "knew no bounds." That mania,
however, was never personal. It was rooted in a larger concern for party
purposes as achieved through loyalty to the cause.

Since he always believed that much was at stake in American politics and that, as a result, real political divisions always existed and
would never go away, he believed that there was only one way for the
adherents of the Jeffersonian impulse to behave. The Republican
Party was a multifaceted conglomerate of many different groups. But
it operated in an either-or situation politically, that is, either they won
or they were defeated. There was no middle ground. That reality obviously did not benefit from the constant maneuvering of uncon-
trolled factions. In such a climate the willingness of others to break
away from the properly nominated candidate of the Republican Party
and to support someone of a different perspective, weakened the
power of the party's larger ideological purposes.

The Bucktails were not always successful. Even as their, and
his, power in state affairs grew exponentially, Van Buren was outmaneuvered by Clinton and his allies in battles over nominations
for office and the party's policy direction. Van Buren made a mistake when he expressed early hesitation about the state financing of
the Erie Canal, which turned out to be very popular as its benefits
to the state became apparent. But he recovered from that misstep,
and supported the canal as an appropriate state-level initiative
when it came before the legislature in 1817.

Concert in Action

Although the Federalists had been greatly invigorated during
the war by the Madison administration's many failures on the

battlefield and homefront, their power ebbed after 1815 on both the national level and in most states, including New York. To Van Buren that was a mixed blessing because as the Federalists faded from the political arena, Republican factionalism significantly intensified.

Although his fears proved to be greatly exaggerated, all but reaching the point of paranoia, Van Buren remained staunch in his belief that the Federalist decline was temporary and that Republican indifference to the threat that they posed would have tragic political consequences. He thought that the growing public claims that the United States was entering a new era of good feelings in which erstwhile enemies would work together for the common good was a dangerous evasion—and distortion—of political reality. He and his Bucktail colleagues repeated, over and over, therefore, that the Federalist threat to American liberties and nationhood through the Hamiltonian willingness to, in Van Buren's words, "destroy the balances of the constitution," had not gone, nor would it go, away. And, as obvious, they could only gain strength from the continuation of party disagreements among the Jeffersonian majority in the state. As he settled in as a strong factional leader, therefore, Van Buren turned his talents even more to bringing order, structure, direction, and above all, discipline, to the political world's swirling disarray.

His answer to Republican factionalism had been germinating in his mind for a very long time: the necessity of developing a new "science of politics," one that would contain and manage the powerful centrifugal forces present in the state's (and nation's) political culture. This meant that he had to go beyond exhortations on behalf of Republican unity and develop a finer weave of managerial institutions, institutions that would firmly stand on the twin bedrocks of policy commitment and the acceptance of organizational direction.

His ideas did not crystallize all at once. Rather they simmered and shaped themselves from 1812 onward, evolving along with his experiences in the state capital, (and, later, in his early years in Washington, D.C.). There were a number of significant marking points along the way. None was more significant to him than when, in 1819, "the Rubicon was passed" in New York politics. The Clin-

tonians supported (for their temporary advantage) a "violent opponent" of the War of 1812 for speaker of the state House of Assembly. He was, Van Buren wrote, "to our friends the most obnoxious
man in the Clintonian ranks." No action could underline more
sharply the danger of faction and the political chaos all of them had
to live with, and suffer from, given Clintonian behavior. Something
drastic had to be done. It was time for new, far-reaching initiatives.

Van Buren's efforts were aimed at breaking the mold of existing
practices, no matter how deeply imbedded they were, not simply to
reform them. Although political parties had existed in America
since the 1790s, neither the Federalists nor the Republicans had
built strong organizations to sustain themselves. Their members
had accepted very little, many of them not at all, the necessity of
submitting themselves to the party will in order to ensure its success, certainly not as a regular, and permanent, aspect of political
affairs.

This would all now begin to change, thanks, largely, to Van Buren's leadership. How conscious he was of how much he was pushing into wholly new areas is unclear. Nor is it certain that he had a
fully formed blueprint in his mind when he started out. But as time
passed in the late 1810s and early 1820s, the logic of his efforts
gave conscious form and shape to a new and powerful political direction; the new science of politics that he sought came into being.

The essence of this new approach went beyond bringing Clinton down, as desirable as that was. It was agreement among like-
minded groups to work together permanently, undergirded by a willingness to compromise on matters that divided them from one
another in the name of the larger Republican triumph over their
common Federalist enemy. To accomplish this he continued to
stress among his colleagues and potential allies that there must be
among them loyalty to something beyond the specific interests that
each had, that there had to be absolute and undeviating commitment to one's national party and to its decisions, once those had
been fairly made. Consultation and negotiations among different elements, the setting of policy priorities, and their acceptance by all,
were the first steps toward effective, purposeful, command of the
state's fragmented political scene. Van Buren was always sensitive

to any local variants of Republican ideology. Each Republican group had its say in party councils. But, then, they had to agree to abide by the decisions of the party majority. To oppose its candidate and policy choices because one found oneself in a minority and unhappy with a particular result was unacceptable. To do so, he numbingly reiterated, would only lead to internal disagreements, fragmentation, and defeat, and the victory of the hated enemy and the enactment of their unacceptable policies. As a Bucktail editor wrote in 1823, "as well might an army expect to conquer without discipline, as a party to preserve its ascendency without concert in action."

To increase the possibility of forging the kind of acquiescence that was needed for party success, Van Buren often sought to deflect, sidestep, or put aside, when he could, particularly contentious, and what he argued were secondary, issues, that were likely to further divide Republicans who otherwise would work together on behalf of the other, more important, matters that were before them.

NEXT TO DISCIPLINE, the principal element in Van Buren's approach was organization. He and his associates sought order and regularity in party affairs through well-understood rules and carefully constructed institutions of consultation and management. As the model was sharpened and implemented over time, what had been the Bucktail faction became, as dubbed by Van Buren's enemies, the "Albany Regency"—a tightly controlled organization, managed from the top, that was the coordinating and directing arm of the state Republican Party. It consisted of a network of local leaders and newspaper editors in the counties, towns, and villages of the state, who carried out the party's purposes as defined by the party's state leadership, at first embodied in the decisions of the caucus of its legislators in Albany, later of a state central committee. Their actions were always regularized and refreshed through the constant holding of legislative caucuses to hear opinions from all sides, consider what policies to support, and choose people to run for office.

Once the party caucus had met, nominated candidates for an approaching election, and publicly set forth its commitments through an address to the voters, the party hierarchy at the state capital began to plan strategy and implement campaign activities. They announced their decisions, and framed their appeals, in the pages of the Albany *Argus*, a newspaper established in 1813, and distributed statewide, which became, and remained for many years, thereafter, the voice of the regular, organized Republicans (later Democrats) of the state. (Its editor was a member of the Regency's leadership.) Distributed primarily through the United States mails, often aided by partisan postmasters, it was at the head of a network of party newspapers established throughout the state to proclaim the Republican message in every election campaign.

The *Argus's* words were recognized as stating the party's law. The local press took their cues from it, reprinting its editorials and other campaign materials it ran in its pages. Supported, as was the *Argus*, by government contracts to publish local laws, and other official documents, the noisy partisan press announced, cajoled, and ordered, all in the interest of Republican victory. At the local level, party leaders holding offices such as sheriff, justice of the peace, town clerks, and the like, supplemented the newspaper onslaught, promoting the party line as they diligently worked among the voters to carry out the needs of the current campaign.

"PARTY IS INDISPENSABLE . . ."

As suggested earlier, what Van Buren and his colleagues were calling for was not simply a variant of earlier political practices and forms. Politics was now to become more of a profession than it had been, with the leader as pluralist broker and with all of the members agreeing to accept, in the name of the common good, what one historian has characterized as "an almost servile worship of organization." Unlike the then current political practices and previous attempts to build such organizations, the Regency worked to make the party apparatus permanent and to routinize the political process through an organizational imperative that all submitted to loyally, something that was very new in tone, in purpose, in content, and in behavior, stressing the hardening of party lines, the clarity of party purposes and direction, and the unquestioned, disciplined loyalty of its adherents.

Van Buren's pursuit of organized, managed, political operations was never uncontested or untroubled. The long-present and deeply ingrained antiparty tradition of eighteenth-century classical Republican ideology still dominated American political culture when he first set to work. Classical Republicanism provided a powerful vocabulary against parties and the management of permanent political conflict. Van Buren's opponents, especially DeWitt Clinton and his allies, called on this vocabulary to argue that Van Buren's insistence on party regularity and organizational discipline was too dangerous to America's civic culture. Organized parties and partisanship, by their nature, traditionalists claimed, particularly their commitment to permanent political warfare, always dangerously splintered the search for social and political consensus to the extreme detriment of the nation.

Further, classical Republicans believed that party regularity and the call for discipline subverted the will of the individual, denying each citizen the right to act as he thought best. Words such as corrupt, oppressive, and the danger of secret cabals, were mainstays of the classical Republican vocabulary and frequently iterated by those opposed to the emerging partisan and organizational blueprint of the Albany Regency. Their articulation underscored the great fear among them of the dangers to be realized from party mechanisms, and the organizing of the masses of voters under the control of a few leaders.

To the Van Burenites, on the other hand, political parties were not threatening to the American nation. They did not corrupt society or its politics. Contrary to established belief, they were necessary, proper, and, in fact, a positive good in the existing political environment. As one of Van Buren's close allies, New York Congressman Churchill Cambreleng, summed up on the floor of the national House of Representatives later in the decade, "party is indispensable to every Administration—it is essential to the existence of our institutions; and if it be an evil, it is one we must endure, for the preservation of our civil liberty. It never yet injured any free country . . . the conflict of parties is a noble conflict—of mind to mind, genius to genius." Such sentiments, while rarely heard previously on the American political landscape, were now constantly put forth by Regency spokesmen in their electoral campaigns and legislative activities. They were, clearly and publicly, the mainstay of the Van Buren–led political revolution underway in New York State in the ten years after the end of the War of 1812.

Van Buren's leadership of this emerging organization was as recognized and as indisputed as his leadership of the Republican bloc in the state legislature. His hard work, clear vision, and organizing talents brought the apparatus together and gave it its structure and purpose. The end result was slower in coming to fruition than he hoped it would be, and it was never perfect despite his attempts at construction, negotiation, conciliation, and compromise. Outbursts of internal dissension and factional warfare were frequent occurrences. Nevertheless, the Regency performed effectively enough in the late 1810s and early 1820s to imprint a blueprint of party development on New York politics and accomplish Van Buren's purpose of securing domination for the Republicans and their core policy purposes in the state while also giving him a solid base on which to build the next stage of his own career.

IN THE MIDST OF ALL OF THIS POLITICAL ACTIVITY, personal tragedy struck Van Buren a number of numbing blows. Hannah had given birth to their fourth son in 1813, but the child, named after Van Buren's friend, General Winfield Scott, lived only a few weeks. Then his aged parents passed away, his father in 1817, his mother in 1818. Most staggering of all, a year later, in 1819, Van Buren's wife died just before her thirty-sixth birthday. For some time she had not been in good health. Always susceptible to a series of debilitating illnesses, Hannah's condition culminated in the onset of tuberculosis. In 1815, she had borne another son, the couple's fifth, in a quite difficult delivery. Her health never recovered from that experience. Doctors could do little for her and she declined rapidly.

As noted earlier, the nature and quality of the Van Burens' domestic relationship can only be guessed at given the lack of evidence about it. He never mentioned Hannah in his published writings set down almost forty years after her death. His comments about her in personal correspondence were sparse, and usually guarded, when they appeared at all. Yet he seems to have been content with her and what she had brought to her marriage with a restless and ambitious man who directed so much of his energy outside of their home. He never married again, although some observers suggested that he was occasionally flirtatious and open to new relationships, at least for a time—probably, some enemies predictably suggested, when such were useful to him. But there is only a little evidence one way or another as to his interests and experiences, and none as to his motivation, in the many years that followed.

Van Buren revealed himself to be a devoted father after his wife's death. Their four sons were always central objects of concern to him as they grew to maturity. Helped by his immediate family, particularly his sister, Van Buren's young children were well cared for in the years after Hannah's death and remained close to their father when they came of age and began careers of their own. The oldest, Abraham, graduated from West Point, served in the army and became his father's secretary when the latter was president. The second son, "Prince" John, attended Yale, practiced law, ultimately served as New York's attorney general, and was a skillful political practitioner in his own right, often compared to his father. Martin Junior and the youngest, Smith, made their way as well, with less ambition and independent direction perhaps, serving their father as assistants and agents, both in Washington and in Albany during Van Buren's active years.

THE POPULAR IMPULSE

Between 1817 and 1820 the political warfare between Clinton and his factional and Federalist associates on the one side, and the Van Buren–led Republicans on the other, greatly intensified. At first, Clinton commanded the field, serving as New York's governor from 1817 to 1822, dominating the legislature, and controlling the two crucial governing councils, of Appointment, and of Revision. (It was his control of the former that led to Van Buren's removal as attorney general in 1819). In response, Van Buren and his colleagues intensified their determination to bring the governor down.

As part of their efforts, the Albany Regency supported the Federalist Rufus King for reelection to the United States Senate in 1819 (in return for the latter's support of Van Buren's candidate, the Republican Daniel Tompkins for governor the following year). On the surface, such support was shocking and seemed to confirm the negative views of "the sly fox of Kinderhook" (one of his recently acquired descriptions), whatever his oft-repeated claims that he was different from New York's other factional leaders.

But Van Buren always made a distinction between the destructive, antiwar Hartford convention Federalists, and those, such as King, the leader of the so-called "High-Minded Federalists." The latter had supported "Mr. Madison's War" despite its Republican roots and were, therefore, much more acceptable to the Van Buren Republicans than were their more rigid, antiwar colleagues. Working with the King group would prove beneficial to the Republican cause, both at a specific moment, and in the long run, when they would be permanently brought under the Jeffersonian wing. Or, at least, so Van Buren argued.

All of this traditional partisan warfare, factional and otherwise, was greatly complicated by the growing surge of political populism in the state, a surge that would have crucial consequences for everyone involved. When Van Buren began political life, the essence of coalition building lay in the negotiating that went on among the leaders of the different factions on the scene. They sought to find common ground among enough of them to build up a winning numerical majority in an election, or in the legislature on behalf of some bill, or on other immediate matters of concern. But things were rapidly changing as the nation and New York entered a new era, one characterized by a growing awareness that the nation's political audience was expanding rapidly and that there was a need for political leaders to heed the roar of the crowd and mobilize these newly articulate masses behind one candidate or another. New York's Republican Party, Van Buren noted in his autobiography, began to be called the Democratic or Democratic-Republican Party around 1818 or 1819, signaling the important crystallization of forces that was underway.

A number of political leaders forcefully pushed the egalitarian impulse forward, arguing particularly for the removal of property qualifications on the right to vote. Van Buren realized that he had to deal with these intense, persistent, and intrusive, impulses. But, how? What emerged at first were the conservative instincts that revealed when confronting what he saw as highly charged changes in standard political practices. He was no political revolutionary. He represented, at one level of his consciousness, a congeries of quite traditional impulses and did not wish to rock the boat when that was not necessary. He later referred to himself, in fact, as "timid in all matters of innovation." That cautioness certainly came out in his behavior in the early twenties.[1]

THE CONSTITUTIONAL CONVENTION OF 1821

The increasingly intense populist surge came to a head in the run up to a convention to revise New York's 1777 constitution. The Constitutional Convention of 1821 was one of the most dramatic moments in the state's early political history. The political egalitarians and their allies, who forced its calling, demanded the modernization of what they deemed an obsolete document, one that embodied, in their eyes, too many restrictive clauses limiting the people's individual liberties, access to economic opportunity, and right to wield power in state affairs.

Although he was, at first, hesitant about calling a convention at all, Van Buren went along with the clamor when he realized that many Bucktails and a majority of New Yorkers more generally supported it. So, eventually, did most New York Republican politicians, however reluctant they may have been. But all of them were determined to shape the document so as to best serve their partisan needs. Whatever the strength of the ideological forces promoting democratization, the various players in the convention also assiduously maneuvered for their own advantage in the proposals that they offered or supported.

The outcome of their efforts was a document that contained many more democratic elements in it than the one it replaced but not as many as might have been included. The right to vote was not extended to all white adult male citizens as many wanted it to be, was more restricted than it had been earlier for black New Yorkers, and did not consider nonmale suffrage at all. The drafters did liberalize much of New York's governing process, making it more responsive to more voters than had been the case. They did away with some of the more obsolete restrictions on the popular will such as the Councils of Appointment and Revision, and eased many of the other restrictions that survived. Other aspects of the new document left in it much of the residue of the less democratic impulses of the past that some delegates had worked hard to eliminate.

Van Buren was largely responsible for much of this balance. His background, and his difficult rise to social status and power, might have made him more open to the growing populist perspectives than many others who started out in a different place in the social scale. And there is some evidence that they did sensitize him somewhat. On the other hand, both his innate caution concerning extreme positions and the pushing of boundaries too far—that is, his conservative instincts—and his acute political sensitives, honed by twenty years of battle, came into play at the meeting. He made it very clear how much he feared the possibility of what he and others called anarchy, and of extreme demands that might have effects far beyond society's capacity to deal with them. He was certainly no leveller. He never had been and he certainly never would be.

He was elected to the convention from the friendly partisan terrain of Otsego County (where he owned some land and was, therefore, eligible to hold office), rather than from his home base, Federalist-dominated Albany. Once there, he chaired the convention's committee on appointments to state offices, giving him great influence on the new document. His power was never unalloyed, however, given the strength of the forces demanding change. He followed, therefore, a middle of the road, balance wheel, position, on the most prickly questions relating to the populist surge, particularly the matter of how far to push universal suffrage. He also proved hesitant, largely for party reasons, to extend the power of the state's voters to include their electing many more state officers than they previously had been allowed to do, preferring to place

appointive authority for these offices in the hands of a governor—
who would usually be, he hoped, a Bucktail.

Still, in the face of populist agitation and egalitarian impulses,
Van Buren proved discerning enough, and politic enough, to advance partway toward the goals of those who he believed to be too
extreme. He tried to restrain and manage egalitarian impulses
where others sought to turn them back, and still others tried to extend them further. As he later wrote in his autobiography, he
worked "to moderate the extreme views" of his friends, seeking,
rather, to change the existing suffrage requirements "on what I
deemed safe and reasonable grounds."

VAN BUREN'S ACTIVITIES AT THE CONSTITUTIONAL CONVENTION, and
his belief in the guidance of the people by party hierarchies, subsequently told against him among many politically involved New Yorkers. His enemies added the charge of his being undemocratic to the
other arguments they so vigorously offered against him in the early
1820s. Historians disagree as to how democratic Van Buren was, with
only a few of them willing to give him the benefit of the doubt by ac-
knowledging that he could claim some egalitarian credentials. At
best, they, as did his contemporaries, have seen him as primarily interested in reinforcing his role as a political tactician, seeking to sustain a particular political situation to his, and his supporters', benefit.

Perhaps the way to sum up Van Buren's position at the convention was that both ideological and tactical considerations always had
much force in his activities. He certainly sought to keep the Republicans firmly on the road to power and the best way to do that was to
move between the different extreme positions on the matters before
the body. But such tactical considerations were not all that was in
play. There was always more to his makeup than that. As a political
leader the important thing about him was his recognition of the impulses present, and his willingness to work with them as he could—
but always for purposes that transcended immediate gain for himself. To protect and enhance the Republican cause, always his main
objective, this combination of caution and sensitivity on the issue of
democratization, seemed to him to be the best path to follow in the
turbulent New York political arena of the early 1820s.

Whatever his original hesitation, his convention experiences were the first steps toward Van Buren's populist political reorientation. He would prove to be as willing as were his opponents to play on the populist surge, learning how to make direct appeals to the voters, and bringing them into the equation of direction, management, and articulation, forging effective linkages between leaders and led, rather than relying only on the assembling of alliances of local elite groups. He came to realize, if somewhat later than others among the populist groups, that he, and those whom he led, could not simply remain rooted in the traditional world from which they had come, whatever their instincts were to do so.

HIS CONVENTION INVOLVEMENT was a fitting capstone to Van Buren's decade-long efforts to bring political order and clarity to New York State. He had distinguished himself as a political leader of enormous talent, the creative progenitor of an approach to politics that was very different in nature from the prevailing norm, more organizational, more ideological, more accepting of permanent conflict, at its core, than had been the practice. Fully formed political parties had not yet emerged. But their blueprint had become quite clear thanks to Van Buren's articulation of it and his intense work on its behalf. Not yet forty years old, he had mastered the rough and tumble of New York's politics, surmounting many obstacles from all sides to move into the very top ranks of the state's political leaders.

NOTES

The Partisan Leader is the title of a novel, clearly about Van Buren, published when he ran for president in 1836, but certainly applicable as a lead-in here.

1. As always in this era, women and nonwhites were not factored into this emerging calculus by any large advocacy group, although some voices did demand, even at this early date, that the electoral revolution be carried further, beyond its present limiting boundaries of race and gender.

Chapter Three

―――――――――――――――○―――――――――――――――

"The Partisan Leader" II
The Senator from New York, 1821–1828

THE REGENCY-CONTROLLED NEW YORK legislature elected Martin Van Buren to the United States Senate early in 1821. He was ready for the change. The many political successes (and occasional setbacks) at the state level of "this enterprising and ambitious man" had primed him for a new stage in his career: more extensive activities and further conquests in the much bigger arena of national politics on behalf of the Jeffersonian cause that he so unstintingly espoused. Once in Washington he would rise rapidly into national prominence. By the end of the decade Van Buren was recognized as second only to Andrew Jackson, Henry Clay, Daniel Webster, and, perhaps, John C. Calhoun, as among the most significant figures in American politics.

TAKING SOME TIME TO WIND DOWN his affairs in Albany, he moved to Washington in early November 1821. (Congress would meet at the beginning of December.) At first he rented living quarters in one of the many congressional boardinghouses that dotted the capital city's landscape. His choice was in Georgetown where his New York senatorial colleague, Rufus King, and a number of other legislators, including several Federalists, also lived. He did not mind the latter's presence. Van Buren usually made a distinction between the dangerous wrong-headedness of his political opponents and the geniality of their company on a personal level— especially if the latter were of the "High-Minded Federalist" persuasion, meaning those, like King, who had supported the War of 1812.

One consequence of his move from New York was its effect on his law practice. Van Buren continued to appear in the state courts when not attending Senate sessions, but he did not expand the reach of his legal activities. Although he now lived in Washington, for instance, he never argued a case before the United States Supreme Court. (A colleague suggested to President Monroe in 1823 that Van Buren be appointed to that body—but more for political reasons than because of his eminence as a lawyer.) More to the point, he began to scale back his practice significantly from 1824 on as his widening political activities more and more filled up his time. An era in his life was drawing to a close. He had acquired enough money from his long and successful legal career so that he and his family could live quite comfortably without his further involvement in the courtroom. He had added to his legal income, as many others who were similarly situated did, through a number of successful land investments, both in New York and in the western states, and by occasionally lending money—with interest—to colleagues and others in need.

Van Buren changed direction in another way as well. He sold his Albany home in 1827 and primarily resided in Washington over the next fifteen years as he held one federal office after another. When he returned to New York for political and family reasons, he stayed with friends, in hotels, or at various resorts in the state, such as Saratoga. He continued to own land in his home state including some in his boyhood home, Kinderhook. But for now, in his forties, he had clearly moved on.

ON THE NATIONAL STAGE

Once comfortably settled in the Senate, Van Buren pursued two political courses: the first, as an active legislator, and, the second, in his familiar role as a party activist and organization builder. From the outset, given his reputation and because he came from one of the most important states, he played a significant role in Senate matters in both its committee rooms and on the floor of the chamber itself. He served on the body's Finance Committee, and chaired its Judiciary Committee from his first days in Washington. In the latter role, he was involved in the reorganization of the federal judiciary, an important initiative that established new circuit courts in the rapidly growing (and legally contentious) western states. He also pushed a number of bills, which were not successful, to limit the jurisdiction of the nationalist Supreme Court, led by the altogether too forceful Chief Justice John Marshall, over state laws.

But his interests and concerns went well beyond the legal world. A wide range of critical policy issues were crystallizing at the national level in the 1820s. The severe financial panic of 1819 had raised serious questions about the ability of the nation's economy to progress further without financial assistance from the federal government. Its structural weaknesses had become all too apparent. The result was an intensified debate on an old issue: the extent of national power in economic affairs, particularly the role of the national bank, the federal financing of internal improvements, and most especially in the early 1820s, the tariff. Congress had rechartered the Bank of the United States in 1816 for twenty years and, for the moment, despite a good deal of continued grumbling against it, the issue of its role and constitutionality was quiescent. The tariff and internal improvements issues, on the other hand, were prominently on Congress's table. Van Buren was involved in both matters from his first days in the Senate.

Most Jeffersonians had believed that the tariffs promoted by Secretary of the Treasury Alexander Hamilton in the 1790s were primarily designed to benefit New England manufacturing against the best interests of the nation's much more numerous agricultural community. These tariffs raised the price of many of the consumer goods needed by a majority of Americans. At the same time, the high duties imposed caused serious tensions in our trade relations with other nations. Republicans had usually sought, therefore, to introduce lower duties as basic national policy in place of Federalist protectionism.

Matters had become more complicated after 1815, however, as some agricultural producers, many of whom were good Jeffersonians in their politics, began to seek protection for their products, especially for raw wool and other agriculturally produced goods. A different policy sensibility was emerging among them on the issue. Other Jeffersonians strongly resisted their efforts, opting, instead, to maintain the parties traditional antiprotectionist position. Republicans were clearly no longer of one mind in favor of free trade or of significantly lowering existing duties on all goods.

The federal financing of internal improvements also loomed threateningly as a potentially divisive matter among the heirs of Thomas Jefferson. The building of the Erie Canal was only one of a number of transportation projects planned, or underway, in the early 1820s. There was a great deal of debate about them in Washington, particularly about whether the federal government had the constitutional authority to pay for them. Congress repeatedly considered bills to appropriate federal money for these projects. Here, too, Republican congressmen divided when the bills were voted on. Some of them, responding to pressures from their home states, aggressively promoted widespread federal involvement as necessary and proper. Others, however, following long-standing states rights' attitudes, resisted any substantial federal role as clearly illegitimate. It was no longer apparent where the center of gravity of the Republican coalition was on this matter.

Although these debates were primarily within the Republican Party, New York's new senator saw the issues with his usual mindset as matters that, at their core, divided good Republicans from their Federalist enemies. Van Buren continued to believe that the latter lurked everywhere and that "the old party feeling," as he called it, drove everything on the scene. His commitment to the primacy of state power over national in domestic policy was sharply etched. His definition of the Jeffersonian political sensibility had little room for the kind of nationalizing policies being so aggressively pushed in Washington. To him, the resurgence of these divisive matters in the committee rooms and on the floor of Congress underscored the need to strengthen the states' rights coalition against the many centralists that he found on Capitol Hill. He was particularly unimpressed by the agitation in favor of nationally financed internal improvements. Always suspicious of such "splendid schemes . . . at the expense of the Federal Treasury," Van Buren brought forward several bills to strengthen state power against that of the federal government, arguing on the Senate floor that federal authority did not extend so as "to make these roads and canals, or to grant the money to make them."

At the outset of his Senate service, Van Buren's position on tariff policy was less clear, although he was always reflexibly hostile to the protection that had been extended to New England's manufacturing interests by previous administrations. Such narrow protection served, as he saw it, neither national nor New York's interests. But he also recognized the increasing political complexity of the issue in the 1820s as many different interests sought protection, now including among them some good Jeffersonians. He searched, therefore, for a legislative position on the matter that he hoped would satisfy those contending elements who usually were his political allies in the continuing battle against Federalism.

MOVING TOWARD A NATIONAL STATES' RIGHTS PARTY, 1821–1825

Van Buren's legislative interests were constantly intertwined with his other major activity in the 1820s, his determination to forge a permanent, unified, and well-organized Republican Party, able to defend the country from the ever-present threat of Federalism. When he arrived in Washington he was no happier about the condition of the Jeffersonians on the national scene than he had been about the political chaos he had previously faced in New York. Despite the efforts of some of their leaders he believed that in Congress, and throughout the nation as well, the Republicans, reflecting a widespread indifference among many of them as to what was at stake, and their lack of reality about the political scene, were confused, highly factionalized, and undisciplined in their actions. To Van Buren, the Jeffersonian movement had fallen on very hard times and, he believed, had to be rebuilt.

The new senator from New York focused much of his energies, therefore, in trying to clear away the factional rubble and to substitute, instead, a clear-cut, anti-Federalist in tone, well-organized Republican coalition. This required, he argued, a different perspective about their behavior than so many of his national Republican colleagues were used to, or practiced. Jeffersonians, he repeatedly emphasized, had to accept the institutions of management, and the commitment to discipline, that he and his Regency associates had originally developed in New York. They had to, in his words, "sacrifice personal preferences to . . . [party] harmony."

His commitment to rebuilding his party as he believed it should be was, at first, not easily achieved. There were many potential allies on the scene but the various factions were not always prepared to practice politics on Van Buren's terms. Many Republican leaders were quite satisfied with the traditional modes of elite maneuvering and bargaining for advantage and the protection of personal and local interests ahead of any larger scale outlooks and commitments. As in New York, they continued to intrigue together, or against one another, moving back and forth as local and personal, not national party, needs dictated. Obviously, there was little discipline among them.

Furthermore, Van Buren believed that his plans were needlessly being complicated by President James Monroe's policy calling for reconciliation between Federalists and Republicans. The president's strongly articulated nonpartisan approach to governing horrified the senator from New York. Early on he tangled with the administration over the latter's naming of a Federalist to be the United States postmaster at Albany. He thought that the president was naive about Federalist ambitions, and was furious that Monroe ignored the harm that such appointments would do to the Republican cause.

Rebuffed by the president when he complained, Van Buren saw the episode as an example of Monroe's extraordinarily wrongheaded understanding of the nation's political scene. Reacting to his frustration, the Regency's bellwether newspaper, the Albany *Argus*, struck out against any belief that it was possible for there to be "the amalgamation of all parties," as the president seemed to desire. Its editor, Edwin Croswell, warned, once again, that "from the first organization of the government, this country has been divided into two great parties." And it would always be so. Too much was at stake—too much separated them from each other. There could never be an "era of good feelings."

"THE PLANTERS OF THE SOUTH . . ."

From his first days in Washington, Van Buren began to reach out to Republican leaders in various states, to establish contacts and make friendships on behalf of his efforts to develop a national organization. He exchanged ideas and plans with, among others, the members of the Concord Regency in New Hampshire, the Virginia congressmen, Andrew Stevenson and John Randolph of Roanoke, and John Forsyth of Georgia. Most critically, Van Buren solidified his close friendship with Thomas Ritchie, editor of Virginia's leading Republican newspaper, the *Richmond Enquirer,* and leader of that state's dominant Republican faction, the Richmond Junto.

These efforts brought him into contact with the divided, often confusing world of Southern oppositionist politics, a world that would constantly affect his plans and hopes, then, and thereafter, as long as he remained active in public affairs. From the first, Van Buren's relations with Southern Republicans were complicated, often tense, and always brittle. He got along with many of them, including the fiercely independent Randolph. But some Southerners, unlike Randolph, Ritchie, Stevenson, and Forsyth, would have none of his approaches and blandishments. They deeply distrusted him as a Northerner, for his overt ambition, and for his championing of partisan discipline and organization. As a result he did not always find his way among them to be as easy as he hoped it would be.

As early as the beginning of the 1820s, problems loomed for him along his southern boundary, the most prominent being the recent intense heightening of sectional sensitivities in the slave states. Many prominent Southerners had been extremely disturbed by the Missouri crisis that preoccupied Congress from 1819 to 1821 and that Van Buren had watched from the state level. While

Northerners and Southerners barked at each other over the admission of another slave state, he believed that the raising of the issue in that form was a Federalist ploy. Downplaying the humanitarian impulses present among the opponents of Missouri's admission, he argued that the "moving springs" of the agitation, "were" as he put it in his autobiography, "rather political than philanthropical." Republicans should not allow themselves to be sucked in by the Federalist strategm and become sectionally divided over the issue. Unfortunately, as he saw it, they had been for a time.

Even after Congress apparently settled the crisis in 1821, fallout from it continued. Tensions between Northern and Southern congressmen remained and challenged the unity of the Republican cause. Van Buren was quite aware of these fissures and was equally determined that they be subordinated to the larger issues that beset them all regardless of section. Unfortunately for his plans, he continued to encounter resistance. No matter how committed he was to overthrowing anti–states' rights forces, men such as Secretary of War John C. Calhoun, and his followers in many of the Southern states, never bought Van Buren's leadership ambitions or his argument for a disciplined partisan coalition. Their immersion in classical Republican values, with their antiparty bias, and the Calhounites great anxiety about the need to protect slave society from outside threats, made them highly suspicious of the kind of alliances Van Buren sought to forge and the specific elements necessary to achieve them. They trusted few outside their own ranks and resisted submission to any discipline imposed by people other than themselves.

At first, Van Buren maintained cordial relations with the politically potent Calhoun. By the early 1820s, the South Carolinian had shed his earlier nationalizing and protectionist proclivities in favor of a powerful states rights' position similar to Van Buren's, interlaced with his growing and unyielding defense of Southern rights against the section's many perceived enemies. But he did not, at first, draw politically closer to Van Buren. The latter kept trying to win him over despite the obstacles. Cooperation with Calhoun remained an important part of his national party-building efforts.

BETWEEN STATE AND NATION

Despite his focus on national affairs throughout the 1820s, Van Buren never ignored the New York State political scene—nor could he given his broader intentions. After moving to Washington Van Buren remained involved in state politics primarily through the able lieutenants that he had left behind, Marcy, Wright, Butler, Croswell, and a rising star among them, Azariah Flagg, a newspaper editor and soon to be state official. He remained in constant contact with them, listening to their reports, hearing their problems, offering suggestions, and when necessary, quietly giving orders.

Every day was a busy one politically for each of them because issues affecting Van Buren's national plans bubbled up constantly in his home state. In 1824, for example, a renewed populist movement, largely embodied in the People's Party, made popular mobilization and antielitism a large part of its fervent rhetoric and campaign techniques in the Empire State. The party crusaded against the political dominance of party leaders, activists, and legislators. Its members focused their opposition particularly on the state legislature having the power to allot New York's electoral votes in the presidential election rather than leaving the choice up to the decision of the people. The ever troublesome DeWitt Clinton joined with them by criticizing the Regency's use of the legislative caucus to nominate candidates for offices in the state as just another form of elitist control of politics. The latter found themselves thrown on the defensive against these populist currents and suffered severely in the state elections of 1824. Clinton was smashingly reelected governor with the support of the People's Party, while, at the same time, many Bucktails lost their races for the state legislature.

It was a stunning defeat for Van Buren and his colleagues. For the moment they had lost political control of New York State. The lesson that they drew from that overturn was clear. Populism was on the march politically. It was not ephemeral and could not be constrained. As at the time of the state Constitutional Convention three years before, the Regency, and especially Senator Van Buren as their leader, had to pay close attention to these democratic yearnings and come to terms with them in some fashion, if possible. The

Van Buren group had not been as attentive to these yearnings as they needed to be. It was time to do so. Van Buren always believed that he could find the means to accomplish that as he thought he had done in the state Constitutional Convention.

In the 1824 presidential election itself Van Buren did not, at first, have a particular candidate in mind to succeed Monroe. His closest associates were divided among the four or five possibilities present, most of whom were members of Monroe's cabinet. Because he was so committed to resisting the powerful nationalizing visions of Secretary of State John Quincy Adams, and House Speaker Henry Clay, Van Buren finally decided to support Secretary of the Treasury William Henry Crawford of Georgia, recognized as a champion of the primacy of state power over federal, as the best counterweight to the nationalists.

As the first step in the campaign, he helped maneuver Crawford's "official" nomination by his party's congressional caucus, where all of the party's congressmen were summoned to the Capitol to meet, consult with one another, and decide on the Republican candidate, as that body had done for some time in the past. Van Buren continued to believe that this legislative caucus was essential, despite the current criticisms of it. Without it, no mechanism existed to discuss, and then submerge, internal party differences, and to bring all of them together on behalf of the larger cause.

But he then found himself outmaneuvered, still on the wrong side of the democratic surge. During the campaign populist speakers and editors assailed Van Buren as the elitist leader of "the caucus party," that "wonderful piece of imposture," as one skeptic called it. In the political atmosphere of the day that was a damning indictment, the charge suggesting how out of step he was with the democratic and antiauthority currents that were loose in so many places in America. The forceful suggestion that the congressional caucus had lost its legitimacy, that the people should nominate their own candidates, the attacks on the caucus that followed, and the resulting range of nominations outside of it made by popular political gatherings and out of control state legislatures, created a very crowded presidential field. To Van Buren's horror, the opposition to

Adams, the most centralizing of the presidential candidates, was divided among too many other aspirants.

As he feared, 1824 proved to be no better for him at the national level than the New York State results had been. Despite reservations and setbacks, he had persevered, and energetically worked, as always, to overcome the difficulties he faced. While in Washington, and after his return to New York when Congress adjourned in late May, he pulled out all of the stops on behalf of Crawford. But his efforts were unavailing. First, his candidate fell seriously ill, thus weakening his appeal. More important, Van Buren found himself once again outmaneuvered, and then defeated. In New York, De-Witt Clinton strongly supported Adams, while a new opponent, the young newspaper editor, Thurlow Weed, assiduously mobilized the democratic currents on behalf of the secretary of state. Together, they beat out the Regency for the state's Electoral College votes. When the election went into the federal House of Representatives for decision (no candidate having received an Electoral College majority), the more successful machinations of the national Republican leaders, Daniel Webster and Clay, on behalf of Adams, added to Van Buren's woes. They won New York's vote, which provided Adams's winning margin, despite his careful, and he thought successful, arrangements beforehand to prevent that outcome.

IN THE AFTERMATH OF THE ELECTION, therefore, Van Buren had a great deal of rethinking and reorganizing to do. The presidential contest had confirmed the disordered condition of those he considered the true heirs of Thomas Jefferson. The states' rights wing of the Republican Party, beset by factionalism, lacked the will to come together and remained without clear and acceptable mechanisms of discipline and direction. The election had also again suggested how much the populist temper, manifested in New York and elsewhere, posed a potent threat to his political planning unless it could be effectively managed by himself and his associates. Finally, Clinton's continuing power in New York, and his repeated successful challenges to the Albany Regency, blocked Van Buren from gaining the upper hand in the state in a manner that would promote the cause and policies he espoused. There was much to do.

THE ASSAULT ON ADAMS
AND THE ELECTION OF 1828

The two sides of Van Buren's political activities on the national stage in the 1820s came together during the tumultuous administration of John Quincy Adams. Once the new president was settled in the White House in early 1825, Van Buren became the main legislative strategist among those Republicans working to thwart his policies. The issues that the president vigorously pushed forward, strongly articulated in his first annual message, stressed the national road to development, that is, the use of the power and resources of the federal government to develop the American economy. To Adams, American greatness, the nation's liberty, and the force of national power, all went together. He firmly rejected the old Jeffersonian truism that the nation's liberty was always endangered by the exercise of national authority except in the most limited spheres of public policy.

Adams's program directly and negatively resonated across the board to the states' rights Republicans, sharply echoing outside the economic realm as well as within it, since it involved the traditional issue of the reach of central authority over the states and individual citizens. Van Buren never let up on articulating those connections and their consequences. To him, the Adams men were clearly Federalists, and he said so repeatedly. Whatever the claims of the administration that they were not, that their notions and commitments derived from Republican sources, Van Buren was having none of it. To him, Adams had come into office "with views of the Constitution as latitudinarian [i.e., Federalist] as were those of Hamilton." In the president's pronouncements and policies, "not one of the followers of the old Republican faith," he afterwards wrote, "no intelligent friend of the reserved rights of the states could fail to see . . . the most ultra latitudinarian doctrines."

Van Buren quickly moved to counter these dangers. There was plenty of opposition to the administration including from Calhoun and his allies, among the angry supporters of Tennessee's Andrew Jackson, who felt their very popular candidate had been cheated of victory in 1824, and from those who looked to Van Buren as the leader of the Republicans. For different, if related, reasons, the president horrified all of them. The problem was that there was not, as yet, unity, nor a single-minded commitment among them to work together. Van Buren moved to rectify the situation. He worked successfully to find common cause among the opposition factions, first in Congress, and then in the electoral arena beyond.

To him the presidential election of 1828 was going to be very different from 1824 and he succeeded in making it so. This time the anti-Adams blocs did become united behind a clear notion of why they opposed the aggressively determined president, and they found, in Andrew Jackson, a candidate able to attract support from the populist factions forcing their way on to the political scene. Of course, success was never simple or easy to come by. Van Buren's efforts began in Congress at its first meeting in 1825 and proceeded from there. After some hesitation and difficulties, Van Buren's states' rights coalition usually was able to control the national legislature and strongly challenge the president on almost every move he made. They proved to be, in Adams's phrase, "as bitter as wormwood in their opposition" to his nationalizing initiatives.

The New York senator introduced congressional resolutions against a range of Adams's proposals including the federal financing of internal improvements, opposed Adams's promotion of United States involvement in an inter-American conference on hemispheric issues—the so-called Panama mission—and did everything else that he could to draw the line against the president and his administration's unacceptable policies and to set the stage for its overthrow in the next election. The Van Buren–led forces successfully hamstrung the president by either not passing or not funding, many of his initiatives. And they went out of their way to defeat his appointments to office, including a Supreme Court nomination.

All of this legislative activity was prelude in Van Buren's eyes. The presidential election of 1828 would be the real testing ground of the future of the Republic and of the power and unity of the Democratic Republicans. In the electoral arena Van Buren supplied much of the planning and energy that created the pro–Andrew Jackson coalition of 1828 from the raw material present. That coalition would encompass the states' rights Republicans such as Van

Buren, who had supported the now seriously ailing Crawford, allied with Jackson's western supporters whose ideological commitments were less clear-cut, and the Calhounites, always very antagonistic to anything that seemed to threaten their particular society of slavery and international trade in cotton, that is, as they saw it, almost everything they encountered from the nationalist President Adams.

VAN BUREN HAD NOT ORIGINALLY FAVORED JACKSON'S candidacy even after the debacle behind Crawford in 1824, and despite the force of the heroic Tennessean's clear popularity in many parts of the Union. He had briefly known Jackson in the Senate in the early 1820s and harbored a great deal of skepticism about his seriousness and capabilities from then on. In addition, states' rights Republicans, in general, were suspicious of the Tennessean for his pro-tariff and internal improvements votes while a senator. But, with that mixture of pragmatism and commitment that always defined him, Van Buren realized that they had to change their minds. There was no one else. (Calhoun had become vice president in 1824 and the Van Burenites supported him for reelection to that office, removing him, for the moment, from presidential consideration.) Jackson was certainly anti-Adams if not quite the committed states' righter that Van Buren and his colleagues hoped for. But they convinced themselves that he had changed and moved a long way toward them since his earlier flirtation with "consolidationism."

Van Buren came out in favor of Old Hickory in 1826, then worked energetically to effect unity behind the Tennessee leader despite the continuing hostility to Jackson among some of his allies. He recognized that in the building of broad-based parties, as against leading smaller factions at the national level, the essence of American politics had to be, as it was in New York, constant negotiation, frequent compromise, and occasional evasion of those matters that had the potential to be destructively polarizing, in order to nudge things along. (From this tendency, rooted in his political realism and subtlety, was to come, once again, the old charge by his enemies, this time on the national level, that he practiced a devious policy of "non-commitalism" as a political leader. In their view he never revealed where he really stood, or where he was going.)

Van Buren's behavior in the run-up to the election of 1828 belied that characterization of him. He made compromises and played some matters close to the vest. But there was no question that the coalition he was building differed from the incumbent president both in its members' general outlook and in the specific policies that they favored—and he and his allies aired these differences publicly, loudly, and frequently.

Van Buren was the recognized political manager of the emerging coalition. He was very good at finding and using rallying cries, first, assailing what others had called "the corrupt bargain" between Adams and Henry Clay that had won Adams a majority in the House of Representatives, and the presidency, in 1825, despite his minority popular vote, and then presenting Jackson as the major embodiment of the new democratic currents at work in America. Jackson believed that he spoke for the people, that they had wanted him for president in 1824, and that they had been denied their wish by the manipulative wiles of antidemocratic forces in Congress. The Democratic-Republican campaign of 1828 made much of that deprivation as well as of, finally, the dangers posed by what had happened to traditional Republican policy commitments under President Adams.

THROUGHOUT 1827, VAN BUREN traveled widely in furtherance of his plans. He first went south, following a leadership strategy for the upcoming contest. At each stop on his southern travels he contacted local notables, shoring up support among them for Jackson, trying to win over the uncertain among them to the cause, and, most of all, prodding the local leaders such as Ritchie to build up their organizations and prepare to mobilize the voters for the upcoming contest that would decide so much. Despite the resistance that he encountered, Van Buren had managed a great deal of headway in the 1820s in overcoming some of the Southerners' suspicions. Irrespective of the demand by some that they should be, sectional lines were not, as yet, all that hardened in America. While there always remained a sense of difference among different regional values and outlooks, Van Buren's argument that there were more important, cross-sectional national issues that had to be addressed, instead of continuing to wallow in regional identity politics, received a sympathetic hearing from many Southern politicians, both his own already committed colleagues there and from many others in the region as well.

His famous letter to Virginia's Ritchie, written in 1827 when he was trying to forge the alliance behind Jackson, summed up his notion of what was politically necessary and the role of sectional blocs in the coalition that he was forging. Van Buren's main theme was familiar, that whatever differences and sensitivities might exist along sectional lines among the groups that he was trying to work with, their common Republican commitments united them no matter where they resided. Political distinctions in the United States were based on the traditional divide between the Federalist and Republican visions of society and government power. That divide, he underscored, was national, not sectional. As such, the heirs of Jefferson had to reinvigorate the famous intersectional coalition of "the planters of the South and the plain republicans of the north" that had brought them victory in 1800 and since. These groups had a natural affinity and the same enemies—in all sections of the country.

Some observers then, and a number of historians since, argue that in this letter, and in many of his other party-building activities from 1821 onward, Van Buren was too willing to subvert Northern interests to the demands of the slave states in his efforts to maintain a North-South Republican alliance. As one historian has written, "the Little Magician of American politics . . . courted successfully the vested interests of the slavery capitalists." Or, to put it bluntly, it is suggested that from the first he sold out something important in order to win an election, or many of them.

Despite such historiographic negativism, however, the truth is, once more, more complicated. An acute awareness (and wariness) of sectional sensitivities such as Van Buren manifested in the 1820s, is not the same thing as commitment to a particular sectionalist position or accepting a particular sectional set of values in their entirety. Van Buren never did either of these. He was not proslavery. Nor was he an antislavery activist as were a number of New York politicians even at this early date. He demonstrated here, as he often did, much circumspection when confronted by a new, contentious, issue, feeling his way and not leading from the front—all in the interest of following the main matter: unity in order to defeat John Quincy Adams.

VAN BUREN WANTED TO CALL a Democratic-Republican national convention to bring the various groups together and sharpen the differences between themselves and Adams. Their aims there would be the familiar ones: the substitution of *"party principles* for personal preferences." No convention was held in 1828, but the desired coming together occurred anyway as Van Buren hoped it would, as the different Republican groups fell into line behind Old Hickory. The Jacksonian Democrats of 1828 were now the identifiable successors to the various Republican factions of four years before, and the clear antagonists of the president as he sought re-election and vindication of his policies.

VAN BUREN ALWAYS KEPT A CLOSE watch on his home state as his plans evolved. In the fall of 1827 Regency newspapers in New York State came out in favor of Jackson and the mobilization of the rest of the energies of their organization followed. Still, New York's politics remained difficult as some Republicans continued to resist the calls for harmony and the discipline that their party leader preached so energetically. Through all of this also loomed the continued and very real presence of DeWitt Clinton, a longtime strong supporter of Jackson, not a late convert to him as was Van Buren. If Jackson won the presidency, which of them would be his choice for leader in New York State? It was a worrisome matter to Van Buren, both personally and ideologically.

Fortunately for his peace of mind—and ambitions—his powerful nemesis suddenly left the scene. Clinton unexpectedly died in early 1828, not yet sixty years old, clearing away the high political roadblock that he had always been to his longtime antagonist. Van Buren eulogized him gracefully in public for his long service to New York State, while silently giving thanks that a seemingly perpetual, and always draining, major political problem was, at last, gone from his life forever.

Finally, as the presidential campaign got underway Van Buren remained in the vanguard of the necessary organizational and other activities to advance the cause, working behind the scenes, as always; calling caucuses to legitimize their activities and speaking on the floor of the Senate against Adams as he deemed it necessary. He and his allies introduced many of the campaign practices that he had developed in New York during the preceding decade. Political committees, including a a central one based in Washington to coordinate activities in the states and nationally, were set up, followed by the establishment of campaign newspapers and the holding of rallies and other popular mobilizing practices. All of these were much more extensive than they had ever been before (although not yet as widespread as they would become). He and Calhoun agreed to designate the *United States Telegraph*, edited by a Calhoun supporter, Duff Green, and published in Washington, as their main national voice, with a range of state-level Republican newspapers picking up signals from it, spreading the Jacksonian word, and extolling the virtues of unity and discipline on behalf of the larger cause.

A NUMBER OF DIVISIVE ISSUES complicated the pursuit of victory in 1827 and 1828. In particular, the tariff continued to bedevil Van Buren and his coalition-building efforts. In 1827 he had supported in the Senate the raising of some rates on raw wool to benefit Northern sheep raisers and in defiance of Southern sensitivities on the matter. However moderate the rates were, they provoked great anger and led to a further confrontation in the spring of the following year when Congress considered yet another tariff bill.

Van Buren's handling of what one historian has labeled the "curious piece of legislation" that became the tariff of 1828 reflected his need to consider the many forces that he was trying to combine and control and the hope that he had found a way to bring them together on this issue. He argued that they had to compromise. There was too much diversity among them, too many different interests involved, for the issue to be smoothly settled in one direction—either full-scale protection at the levels demanded, or free trade.

The result that he offered sought a middle way. Despite claims to the contrary by his enemies, there was coherence to what he shepherded through Congress, a bill whose provisions fell somewhere between the kinds of protection, largely for manufacturing enterprises, favored by Adams's national Republicans, on the one hand, and the free trade longings of the Calhounites and many Northern merchants, on the other.

Despite its roots in Van Buren's strategy, the bill drew support from some New Englanders. More critically, it also drew expressions of abomination from many Southerners. Van Buren expected that. But, as he successfully moved to shore up support in the western and Mid-Atlantic states by agreeing to their moderate duty demands, he believed that the Southern opponents of Adams would remain loyal to Jackson despite their anger toward any increase in tariff rates. They would not support Adams. They had no place else to go but to Jackson.

THERE WERE MATTERS THAT VAN BUREN could not always finesse. The growing and very intense Anti-Masonic agitation in western New York, parts of New England, Pennsylvania, and elsewhere, and its effective politicalization behind the national Republican state leaders, Thurlow Weed and William Seward, among others, posed a significant threat to ensuring that New York and other states would be in the Jackson column. The Anti-Masonic explosion, which had a particular target, but which also included a range of tensions, hatreds, and paranoid fears about the direction of American society, was just the kind of popular uprising that Van Buren hated. It was rash, rabid, and uncontrollable. But it was widespread and very popular in certain places, and, therefore, electorally important. It successfully energized many people against long-established practices and conditions that were allegedly elitist and antidemocratic and, therefore, no longer tolerable.

Weed and Seward did their work well. New York's Anti-Masons supported Adams in 1828 even though many of the president's national Republican supporters were themselves Masons. All that the Jacksonians could offer in rebuttal to that commitment to Adams was their claim that they, not the national Republicans, represented the true spirit of democratization abroad in the nation, a claim that was not easy to sell to the hostile Anti-Masons. Van Buren could only hope that their numbers would be less and their influence more limited, particularly in the electorally critical Empire State, than the hoopla that they were making in New York's western counties suggested.

THE FINAL ELEMENT IN ALL OF THIS PLANNING for national victory was Van Buren's agreement to run for governor of his home state since Regency leaders argued that his presence on the ticket would significantly bolster their party's chances there. They believed that, despite the anger of his enemies toward him, he was quite popular in many parts of the state and represented the interests of many New Yorkers. He accepted their call, with some reluctance at first, but, not unexpectedly, then followed the route of political duty. When the Senate adjourned in May 1828, he returned to the state to carry the Jacksonian banner in the upcoming election on behalf, as he saw it—and publicly claimed—of states' rights, the rule of the people, and the decisive overthrow of Federalism.

In all of this effort he and his associates were successful. After a bitter campaign, Jackson handily won the presidency and Van Buren was easily elected governor of New York. The presidential and congressional elections were very close in the Empire State, however. Jackson's majority was about 8,000 votes there, out of 270,000 cast. He won twenty of the state's thirty-six electoral votes (which were chosen in individual congressional districts in 1828). While Van Buren won the governorship by a substantial margin, his colleague and lieutenant, Silas Wright, was reelected to Congress by a majority of only 45 votes in his home district along the Canadian border. Clearly more work needed to be done on behalf of the Democratic-Republican coalition.

POLITICS AND CONVICTION

Van Buren moved through the political wars of the 1820s with his usual dexterity and a clear purpose. His political intelligence and tactical nimbleness were as noticed by observers on the national scene as they had been in New York a decade before. His reputation as a political magician continued to grow, not always with a positive twist to it. His many enemies among the Anti-Masons, the national Republicans, and the always suspicious Southerners were not impressed with his emergence into national prominence and authority.

Their resistance to him was almost always couched in personal terms. His enemies unimaginatively repeated the familiar charges against him of Machiavellian intrigue and lack of principle, so loudly and relentlessly proclaimed against him earlier throughout his state career. He was, to them, nothing but "a cunning, managing man." When he and DeWitt Clinton came together in 1827 on behalf of Jackson's election, one friend of Henry Clay referred to it as "open prostitution." To another opponent, he was "as slippery as an eel," always looking "for place and preferment." In one of their many unfriendly moments before 1827, Clinton referred to him as "that prince of villains," at another time, as "a scoundrel of the first magnitude."

As already noted, there is no question that Van Buren was ambitious and determined to advance himself as he could. His whole life indicated that. But his behavior remained consistent. His managerial and, yes, manipulative talents were primarily used to achieve purposes beyond himself, embodied in his sustained devotion to certain values and principles. As he had in New York State, he clearly demonstrated, when he came onto the national scene, his fear of too much central government authority, a perspective intensified in Washington where he and his allies continued to hear the nationalist Hamiltonian echoes they so greatly feared.

In their resistance to all that the new Federalists were pushing, Van Buren and his allies came to represent, at the national level, an alternative vision of their society and its future direction, one embodying a very traditional core drawn from the preindustrial, highly localist, agrarian culture of the South and much of the middle states, as well as from urban artisan values opposed to what they saw as the rapacious power of the industrial and commercial classes. It was a vision that the Van Buren Republicans wanted to preserve and enhance as the singular embodiment of the nation and its virtues. That vision was under attack from its powerful enemies in the Federalist camp of John Quincy Adams and Henry Clay and had to be aggressively defended. In short, in their view, there was a clear and important economic, social, and political agenda in the 1820s, and a great deal for Americans to fight about, or guard against. Van Buren and his allies took up arms in response.

As to his own avowal, or nonavowal, of particular positions, one contemporary, not always friendly, said of Van Buren's alleged non-committalism on important issues that "he was wary in committing himself upon any quest, until the time came for action, and when that moment arrived, he was as prompt and decided as Napoleon himself." To another Van Buren contemporary, the political historian James Jenkins, this added up to "the prudential foresight with which . . . [the Republican leader] guarded against all possible contingencies." Such comments are, I suggest, a fair evaluation of the man at the moment of his first great national electoral triumph.

Van Buren believed—and he calculated. He was adept at maneuver, management, and compromise when necessary. He saw nothing wrong in such qualities or techniques because they were necessary in a pluralist nation of many different conflicting interests all set in a foundation of a deep ideological divide and widening popular involvement. He and his colleagues lived in two worlds, the traditional and, most comfortable to them, elite centers of political bargaining, agenda-setting among different groups, officeholding and electoral management, and, at the same time, in a new world, "the local and particularistic universe of the electorate."

The importance of the latter continued to grow throughout the 1820s and whatever Van Buren's caution about the impact of the unleashing of populist energies in politics, he and his colleagues were learning how to deal with the democratic surge under way. They had to. What they had come to recognize as the primary political lesson of the current day was that the two political worlds— of management, and of democratic expression—were not separate spheres. Rather, they were always intertwined and constantly interacting with one another, even though they dealt with different political elements, and their basic essences called for quite different talents. If the Van Buren–led party leadership carried on successfully in dealing with that popular element, then the emerging Jacksonian Democratic coalition would not be just another faction in a sea of them, but something much greater and less ephemeral: a permanent national force, organized and acting on behalf of the people through the realization of the clearly understood, strongly stated, and always relevant principles inherited from the Jeffersonian Republicans of an earlier generation.

Chapter Four

─────────○─────────

The Seats of the Mighty,
1828–1832

IN THE WORDS OF THE HISTORIAN William Freehling, Andrew Jackson, the seventh president of the United States, "marched on Washington" in 1829 filled with a reformer's zeal to cleanse the nation's stables of what he and his colleagues saw as their odious Federalist encrustations, thus restoring republican liberty to the American people. To do this, he brought Martin Van Buren with him. The "pudgy, pasty . . . politician" from New York (he had gained much weight and lost much hair in middle age) served only forty-three days as governor of his home state before resigning to accept Jackson's offer to be secretary of state in the new administration. His appointment was not unexpected. The new president, recognizing the New Yorker's useful talents and political power, and grateful for the critical services that he had rendered in the 1828 election, had made it clear that he wanted him to join his administration as soon as possible. Van Buren was certainly willing to do so.

The newly elected governor of New York did not, therefore, remain long enough in Albany to make much of an imprint on state affairs. He did champion a banking law that created a state safety fund, a financial reserve from which banks could draw at moments of economic difficulty. It was an original idea that provided opportunities to safeguard New York's continued development without creating a central bank to regulate and direct monetary affairs, a notion that was anathema to the state's Democratic-Republicans. Beyond that, there was little time for Van Buren to accomplish anything else.

The new secretary of state returned to the nation's capital in late March, leaving the fortunes of the state in what he believed were the good hands of his Regency lieutenants. He was accompanied by his oldest son, Abraham, recently graduated from the United States Military Academy at West Point, who would serve as his father's secretary. Martin Junior also came down to live with his father while John, who had just graduated from Yale and was living in New York City, and Smith, still in school in Massachusets, visited as often as they could. At first, the Van Burens settled, as Martin Senior, had before, in one of the Pennsylvania Avenue boardinghouses that catered to officeholders. But he soon bought a house on Lafayette Square across from the White House, one recently vacated by Henry Clay and his family. The Van Burens lived there until the head of the family departed for England in 1831.

EARLY JACKSONIANISM

The secretary of state quickly found out how much there was to do. Andrew Jackson's two terms were going to be anything but a placid time politically in the United States—again confirming Van Buren's notions about the inevitability of constant political warfare. A great deal of heat had been engendered in the run up to and during the election campaign. The national Republicans had lost the presidential election but they remained a powerful force in Congress. Everything that Jackson and his lieutenants did after 1829, therefore, fueled intense resistance from them and ongoing confrontation and conflict while contributing, as well, to the clarification of the issues at stake.

VAN BUREN WAS, INEVITABLY, CLOSELY INVOLVED in the public contentiousness. During Jackson's first administration he was once again engaged in the two very different tasks he had undertaken while in the Senate. He continued as party builder and partisan leader while carrying on, as well, his official duties as secretary of state. He had brought the Republican Party far in the 1820s. But it was not yet the fully formed partisan organization that he hoped it would become. While not as ramshackle a collection of disparate groups as their opponents claimed they were, the president's allies hardly constituted a monolithic ideological body with a clear perspective and policy agenda when they entered office in 1829. Old Hickory had won the presidency at the head of a coalition united largely by its members' opposition to John Quincy Adams. In office the fissures in the Jacksonian alliance became evident. Many of those who had come into office with him were not there to promote the president and his policies, but, rather, primarily to pursue their own interests and ideas.

As for Van Buren, despite his articulation of the movement as committed to states' rights Jeffersonianism, that is, the "old party feelings," he led only one portion of the whole. At the same time his commitment to orderly managerialism and self-sacrificing discipline in political affairs remained widely resisted among his putative allies. The different Republican groups still did not easily accept the necessity of the type of unyielding commitment and individual subordination to a larger entity that his vision of a national party demanded.

As a result of these differences among the people now in power, the political situation in Washington had an unsettled quality to it in 1829. Few of the various interests and regional groups jostling with each other for favor were satisfied by Jackson's early appointments to office, or many of his other decisions. Van Buren heard a great many complaints about the president's initial moves, and the uncertain nature of affairs, from his Republican friends in various stops on his way down to the capital from Albany, complaints that did not let up after he arrived in Washington.

The new secretary of state did not himself start out as particularly close to the president. When he first entered the White House Jackson was surrounded by the Tennessee colleagues with whom he had been working for a long time, men such as William B. Lewis and John Eaton. They were intensely loyal to him, supporters with whom he felt comfortable and who, while avid seekers of power themselves, did not have the reputation for political sharp practices that was associated with Van Buren, practices that Jackson had long publicly deprecated despite his apparently positive feelings toward his new colleague from New York.

Jackson and Van Buren particularly differed at the outset over the president's naming of a New Yorker, Samuel Swartwout, whom Van Buren strongly distrusted, to the important patronage plum of Collector of the Port of New York. Jackson had also already named ministers to England and France without seeking his secretary of state's advice. Van Buren protested, but lost on the Swartwout matter before he came to Washington. He was able to change the ministerial appointments once he arrived on the scene and convinced the president to withdraw the nominations. Still, none of this indicated an auspicious beginning to their relationship.

These initial differences, the apparent distance between them, and the effect of what one historian has referred to as the "byzantine intrigue" of the early Jackson presidency, did not last very long nor interfere with Van Buren's emergence into Jackson's favor. Old Hickory was quite cordial toward his new secretary of state from the first and Van Buren skillfully developed their relationship into one where he became the most trusted of the president's counselors. It began on the night that Van Buren arrived in Washington in late March. Going over to the White House he found a quite friendly Jackson happy to see him. The president seemed more open and accommodating than he had been up until then in their correspondence and anxious to discuss pending matters with his secretary of state.

That first meeting began the long and fruitful relationship between the two very different men that was to advance American political life far beyond what it was when they began their friendship. In the first two years of the administration Van Buren and Jackson saw a great deal of each other, usually at the president's behest. Among other encounters, they took daily horseback rides together where they discussed the nature of the administration and during which advice was sought and given. As a result, Van Buren and Old Hickory developed a closeness that has been often been seen as that of mentor and favored acolyte. It certainly became one that redounded to the New Yorker's benefit then and later.

The friendship had much more to it than its personal dimension, as important as that was to both men. Jackson's warmth toward him did not mean that Van Buren dominated the affairs of the administration from his first appearence in Washington. But as their association deepened, the two leaders discovered how much they agreed on policy matters, about the personalities that surrounded them, and about the direction that the government should go. Out of their personal and policy synergy something more ideologically unified ultimately emerged to distinguish, with increasing sharpness, the movement they led.

SECRETARY OF STATE

During these first years of the Jackson administration Van Buren officially spent his time in the State Department, located, in 1829, in a building near the White House at Pennsylvania Avenue and 15th Street. At first glance his activities were not all that numerous. He had responsibility for a quite small-scale operation, similar in size to the, as yet, little developed rest of the federal government. The Washington-based staff of the State Department consisted of a dozen clerks or so, and two messengers, and had charge of less than twenty foreign missions, eight in Europe, seven in Latin America, and four accredited to the Barbary States in North Africa. (There were also several dozen consuls stationed in many parts of the world looking after American interests.) In addition, the department had a number of domestic duties assigned to it, for example, record keeping for the national government, the transcription and publishing of the laws of Congress, and the supervision of the Patent Office.

Whatever the smallness of the enterprise he headed, Van Buren was never idle. He found plenty of matters to deal with in the foreign realm and went immediately to work. He followed two skilled and experienced diplomatists in the office of secretary of state: John Quincy Adams and Henry Clay, both of whom had been negotiating complex trade and boundary issues with Britain and Spain for a decade and more. But he did not particularly suffer from his relative lack of diplomatic experience. In addition to the important matter of appointing ministers to various foreign capitals, he, as he remembered his early days in office, "entered upon a very full examination of the condition of the public business at the different points to which new Ministers were sent, the actual state and past history of unfinished negotiations and the collection of materials for new instructions [to the American ministers abroad]. Upon this work was bestowed between two and three of the most laborious months of my whole life."

In all that occurred, there was never any question about his recognition of the president's primacy of place in shaping what was accomplished in the administration's name. That reality did provoke some wariness in Van Buren at the outset as to the direction that the government would take in foreign affairs. The new president had a reputation for marked contentiousness in diplomatic matters. He had been distinguished throughout his military career on the American frontier by what one historian has labeled his "belligerant nationalism." That reality created much concern in the State Department especially since the president made it clear that he would be closely involved in the working out of American strategy toward the world even as he carried it on through his loyal deputy, the secretary of state.

But it was also became clear fairly quickly that, despite Van Buren's initial apprehension, the president was willing to pursue a less bellicose policy than his reputation suggested in order to expand overseas opportunities for American commerce. In fact, there was little evidence of belligerence in Jackson's attitude toward the world abroad, and much attempt at conciliation in the interest of promoting both advantages for the United States, and peaceful relations, particularly with two long-standing powerful antagonists, Great Britain and France.

Together, the two men enjoyed a number of significant diplomatic triumphs from 1829 onward, each achieved by calm negotiation, and the compromise of outstanding differences. First among these initiatives was the long-standing dispute between the United States and Great Britain because each nation had allowed only limited access to each other's ports in the interest of protecting its own shippers from competition. The particular focus in 1829 was on the West Indies trade. American ships had long been shut out of the British-controlled Caribbean islands. In the previous administration

President Adams had taken a very hard stance against the British even when the latter seemed to indicate to American officials some willingness to resolve the matters in dispute.

Van Buren's tack was different from what had gone before. From the beginning he demonstrated the administration's interest in the opening of trade opportunities and flexibility about the issues dividing the two countries. He began by accepting, for example, some continued limitations on American access that the British insisted on. As a result, negotiations between the two nations moved along fairly rapidly and, in October 1830, the West Indian ports were opened to American merchant ships for the first time since the War of 1812.

Second, there were long-standing tensions between the United States and France to which Van Buren successfully turned his attention and skills. These involved the claims of American citizens against the French government for property losses they had suffered during the Napoleonic wars. The spoliation claims, as they were called, had bedeviled relations between both countries for twenty years. Now Van Buren moved to settle them as soon as possible. Working through the new American minister in Paris, his close political friend, William Cabell Rives of Virginia, the two governments soon forged a satisfactory settlement. A treaty was signed in 1831, although some problems remained in carrying out its provisions, issues that were resolved only after Van Buren had left office.

Third, the administration initiated a number of efforts that were ultimately successful, to increase trade opportunities, and to settle outstanding issues, with other European nations, including Spain and Portugal, and began efforts, as well, to improve U.S. relations with Russia. At the same time, America's continuing interest in the Mediterranean basin led to agreement on a commercial treaty with Turkey, and to the further improvement of the nation's habitually difficult relations with the Barbary States.

American foreign policy also looked across our immediate borders to both the south and the north during Van Buren's tenure in office. To the south, Mexican-American relations had not been very warm for some time, and under John Quincy Adams there had also been tense moments with the other newly liberated republics of Latin America. When Jackson and Van Buren took over in 1829 these tensions began to be eased significantly except in the case of Mexico where Jackson pushed vigorously to make the northern Mexican province of Texas part of the United States—an initiative that the Mexican government firmly resisted, and that, as a result, went nowhere for the moment.

In the north Van Buren worked very hard to resolve the long-standing border dispute over the boundary between the state of Maine and British Canada. Previous treaties, going back to 1783, that had dealt with the matter had been based on faulty maps, a fact that did not deter each side from developing nonnegotiable positions about the territorial claims that they drew from them. Van Buren tried to break through the perennial stalemate by finding a reasonable compromise. His determined efforts advanced matters a certain distance, but the issue, as always, repeatedly revealed the depths of its intractable side and remained unresolved for another decade.

MARTIN VAN BUREN was not a great secretary of state. His brief tenure revealed no overarching vision on his part—no Van Buren Doctrine—about the nation's diplomatic future except the desire to settle long-standing disputes and to foster Jackson's hopes of opening up additional trade opportunities for American commercial enterprise. The best that his close friend, political ally, and future biographer, George Bancroft, could later write about his record was that Van Buren's years in the State Department "were distinguished by his effective industry."

That estimation is not entirely fair. He was not a professional diplomat and his primary interests always lay elsewhere. But Van Buren held the office and acted forcefully, and with some skill, while he was there. It is not possible to determine with precision the exact contributions of either the president or his secretary of state to the formulation and carrying out of the policies undertaken in these years. Still, whatever the balance between the two, Van Buren certainly played a major role. Through all of the trials of foreign policy, the neophyte secretary of state demonstrated a good deal of shrewdness, much common sense, his ingrained political intelligence, and a certain unexpected expertise about international relations. His cautious balancing of the possibilities present in each situation, and his sense of timing about the issues they confronted, were important in shaping what occurred in the years that he led the State Department.

THE PETTINESS OF INTRIGUE

Van Buren could not focus his entire attention on foreign affairs during the years that he was secretary of state, nor was he inclined to do so. As noted, the nation's political arena, with its intense disagreements over policies and people, continued to bubble as vigorously as ever in the early Jackson years. The defeated national Republicans, led by Henry Clay, who was now in the Senate, unrelentingly criticized the new administration for its policies, over the way the president governed, and about who his associates were, particularly sniping at the president's emerging close confidant, the despised party manager, Van Buren.

At the outset, the Jacksonian administration's appointments policy, which placed close friends and loyal supporters in government positions, drew particular fire from the national Republicans. They argued that the appointments were the onset, at the national level, of the partisanly driven "spoils system," which would place the ordinary activities of the government in the hands of men distinguished only by their partisan involvement, men who were inexperienced in affairs of state and likely to be ineffective, all to the nation's detriment. Much of their hostility to the policy was directed against Jackson's secretary of state since such partisanly driven behavior was already associated with Van Buren and could be effectively used, the opposition believed, against him and the president.

The president and his men lashed back. They assailed the opposition's exaggerations and their undemocratic attitudes about who should administer the government. Their patronage policy was necessary, Jacksonians argued, for a number of good reasons. First, the rotation of officeholders was, as Jackson put it, "a leading principle of the republican creed." Government positions should not be confined to only a few long-serving officers but open to a wide range of Americans who could do the job equally well. Moreover, officeholders who remained too long in place were always in danger of being corrupted under the pressure from private interests. Finally, fresh appointments were necessary so that the officers of the government would be true supporters of the administration's policies, men who could be counted on to carry them out as directed to.

But the Adams-Clay people never allowed themselves to be persuaded that Jackson's appointments policy was something more than a partisan ploy to enhance Democratic strength. They kept up their fire unrelentingly. More to the point, their noisy eruption over appointments, and over so many of the other things that came up, clearly indicated that nothing that this administration undertook would escape their assault, and that everything in view would be used to keep the partisan pot briskly boiling.

At the same time, political dissidence did not come only from the opposition. The factionalized nature of the Jacksonian movement continued to provoke intense infighting even after the new administration had settled in. Van Buren remained deeply involved in trying to smooth things over among the contesting groups making up the Democratic-Republican majority. He saw himself, at first, as a conscious balance wheel among the various skirmishing Jacksonians, a position that was not always easy to maintain given the differences and rivalries surrounding the president.

Most critically, Jackson and Van Buren had to deal with the formidable vice president of the United States, John C. Calhoun of South Carolina, still the leader of one of the powerful political factions that had supported Jackson in 1828, and a man who fully expected to be the latter's successor as president. (At the outset it was widely believed that the aged and worn Jackson would serve only one term.) Calhoun had been a prominent national figure since the War of 1812, first in Congress and then as secretary of war during the Monroe administration. By the time that Jackson became president he had become the leading figure among those who were even more skeptical than was Van Buren of extending the reach of national power in any area, and much more concerned than anyone else, to preserve the dominance of state authority in the many questions that raised the question of the appropriate balance between the central government and the states.

At the outset of the administration, Calhoun and his allies believed themselves to be the dominant element among the Jacksonians. Several members of the new cabinet were close to the South Carolina leader and presumably were watching out for his interests within the Jacksonian circle. Furthermore, the editor of the main administration newspaper in the capital, *The United States Telegraph*, was still Duff Green, who remained a close confidant of Calhoun, and an avid promoter of his claims to be Jackson's successor in the White House.

Nevertheless, whatever their apparent political strength, the Calhounites were rarely happy, or confident, about their position. They were particularly suspicious, actually intensely jealous, of the increasing power of, and growing role played by, others inside the Jackson camp. Calhoun's unhappiness increased mightily when he began to believe that the adroitness and skills of the emerging Van Buren group, and especially its leader, might reverse the original order of future preference between the two of them, where such counted—in Jackson's eyes. There was an uncomfortable amount of public speculation from the first about the potential rivalry between Van Buren and the vice president over the presidential succession. Congressman James Buchanan of Pennsylvania was quoted as saying, even before Van Buren arrived in Washington, that "disguise it as we may, the friends of Van Buren and those of Calhoun are becoming very jealous of each other."

VAN BUREN NEEDED NO PRODDING to be on guard about Calhoun. He believed that the South Carolinian was, in ideology, commitment, and probable behavior, not a loyal Jacksonian, would never be one, and would probably do things that would be detrimental to the emergence of the party that he, Van Buren, was hoping to build behind the president. Van Buren and Calhoun had managed to work together to elect Jackson in 1828. But from then on there were serious difficulties between them since it became very clear that, beyond personal ambition, each one's political outlook was at odds with the other's, ideologically and organizationally.

The differences manifested went beyond the principal protagonists at the top of the government. Many of the Southerners who supported Jackson in 1828 remained as restless as ever. The internal dynamics of their section, shaped by the existence of slavery, as well as by economic and regional differences among them, continued to affect them in different ways as Van Buren had discovered from his first days in Washington. He remained close, after 1829, to the group of professional politicans in the region with whom he had worked since 1821, who shared his traditional Jeffersonian states' rights philosophy, and who also accepted the discipline called for by the dictates of the emerging national party system associated with Van Buren. While often sensitive to sectional concerns, these Southerners also found ways to work closely with political leaders from other states in pursuit of common goals. In addition, Van Buren became friendly with the Jacksonians' strongest, certainly their loudest, congressional voice, Senator Thomas Hart Benton from the slave state of Missouri. Benton was out of the same mold as Jackson: his commitment to nationalism over sectionalism, and to a Democratic-Republican movement that crossed sectional lines, outpaced all other considerations in his mind and makeup.

In contrast, those Southerners who supported Calhoun were growing more particularistic in their views as time passed; that is, they were increasingly adopting extreme states' rights positions that indicated their consistently high sensitivity to any threats of centralization in the United States even from their Republican friends now in power. They combined this sensitivity with their equally intense sectional touchiness that erupted once again in the years 1829–1832, and that continued to grow and fester throughout the rest of the decade because of their resistance to the policies pursued by Jackson and his associates. Finally, Calhoun and his allies continued to despise the partisan notions that distinguished Van Buren politically. The South Carolinian was always suspicious of such, continuing, rather, to celebrate independence from pressures associated with the demands by political parties for unquestioned loyalty, and to see party politicians in the traditional way, as a major cause of civic decay in the Republic because of their insistence on such submission and their vulgar demagogic notions of electoral politics.

Still, despite the imperatives that drove these Southerners, fostered by their many fears and hyperwariness about what was going on in national politics, most of the Calhounites remained convinced that they were in positions that prevented their claims to preference from being effectively sidetracked for very long. To do so would cause enough of an embarrassing uproar in the South, and elsewhere, to severely hurt the emerging Jacksonian party. Calhoun, his friends believed, was too eminent, and too strong politically, not to win out in any showdown against the upstart secretary of state from New York.

Whether Van Buren had serious presidential ambitions early in the new administration, as the Calhounites feared, is a matter of speculation. His outward demeanor and behavior were, as always, extremely cautious and noncommunicative on the matter. There were many other Jacksonians that he probably ranked as more likely to rise to that particular eminence than he. His reputation was, at the moment, that of an adept state-level politician with some important national experience, but with little of the stature that was attached to others who had been involved in national affairs far longer than he had been.

On the other hand, as the acknowledged leader of his party in the largest state, as the chief minister in Jackson's cabinet, for his role in the president's victory in 1828, and his efforts to shape the movement thereafter, he drew not only a great deal of attention, but also much support. There were plenty of people, including some in the president's inner circle, who believed that Van Buren had an excellent claim to be considered for the succession, and who took that claim seriously. He was certainly not unaware of their attitudes, but was always quick to try to hold back their enthusiasm on his behalf, downplay their notions in correspondence, and prevent their inside gossip from becoming too public. He feared that too much speculation about the future would intrude on his relationship with Jackson and cause unnecessary difficulties with the president's other supporters.

"THE EAR AND CONFIDENCE OF MAJESTY"

Van Buren did rise to the top of the Jacksonian movement at the expense of Calhoun, helped by an unexpected and precipitate fall from grace by the vice president. That fall was all but inevitable anyway, given all of the elements that were in play after 1828, but it began in farce. From the beginning of the administration the Washington political scene was roiled by the "petticoat politics" of the Peggy Eaton affair. Throughout 1829 and into 1830, the reputation of the new wife of Jackson's secretary of war and longtime Tennessee friend, John Eaton, was the subject of much gossip in high circles, none of it favorable to Mrs. Eaton. Her reputation was sullied, in the eyes of much of official Washington, by her alleged record of sexual promiscuity with a range of suitors before her marriage to Eaton, and because of her husband's subsequent indifference to the stir they were causing as they flouted the demands of respectability in official Washington. They were not behaving as the social dictates of the time demanded of them.

Mrs. Eaton was met, therefore, with great coldness and outright rejection by the leaders of the Washington society, especially the wives of high government officals who were led, it was clear to most observers, by the vice president's wife, Floride Calhoun. Believing the worst about Mrs. Eaton, and affronted by her presence, they refused to attend official functions where she was likely to be present, seriously embarrassing the president as they did so. Vexed at their behavior, and seeing in it the same kinds of unfounded charges and subsequent insults that had been directed against his beloved late wife (who had been called a "whore" in national Republican pamphlets and editorials during the recent presidential campaign, and who had died only weeks after his victory), Jackson engaged in bitter recriminations with members of his offical circle.

In particular, this "plague spot of the Administration," as Van Buren characterized the matter, provoked a serious conflict between Calhoun and Jackson. That confrontation was intense enough on its own merits, only to be much further exacerbated by Van Buren's cordiality toward the Eatons, and his willingness to socialize with them in company with some of his friends in the diplomatic corps in Washington. All of them were either bachelors or widowers, and were presumably less susceptible to the kinds of social pressures being directed against others on the scene. "The sharp sighted secretary of state," one congressman summed up in a letter to his wife, "saw the attitude in which the respective parties stood and stepped forward in a manner the most courteous and civil and made his bow to Mrs. E. and on all occasions devotes himself to her. This has won the ear and confidence of majesty and gives him the lead in the counsels."

Looking back, all of this may seem, in retrospect, to have been a silly and demeaning matter for politically seasoned adults to be so concerned about and to fight over so viciously. But in the social culture of the time, "the Eaton malaria" clearly was a real concern to those involved, much discussed, serious and quite damaging to relations at the highest level of the administration. "If no blood was spilled" over it, Van Buren later wrote, "a sufficient quantity of ink certainly was shed upon the subject." All of it, it was noted then, and since, was to his ultimate benefit. Van Buren's attitudes and actions in accepting the Eatons, and consorting with them socially, stood him in good stead with the president, while, at the same time, further raising the already unusually fierce ire of their opponents.

VAN BUREN MOVES TOWARD PREEMINENCE

The Eaton affair was only one element in the rise of Van Buren in Jackson's esteem accompanied by the reciprocal fall of Calhoun from favor. More of the many things that drove Calhoun and Jackson apart soon emerged, with the secretary of state continuing to benefit from each of them. Accompanying his jousting with Calhoun were Van Buren's related efforts to give ideological focus to the Jacksonian administration, a focus that ultimately proved inimical to the vice president's position. As the Jacksonians took firm hold, and began to implement their plans, Van Buren moved with his usual mixture of caution and commitment. He was not always in the forefront of the policy matters that came to the fore, but, along with Jackson's other close advisers in his "Kitchen Cabinet," and, unlike the vice president, he always publicly supported the president, and worked closely with him on the range of matters where their attitudes were so congruent.

There were many opportunities for him to do so. As he grew close to the president throughout 1829 and into 1830, Van Buren helped to write many of Jackson's state papers and give them the firm stamp of the general ideology that they both shared. Both of them believed that the purpose of government was not to engage in unwarranted intrusion into, and needless regulation of, people's activities, or to expand the reach of its authority. Rather, the American government should use its power to end restrictions on the rights and opportunities of the people, restrictions that infused American society, and that too often stemmed from monopolistic economic institutions such as the Bank of the United States, and from policies that favored only one segment of the people at much cost to the rest—for example, the protective tariff. The president's and secretary of state's discourse, and their behavior, underscored these commitments at each step along the way from 1829 on.

There was no lack of policy issues for them to fight over with their opponents and to provide the opportunity, as Van Buren afterwards claimed, for the administration to win "the highest and most enduring honors." Translating the Jacksonians' general ideological commitments into specific policies was never easy. But it had to be done. A number of these emerged (and were settled) during the president's first term. Other issues appeared then, but remained unresolved, to become the cause of continued contentiousness well into Jackson's second administration.

The first two of these policy matters, involving Indian removal and the federal financing of internal improvements, united most of Jackson's supporters and clearly indicated the direction that they intended to go. The president never wavered in his belief in the need to separate the Indian and white populations on the nation's frontiers and to open up the former's land to settlement by the latter. In order to accomplish this, he insisted on pursuing a policy of removing the Indian tribes from their established homelands in Georgia and Alabama, in particular, to their own demarcated territory farther west, far from contact with the white settlers moving into the contested, that is Indian, lands.

Jackson's determination in the matter was accompanied by its accomplishment: the successful transferance, by federal officials, of most of the affected eastern Indian tribes across the Mississippi River into Oklahoma, although it took a long time to carry it through to completion. In beginning the process of Indian removal Jackson followed his own, and his supporters', racialist and expansionist instincts, despite loud opposition from humanitarian groups, while heeding, as well, the strong pressures on him emanating from local politicians in the South and West who were determined to force the tribes out of their states, even without the sanction of law and, if necessary, in defiance of it.

PRESIDENT JACKSON USED HIS OFFICE'S VETO POWER more than any of his predecessors had done, most of the time over questions of internal improvements construction. The most famous of these was his veto in 1830 of a congressional bill that sought to use federal funds to continue the building of the Maysville road in the state of Kentucky, a road that, despite being a spur of the larger in scope National Road, lay entirely within that state. It was, in the eyes of many Democratic-Republicans (but not all), therefore, a local, not a national, project. In his refusal to sign the bill, Jackson demonstrated the essential states' rights commitments that defined himself and his secretary of state. Van Buren wrote the president's veto message, stressing, in powerful language, the unacceptability of what he referred to as "the abuses of the powers of the Federal Government in regard to internal improvements."

The issues that followed upon these, first, the tariff, and then the recharter of the Bank of the United States, further clarified what the administration was about, while, at the same time, opening critical fault lines in the Jacksonian coalition. John Quincy Adams's expansive notions of the power of the national government were now being pushed forward under the leadership of Henry Clay in the Senate. At the center of the Kentuckian's "American System," was the protective tariff, an issue that continued to be a difficult problem for Jacksonians and that was to bedevil politics after 1829, as it had throughout the middle and late 1820s.

Many free traders, primarily, but not exclusively, in the southern states, wanted the president to move vigorously, from his first days in office, to lower tariff rates. But the Jacksonian coalition was still divided over how far to go in setting such rates. Few, of course, wanted as much protection for American industry as the national Republicans deemed to be necessary. Nevertheless, the distance between moderate protectionism, as advocated by Van Buren, among others, and the free trade policy demanded by many Southerners in particular, still provoked strong disagreements within the coalition. It also threatened a much more far-reaching confrontation.

By late 1829, the national press began to link Vice President Calhoun to an extreme antiprotective position that was emanating from his home state. The year before the vice president had secretly written, and his associates had publicly issued, the South Carolina "Exposition," powerfully asserting the state's grievances—and its attitude of defiance—concerning the tariff issue. The version of states' rights pushed by the South Carolinians, included the right, they insisted, to nullify a federal law that they found harmful to South Carolina. That is, they claimed that they had the power to prevent its application inside the boundaries of their state.

They had something quite specific in mind at the beginning of the 1830s. Calhoun and his supporters, violently hostile to the existing level of tariff duties embodied in the act of 1828, and unappeased by a new tariff working its way through Congress, made it known that their state would formally refuse to permit the provisions of the existing law of 1828 to be carried out within its borders. In response, President Jackson made it equally plain that he rejected such defiance and would meet any nullifying action head on and decisively.

The simmering tensions remained covert for some time but publicly exploded—in Washington, at least, at the Jefferson Day dinner of political leaders, allegedly Jacksonian supporters, in April 1830. Both the president and Calhoun attended the event and made clear by their public toasts that they were heading toward a serious confrontation on the issue. The dinner had originally been organized by some of the pronullification forces who saw it as an opportunity for them to shout out their position in the presence of the president. Jackson did not give them much slack when they did. In his toast to the assembled guests he added to his essential states' rights position the notion of democratic nationalism. "The Federal Union," he said. "It must be preserved." The meaning was clear to everyone there. Appropriate federal authority could always overcome, when necessary, local attempts to subvert the will of the many, personified in the president who held office by virtue of a popular national mandate that could not be ignored, even by a sovereign state.

In his toast, which followed Jackson's, the unabashed Calhoun swung back at the president directly, and with great force, a fact not lost on anyone present, including his target. "The Union," he declared. "Next to our liberty the most dear." It was a tense moment not lightened by the secretary of state. Typically for him, Van Buren's toast, which followed those of the main protagonists, reflected a more cautious notion than the president's, stressing his belief that matters, even those as divisive as this, could always be worked out through a commitment to moderation in public councils, that is, through "mutual forbearance and reciprocal concessions." Neither sentiment was much in evidence, however, either that night or in all that subsequently occurred.

His temper aroused by Calhoun's aggressive behavior toward him, the government he headed, and the mandate that he held from the American people, Jackson was further infuriated by the discovery of earlier Calhoun hostility toward him. Over ten years before, Jackson had commanded the American troops on the Florida frontier, and behaved in a most aggressive manner in carrying out his mission there. Secretary of War Calhoun had suggested then that Jackson's vigorous forays into Spanish Florida against the Indian tribes ignoring, as he did so, the diplomatic consequences of such actions, should lead to his official chastisement by President Monroe. When President Jackson learned of that long-ago unfriendly advice, he demanded an explanation from the vice president. He received one back that was offered in Calhoun's usually starchy and unrepentent style. The explanation found its way into print, a fact that hardly soothed matters between them. It led, instead, to the verge of an open split between two most powerful and resolutely inflexible men.

THE TENSIONS REVEALED in the episode only added further provocation to a relationship between the two top elected officers of the national government already rubbed raw by the Eaton affair and further complicated by the other matters developing in 1829 and 1830. Because of all of this agitation Van Buren's stock continued to rise within the administration. He had rarely pushed himself forward in many of these domestic concerns, given the differences within the Jacksonian coalition, differences that he cautiously hoped would be sorted out without too much damage to the movement as a whole. Jackson's forceful assertion of presidential power troubled many of his original supporters in addition to the president's enemies in South Carolina and elsewhere. That negative reaction included Van Buren to some degree. He was, at first, wary of Jackson's assertive, confrontational policy toward the Indians and Calhoun. But, given Old Hickory's determination to act forcefully, and the many things they had in common and were fighting for, Van Buren quickly came around to subordinate his will to the administration's leader, and stand firmly with the president.

By the beginning of the 1830s, the once powerful Calhoun was clearly on the political defensive on all fronts. One sign of this, in addition to the other indicators present, was Jackson's commitment to the establishment of a new Democratic newspaper in the capital, one more favorable to him than Duff Green's had become since 1829. The *Globe*, edited by a fervent Jacksonian, Francis P. Blair, brought to Washington from Kentucky, and who was personally warmly supportive of Van Buren, became the dominant Democratic newspaper voice of the next generation. While Van Buren was not yet fully in control of the party in the national capital, or elsewhere, this, and the other actions together, suggested that he was clearly emerging into a position of increasing power, much more than the first among equals. Certainly, the president had come to see him, as he put it in a letter written in late 1829, as "*able* and *prudent*," and "firm to the core," that is, loyal to Jackson and his crusade.

In all that he had been involved with in Jackson's first administration Van Buren continued to reveal himself as the embodiment of a new political breed: he represented the ordered in-
terplay of interests within a managed system, not the leadership
of a crusade, or the fervent spokesman of a mighty ideology that
he championed. At the same time, to him the practices of everyday politics—coalition building, horse trading, and compromise,
continued to be rooted firmly in the holding and articulation of
strong policy commitments, rooted in the powerful ideology of
Jeffersonian republicanism, as had been the case throughout his
political career.

PAUSE: TO ENGLAND, 1831–1832

Jackson appointed Van Buren as minister to England in 1831 as the
result of the political machinations that had been so prominent a
part of the administration's first two years. The move was, in fact,
initiated by the secretary of state, and was, at first, resisted by the
president. As the internal tensions within the administration increased in force, Van Buren thought that it was time, and tactically
useful for him, to resign from office, get out of the line of fire, and
deflect widespread public notions, spread by their enemies, that
Jackson was completely under his influence. Such personal removal
from the scene would, he believed, benefit the president, himself,
and the cause that both of them sought to advance.

Van Buren convinced the president that the move would clear
the politically befouled air, allow Jackson to ask those other cabinet
members who were too close to Calhoun to resign as well, and stop
the allegations fostered by the Calhounites and the national Republicans about Van Buren's nefarious hidden role in what its enemies saw as the excesses of the administration. When Jackson finally reluctantly assented, accepted his cabinet's resignation, and
then nominated Van Buren for the London mission, the New Yorker
left the State Department, packed his goods, and, accompanied
by his son John, sailed for England as soon as he could, arriving
in September 1831. He left, in his wake, a great many political

heartburnings among his enemies that were to reappear, and affect him one more time, even as he settled down in London.

FROM HIS FIRST DAYS AS MINISTER he found himself in quite congenial circumstances. In his official role Van Buren made a good impression on the originally skeptical English and took full advantage of the warming up in the two nations' relations with each other that had been going on since the settlement of the West Indies trade dispute. He found an amiable companion in the person of the incumbent secretary of the London legation, the novelist and essayist Washington Irving, the son of a prominent New York editor and politician, whom Van Buren knew well. The author and Van Buren became quite close in London and were to remain good friends thereafter.

Van Buren's life in the British capital was not as busy for him as it had been in the situation that he had just left. It was a time, rather, of many social engagements with members of the English political class, including the new king, William IV, the son of George III, all of which he thoroughly enjoyed. The poor boy from the "Dutch counties" of New York, and the suspect—to his enemies—national politician of less than honorable ambition, had found another niche for himself that he occupied comfortably, ably, and, as usual, with a great deal of grace. And, in the business that he did carry on, Van Buren turned out to be a most effective representative of his country in the time that he was able to spend in London.

But his stay in the British capital was cut short by the savagery of the political divisions at home. The Jacksonians had never clearly controlled the United States Senate after 1829. There were a number of legislators who regarded themselves as independent of both of the contending coalitions on the scene, and who frequently resisted the president's attempts to win their sustained support. They sometimes voted with Jackson, other times not. As a result, the administration's enemies in the Senate were able to defeat a number of his appointments to federal office. When Van Buren's nomination as minister came up for confirmation by the Senate in January, 1832, the vote on it resulted in an even split between the yeas and nays. The tally had been deliberately maneuvered by the anti-Jacksonians, led by Daniel Webster and Henry Clay, so that the tie-breaking vote against confirming him could be cast by the presiding officer of the Senate, Vice President Calhoun. He did so with all the malice aforethought for which the South Carolinian was noted, ringingly declaring to another senator, "it will kill him sir, kill him dead. He will never kick, sir, never kick."

Van Buren lived to kick again. Despite the defeat, his friends were delighted by what the Senate had done since they believed that the action, "by a motley band of Senatorial factionists," would make him a martyr in the eyes of Jackson's supporters, propel him forward politically, and guarantee his selection for the vice presidential nomination in 1832. "You will be our V. P. in spite of yourself," his old New York associate, Congressman Churchill Cambreleng, wrote from Washington in the immediate aftermath of the Senate rejection. And he was right. The Senate's action did propel Minister Van Buren well forward at several levels. First, Jackson became even more deeply committed to him as an ally, as his next vice president, and as his eventual successor, as a means of confronting and confounding all of his hated enemies from the national Republican Henry Clay to the nullificationist John C. Calhoun.

Calhoun, in the meantime, had done himself little good if he still harbored any hope that he would be Jackson's successor. The nullification crisis between South Carolina and the United States burst forth while Van Buren was in Europe when South Carolina confronted—and defied—the federal government. Its legislature passed an ordinance announcing that the state had formally nullified the tariff law and would not carry out its provisions at the port of Charleston. The tense confrontation that ensued escalated fiercely, culminating in Jackson's threat to use troops against the recalcitrant state, and his suggestion that he would gladly hang Calhoun, who had resigned as vice president to return home and lead his state in its defiance of federal law. The relations between Jackson and the leader of South Carolina's resistance had reached their lowest point to date.

All of this confrontation and maneuvering came to fruition when, stimulated by local Democratic leaders friendly to Van Buren, mass meetings of Jacksonians in New York and in a number of other states demanded that the New Yorker be brought forward for vice president on the Jackson ticket in 1832, demands that provided proof that there was a significant popular impulse behind his friends' claims for his moving into higher office. That impulse was politically useful when the first Democratic national convention met in Baltimore, Maryland, in late May 1832. The assembled delegates enthusiastically named Van Buren as their candidate for vice president under their new rules mandating that a party nominee had to receive two-thirds of the votes in the convention to be nominated. Van Buren received more than was required, demonstrating his widespread support among Democratic activists. He now occupied the slot that the Jacksonians had previously filled with the name of John C. Calhoun.

VAN BUREN DID NOT RETURN HOME until July so that his enemies would have little justification to claim, as they already were unstintingly doing, that he was coming back to connive on his own behalf to win the nomination. Staying on in Europe, he took his farewell of his many English friends, and, crossing the Channel, he leisurely visited a number of places on the continent including making a short trip to his family's original home in the Netherlands. He thoroughly enjoyed his sojourn and, as astutely, realized that he was remaining out of the direct line of fire while the presidential campaign evolved at home. But he realized that this would be only a short respite from the angry political warfare that had characterized so much of Jackson's first term in office and that Van Buren knew was sure to continue.

Chapter Five

―――――――――◯―――――――――

The Democracy's Heir Apparent, 1832–1836

WHEN VAN BUREN RETURNED FROM ENGLAND in early July 1832, he traveled first to Washington to reestablish contact with Andrew Jackson and be brought up-to-date on political affairs. To be sure, he was well aware of the current state of matters thanks to his assiduous reading of the Democratic newspapers that had been sent to him in London, and his extensive correspondence with political friends in New York and elsewhere. An always turbulent public arena had grown even more so during his absence abroad. President Jackson had continued to stir up violent opposition—because of his policies, and for the manner in which he governed the country. As he did so, party lines were becoming sharper and more deeply etched than they had been. The unwieldy Jacksonian coalition of 1828 continued its evolution into the more ideological Democratic Party of the next decade.

In particular, the relentlessly pressing and extremely polarizing issues of South Carolina nullification, and the Bank of the United States, powerfully agitated the nation's political waters, as the president began his reelection campaign. The two were, in Van Buren's words, "the most important resources on which the opposition relied to win the great game they were playing for the government."

During Old Hickory's first administration, the bank's aggressive president, Nicholas Biddle, had pushed hard for its rechartering, somewhat earlier than necessary. (Congress had chartered it in 1816 for a twenty-year period.) Finding the president unforth-coming, Biddle sought support among the national Republican leaders, Clay and Webster, to effect that end. They responded willingly. But the working out of the matter had only begun when Van Buren left the cabinet in 1831. It developed over the next year into a full-scale confrontation between the executive and members of Congress over both what should be the nation's financial policies, and about the nature of the actions that Jackson took during the controversy.

To the president's fury, and Van Buren's dismay as he learned about it, some Democrats also supported recharter. More and more caught up in the powerful national economic expansion that was under way, these Jacksonians had become convinced of the need for banks to further that development. Some of them supported the strengthening of state banks. But others believed that a national bank was an economic necessity. Other Democrats remained with Jackson at the opposite end of the policy spectrum, unhappy about the way national financial policy was becoming hostage to such institutions generally, as well as, specifically, the unchallenged control of the Bank of the United States over the economy.

VAN BUREN'S RETURN TO THE UNITED STATES coincided with the president's controversial veto of the bank's recharter by Congress. Jackson pulled his friend into the battle from the latter's first moments back. "The bank, Mr. Van Buren," he exploded when they met, "is trying to kill me, but I will kill it." He asked Van Buren to read his impending veto message (which had primarily been written by one of his close advisers, the populist Westerner, Amos Kendall). The stinging veto contained a powerful assault on an aristocracy of wealth, enunciating an intense distaste—and fear—of the power of the bank over the American economy and the threat that an institution of its size and wealth posed to the well-being of the people of the United States—as represented by the nation's president. Van Buren responded to the president's request for advice with much approval of the message's sentiments, and some suggestions about wording. It was like old times.

AFTER HIS VISIT TO THE PRESIDENT, and a trip to Capitol Hill to renew acquaintances, Van Buren returned to New York and remained there through the election campaign, and the period following, until his formal assumption of office in March 1833. Staying in Albany hotels, and in the homes of friends in several different upstate towns, he directed his attention to mobilizing the party in the state behind the president and his policies, and finding all possible ways to win the upcoming election. As always, there were a number of personal and factional disagreements among his Regency associates that needed to be attended to—which he did with his usual skill— as preliminary to a well-organized, thorough, and effectively run electoral contest.

Even as he became fully absorbed in party and election affairs during the summer and fall, Van Buren remained in regular correspondence with Jackson over the reigning policy disputes in Washington. The president continued to rely on his advice on the issues before him alongside that from such men as Jackson's confidants during the recharter battle, Kendall, and Attorney General Roger Taney, to whom Jackson had turned for assistance while the New Yorker was in London. Van Buren was certainly willing to respond to the president's requests. As always when dealing with him, even when he felt somewhat uncomfortable about the president's aggressive policy actions, and his rhetorical, and real, muscle flexing, he was deferential, committed—and quietly cautious in the suggestions that he offered.

ONCE AGAIN VICTORY AT THE POLLS

The campaign developed as expected. The opposition forcefully pushed the bank issue during the months leading up to Election Day as an example of the president's lack of understanding of what was necessary and proper for the continued economic health of the United States, and of his imperious, overreaching behavior unbecoming to the nation's chief executive. Obviously neither Jackson nor Van Buren agreed with that assessment. They remained determined, instead, to prevail against what they believed were the bank advocates' aristocratic heresies that threatened the people's rights on behalf of a narrow, selfish, institution, always promoting its own special interests, whatever the national good demanded.

The maneuvering over South Carolina's resistance to federal authority boiled along as well as the election approached. Most Democrats, following Jackson's lead, had supported him in his resistance to the nullifier state's implacable challenge to national authority, as they were aligned with him over Jackson's resistance to the recharter of the bank. But there were the usual range of internal party complications. Democrats were not fully united on the nullification issue as they were not about the bank. Many of them were, in fact, especially uneasy, or even in disagreement, with the president, about his thunderously asserted, very strong, policies for dealing with each of his opponents. Little of this disagreement came out during the campaign, but Van Buren and his associates were aware of some Democratic restiveness about the way the president went about his activities and quite sensitive to their potential importance in a second Jackson administration.

Jackson's enemies did not ignore Van Buren during the campaign. He was a central focus of their assault, accused by them, with great venom, of all kinds of misdeeds against the American people, misdeeds that were always, to be sure, hidden from public view. He was unseen but culpable. Both the president's anti-bank, and anti–South Carolina, policies were laid at his door. Nor did the anti-Jacksonians forget Van Buren's narrow partisan outlook and behavior, which, in their view, so debased American politics. The charges were, of course, familiar, and to be expected, given the powerful antagonism that he generated on most matters from the Adams-Clay national Republicans, and the Calhoun Southern Rights faction, both of whom he had confronted, and helped defeat, during the first Jackson administration.

A number of Democrats became extremely uncomfortable about the attacks on their vice presidential candidate as the opposition's campaign unfolded. Some came to believe that the assaults on Van Buren could make him into a serious drag on the party ticket despite Jackson's wide popularity. Late in the campaign, there was, in fact, an attempt by Southern supporters of the president, feeling the heat generated by the Calhounites against Van Buren in their states, to substitute a Virginian, Philip Barbour, for the New Yorker, when their states cast their electoral votes for the office of vice president. The effort did not get very far but demonstrated the reality of current irritants and presaged future difficulties.

DESPITE THE FEARS EXPRESSED by nervous party leaders, and the intensity of the Clay-Calhoun-led assault, the Democratic-Republican national ticket won a convincing victory in the presidential election of 1832. In New York, Jackson and Van Buren took all of the state's forty-two electoral votes with a slightly larger popular vote margin than Jackson had received there four years earlier. Completing their triumph, Van Buren's friend and Regency colleague, William Marcy, was elected the state's governor. In the rest of the nation, the party's overall winning margins were as impressive as four years before, even though Jackson lost some support in the South, and the opposition made strong efforts everywhere behind its candidate, Henry Clay.

Vice President–elect Van Buren returned to Washington just before his inauguration, this time renting a house on 19th Street near the White House. Once again, two of his sons were with him. The oldest, Abraham, stayed only a short while since he was still in the army and was soon ordered to duty elsewhere. His third son, Martin Junior, continued to live with his father and assist him in his political work as he had done for some time. Van Buren's second son, John, and his youngest, Smith, remained in New York. John's career as a lawyer and politician, very much in his father's mold, was in full gear in Albany, while Smith served as his father's local eyes and ears, keeping him aware of what was going on in the bubbling cauldron of New York politics. Over the next four years, whenever Congress adjourned, Van Buren, more often than not, returned to New York, spending much time in Saratoga and in other resorts in the upstate area, relaxing with whatever members of his family were with him, and, as always, closely attending to the state's political business.

IN OFFICE AS JACKSON'S RIGHT HAND

The new vice president was sworn in and took up his official duties on March 4, 1833. Those duties were rather light, consisting primarily of presiding over the Senate during the several months that it sat each year. Some earlier vice presidents, such as Thomas Jefferson, Aaron Burr, and John C. Calhoun, had been involved in a great deal of politics and drama while in office. But few of the others who had occupied the position enjoyed similarly memorable times. Van Buren, everyone agreed, would. Finally, two of his predecessors had subsequently ascended to the presidency, but none had done so since Jefferson in 1801, although Calhoun had entertained high hopes to reverse that discouraging pattern—as yet to no avail.

But, of course, Van Buren's situation seemed to be much more promising as his role as Jackson's right hand and apparent successor increasingly solidified throughout 1832 and into 1833. With that in mind, the opposition continued to ratchet up their bitter assaults as the administration settled in, demonstrating how much more determined than ever they were to stop Jackson and his second-in-command. And there were always many opportunities for them to do so.

By the winter of 1832–1833, the nullification controversy had come to a head in both South Carolina and Washington and had been defanged by some agile maneuvering in Congress even before Van Buren returned to the Capitol for the inauguration. At first, he, from afar, and his New York colleagues on the scene in Congress, tried to seize the initiative by reworking the controversial tariff laws to which South Carolina had taken such exception. But, led by Henry Clay, the opposition forestalled that effort, and pushed their own settlement, with Calhoun's (and ultimately, Jackson's) acquiescence. Congress passed a new, somewhat lower, tariff, in 1833, one largely drafted by Clay and his allies, which the president accepted, although some Democrats, including a few from New York, opposed any rate reductions at all, even to resolve the crisis. Jackson then stood down his threat to use force against the nullifiers. The South Carolina legislature ended the drama by symbolically nullifying the now unnecessary Force Bill that Congress had passed during the crisis, at Jackson's insistence, to give him the authority to coerce the state if it proved necessary for him to do so.

CONTINUED POLITICAL TUMULT

The settling of the nullification crisis through unusual interparty cooperation did not quiet the national political scene much, if at all. The disparate group of national Republicans, Calhounites, Anti-Masons, and those original Jackson supporters who had been driven off during the first administration, had begun to work together in a somewhat more disciplined fashion, first during the presidential election, and then on the floor of Congress, finding their voice and energy in their determination to stem the tide of what they claimed was "executive usurpation," and Jackson and Van Buren's manipulative partisan intrigue against the national interest.

At first, they bore a number of different party names, especially being referred to as the "Opposition" in 1833. They came to settle on the name "Whigs" by the following year in conscious echo of those who had opposed an overreaching, despotic, king in seventeenth- and eighteenth-century England. They were determined to erect formidable barriers against "King Andrew" and his policies, whatever their own internal differences might be. Not yet an organized political party, the coalition had great strength in the United States Senate where the hated Van Buren sat as its presiding officer. That body became, in Van Buren's words, "the headquarters of the opposition," the place where they raucously mobilized their unflinching anger against the administration. (The House of Representatives, led by the stalwart Democratic Speaker, Andrew Stevenson of Virginia, ably assisted by Congressman James K. Polk of Tennessee, had an administration majority.)

As a result of the Whig determination, whatever Van Buren's wish might have been, it was impossible for him to keep a low profile and work quietly behind the scenes to shape administration policies and secure his own future. The vice president continued to be much in evidence in the turmoil of the partisan battles of the

second term as his enemies went after him in their speeches, editorials, and campaign pamphlets, in the most relentless and ven-
omous way.

Why was he so disliked by his enemies? Van Buren had always
tried to maintain cordial relations with his political opponents, to
uphold, in his words, a "line of separation between personal and political differences and to protect social intercourse from the delete-
rious influence of partisan illiberality or violence." But he was never
very successful in doing so, albeit through no lack of effort on his
part. Calhoun and Daniel Webster publicly snubbed him when he
first returned from England and visited the Senate. Although Clay
and he were usually cordial toward each other, most of the other
Whigs followed the paths of Webster and Calhoun, not only dis-
daining the new vice president for his political role, but actively and
continually expressing their personal hatred of him as well.

Surely, his successes and rise to power, as well as his perceived
involvement in the president's actions, infuriated the opposition,
and made him a particular object of loathing. He also continued to
be denounced for his success in his championing of a style of political warfare that so many Whigs found distasteful, and that they
continued to assail fiercely with all of the energy they could muster.
As in New York State ten years before, the new reality of organized,
disciplined, political parties managing everything was becoming
more and more evident, even if development was still incomplete.
And their growing role continued to offend those still caught up in
the long-established truths of a preparty political culture. Van Buren's opponents never let go of their belief that his artfulness in the
deceit-filled milieu of partisan operations, not his talents, was what
had brought him almost to the top of American politics, and to his
place as Jackson's choice as his successor. That kind of success was
simply not acceptable to them.

Even as the Whigs pressed ahead against him and his cause,
Van Buren was becoming increasingly concerned about internal divisions among the Democrats. Echoes of the nullification episode
still lingered. It had provoked a great deal of opposition to the president among some of Jackson's original supporters in addition to
all of the challenges emanating from his long time opponents. Jack-

son's nationalist notions and behavior, embodied in his assertion in his public messages of presidential authority over a defiant state, had continued to grow in power and continued to go too far for others in his coalition. While not joining them, Van Buren's own Jeffersonian commitments to the primacy of states' rights in the federal Union, and his alliance with many Southern political leaders, made him wary, as he had often been on other matters, of Jackson's intense, belligerent, roaring against South Carolina—however deserved it was.

What particularly disturbed Van Buren was that Democratic restiveness about Jackson's impulse to move from loud public denunciation to the possibility of armed coercion against a sovereign state, a restiveness that was particularly notable among Van Buren's Southern allies, had the potential to disrupt the successful coalition against their opponents, damage the Jacksonian agenda, and threaten Van Buren's next step up the political ladder. While he agreed with the president on the ultimate outcomes to be desired on the controversies that surrounded them, he worked assiduously, and tactfully, when he could, to tone Jackson's belligerence down more than the president seemed at first inclined to do, including getting him to accept the compromise on nullification worked out by Henry Clay.

THE BANK WAR, which flowered throughout the year after the presidential election, was as controversial and as rending both between the Jacksonians and the Whigs and between different blocs of the president's supporters as well. In Democratic circles in New York and in other states, the split over banking policy had, inevitably, continued to grow, even as the battle moved on from whether or not to recharter Biddle's bank, to one about the propriety—and constitutionality—of Jackson's next step in his campaign, the removal, by presidential direction, of the federal government's deposits lodged, by law, in the Bank of the United States.

Van Buren, while, as before, agreeing with the thrust of Jackson's policies, again urged caution on the president. He pointed out how much his use of his power against the bank, as with his threats against the nullifiers, frightened loyal states' rights Democrats and led them to believe that Jackson was making demands and asserting powers that they could not comfortably support. But Old Hickory followed the advice of another close adviser, the more radical, antibank, Amos Kendall, who disagreed with Van Buren's caution. In mid-1833, the president ordered the removal of the deposits, convinced that, otherwise, Biddle would make use of these federal monies against the administration.

The removal policy provoked a storm that gave an intense surge of energy to the Whigs, if they needed one. Led by Henry Clay, the opposition lashed out against the president in their newspapers, and in particularly sharp speeches on their home grounds while Congress was not in session, lashings out that usually focused on Van Buren as well, chastising him for his alleged role in abetting the president's dangerous economic policies.

Whig assaults on the administration increased in fury and intensity when the first session of the Twenty-third Congress convened in late 1833, again led by Henry Clay, seconded by Daniel Webster and John C. Calhoun. There were few epithets that opposition spokesmen did not aim at the president and his associates for their unintelligent policies against the mainstay of the nation's financial system. The Jacksonians responded in kind, and as fiercely. Finally, the Whigs in the Senate gave sharp point to their furious attacks on Jackson by passing, in early 1834, an unprecedented formal resolution of censure against the president for his deposit removal policy. They did so despite the roars from the White House and the vigorous attempts of Van Buren and Democratic senators to prevent its passage.

The battle intensified further when Biddle also counterattacked against the president. From the bank's headquarters in Philadelphia, he began to apply screws to the financial system and through it, to the economy generally, by calling in the bank's extensive loans to private and state banks throughout the country. This forced the latter, in turn, to call in their own loans to individuals. Not everyone could meet such demands for repayment, and a round of bank failures, and bankruptcies, began exploding, by mid-1834, into a full-scale economic downturn. In consequence, the nation's political atmosphere continued to overheat in bitter colloquy, personal vituperation, and everyone's increased determination to destroy the other side.

THROUGHOUT THIS "PANIC" SESSION of Congress, Van Buren made every effort to maintain his outward imperturbability as he sat in his chair presiding over the Whig assault. Closely working with colleagues from other states such as House Speaker Stevenson, Congressman Polk, and Senator John Forsyth of Georgia, as well as his friends and New York lieutenants, Senator Silas Wright and Congressman Churchill Cambreleng, he publicly ignored the attacks on himself while working hard to keep the Jacksonians on Capitol Hill fully on guard, united, and well prepared to resist the onslaught of the Whigs. At the same time, he remained in close proximity to Jackson, offering his counsel and continuing to try to prevent any rash outbreaks from the president.

But these were difficult days for the vice president. Even when Biddle began to back off in his credit-tightening activities in reaction to the cries from some Whig supporters that the actions being taken by the bank president were hurting them as well as the Democrats, the intense confrontation continued. In addition to everything else dividing him from his Whig adversaries, Van Buren was having an unusually hard initiation into the bitter intensity of presidential succession politics in a situation where he was the main player visible, and the particular point at issue in the minds of many of those engaged.

A DEMOCRATIC PARTY AT LAST

The Bank War shifted focus as the administration turned to finding alternative locations for the deposit of the public monies received from the collection of customs duties and the receipts from land sales that had been previously lodged in Biddle's bank. Kendall and Taney took the lead within the administration on these matters, sometimes in conflict with Van Buren's advice and wishes. Like everything else in these years, their solutions proved to be exceedingly contentious. For one, Van Buren was severely criticized for his alleged pressing for certain New York banks to be selected for this rewarding task. The Whigs argued that the choices of these "pet banks" by the administration were still another example of the corrupting spoils system by which the Jacksonians, led by the vice president, always operated. Their criticism was undeserved in this case, the selection of deposit banks had sources beside that of political preferment. But the issues of financial control, the location of the federal monies, and the way that state banks operated, no longer supervised by the regulative muscle of Biddle's bank, remained unresolved and intense areas of contention to the end of the Jackson administration.

The congressional Whigs claimed another victim during this ongoing battle when the Senate refused to confirm Jackson's appointment of the rabidly antibank Attorney General Roger B. Taney as secretary of the treasury—an action that further roused the president and poisoned the atmosphere in Washington even more than it already was. Taney's rejection did have one positive effect so far as Van Buren was concerned. The attorney General's abortive move to the Treasury Department allowed Van Buren to push successfully for the appointment of his old associate and law partner, Benjamin Butler, to replace Taney as the administration's chief law officer. When that appointment went through, and Butler came to Washington, Van Buren invited him and his family to live with him in his house in place of his departed son, Abraham.

OTHER POLICY MATTERS, large and small, also arose and held the stage briefly to the end of Jackson's presidency. One of them, the revival of the dispute with France over the claims of American citizens rising out of French trade depredations during the Napoleonic wars, flared up once again when the French government found that it lacked sufficient political muscle at home to meet its obligations under the treaty negotiated when Van Buren was secretary of state. The vice president was drawn in to help sort out the situation before a fuming Jackson unloosed one of his rhetorical bombshells against still another enemy, a mollifying task that Van Buren accomplished with some dispatch.

At the same time, as noted, there continued to be powerful debate over the nation's financial policies as the Jacksonians sought to rationalize their banking and credit policies in the absence of a national bank. Like everything else, these financial matters, and all of the other issues that arose, quickly became the subject of bitter partisan contention in Congress, moving Van Buren to remember, in uncharacteristically sharp fashion, the sight from his seat on the Senate rostrum of "grave Senators making vehement speeches about nothing." Clearly, whatever the objective importance of the matters under debate, what was moving to the forefront in everyone's minds in each of these episodes was the impending presidential election and how to reap some advantage for their party in preparation for it.

THE TUMULT OF THESE YEARS, particularly the successive domestic crises, helped the protean political parties' continued evolution, with all of their increasingly well-defined positions, and their emerging mechanisms for selecting candidates, establishing officeholding successions, and responding to the needs and demands of their leaders and those whom they led. But they had not yet fully matured. At the outset of the second Jackson administration neither party was fully formed structurally or ideologically, nor was either a well-disciplined institution. Each of the partisan coalitions continued to contain contradictory impulses within it, nullifiers and nationalists side by side in the anti-Jackson group, a number of old Federalists, with their aggressive nationalism, alongside Jeffersonian Republicans offering quite differing notions about the correctness of Jackson's actions, among the Democrats.

In addition, the tensions between a range of special interests, for example, Democratic supporters of banks and banking, or tariff protection, and, in contrast, others who cherished a deep ideological commitment to an agrarian, states' rights, limited government reach vision of the world, were always present in the coalition that Van Buren was building, further complicating its operations. The Jacksonian movement remained home to different priorities, conservative, even reactionary, agrarian Republicanism, and populist striving confronting small-town entrepreneurial notions, devout states' rights champions against those who accepted the need for effective and increased national power embodied in the president, political insiders, and antipartisan organization resistants, as well as an array of local differences that were always simmering beneath the surface of party activities.

As Van Buren wrote in reference to the tariff, Democratic administrations had always found it to be "a perplexing question" because, he went on, "the protective system was not in harmony with the unbiased feelings of a large majority of the democratic party but portions of it, too important to be neglected, were so hampered by the pressure and clamor of local and special interests as to make decided hostility to it on their part very hazardous and in some instances necessarily fatal to their power." The same comments could be appropriately made about banking and internal improvements. Van Buren had always been disturbed that Jackson's official family included people whom he believed leaned much too far in the nationalist direction. They were, in his mind, not really Jeffersonians, but, rather, dangerously reeking of Federalism. The critical mass of Democrats saw themselves as Jefferson's successors, but that, apparently, still meant several things in the still emerging partisan definitions of the early 1830s.

What had held the Democrats together through such ambiguity and differences was, first, their deep loyalty to Andrew Jackson. Beyond that, they were also aware of how much most of them had in common, especially their deep sense of how far beyond anything that they wanted to do in policy terms the Whigs were in their willingness to expand the national government's authority in domestic concerns. And, most critically, there was always an ideological center of gravity to the coalition behind Old Hickory and his chosen successor. Whatever differences there were among its members, the party still primarily rooted itself in Jeffersonian notions of the limited state, followed by the kind of agrarian nationalism that had doubled the size of the nation, coupled, finally, with a strong populist streak growing out of the battles against privilege and overweening power that had characterized so many political episodes since the Panic of 1819, the presidential election of 1824, and their intense aftermaths, culminating in the Bank War.

The Jacksonians' embrace of populism was well articulated by this time as well—no more so than during the confrontation with

Biddle's bank. In their own view, the president and his fellow Democrats believed that they spoke for the people, their policies were those of the people, while their enemies were drawn from the ranks of those who always had and who intended to continue to oppose the people in achieving their full political rights and, through that, social and economic improvement. Unlike their adversaries, the Democrats sought, they said, to remove restrictions hindering the people's efforts to better themselves—to level the playing field of Americans life so that no one had an advantage over another. To be sure, to build on an earlier comment, this commitment to democratic values, as it matured in the first half of the 1830s, was a restricted one in line with the dominant notions of the time. The people, to Jackson and Van Buren (and to many—but not all—of their opponents, as well) consisted of the white male population of the United States. Democrats were reaching well beyond previous boundaries in their democratic rhetoric and commitments, but still would not step as far outside the assumptions of their culture as they might have and that future generations ultimately did.

Within such limits, however, they were sincere in their beliefs and articulated them strongly in all of the political battles that had erupted since Jackson had assumed the presidency in 1829. In the White House and in Democratic club rooms, Jackson had become, over the past eight years, the "tribune of the people," speaking for them and working on their behalf. And the Democratic Party and Martin Van Buren were with him on this. Whatever hesitations Van Buren may have had about the populist zeal so often expressed in Jacksonian rhetoric because of the unpredictable nature of the people in any given election or policy dispute, he was closely aligned with Jackson in believing that they truly served the American people while their opponents did not.

JACKSON'S AND VAN BUREN'S UNDERSTANDING of themselves was, of course, not alone on the scene. To their enemies all of these claims, and apparent submission to the popular will, remained, in the language of the day—"buncombe," that is, deceptive. The president was, the Whigs constantly argued, manipulating the populace in the interests of a new "Caesarism" that was intended to maintain himself in office through wily maneuvers and the deception of the easily gulled. The "tribune of the people" and his right-hand man were not only engaging in wrong-headed policies but paving the way for a devastating and unacceptable transformation of the American political scene.

"VAN BUREN'S CABINET"—AND PARTY

Van Buren fretted constantly about the strength of the opposition and the threat posed by his party's internal disagreements. Such fretting was part of his makeup. But, as 1836 drew nearer. matters were never as desperate as Van Buren and other worried party leaders feared. Political portents increasingly looked better than they had during the uncertainties of the Bank War in 1833 and early 1834. After the mid-term congressional elections of 1834, Democrats elected the astute, committed, and partisanly combative Polk, as Speaker of the House of Representatives. His leadership was expected to be a plus for the party's legislative prospects. The Democrats' situation in the Senate was improved as well.

More to the point, party lines had further clarified and partisan discipline had hardened significantly. Nonpartisan approaches to political questions had ebbed, and factions had become more and more subject to party leadership. While some minor parties remained active on the local level, most such dissidence had quieted significantly when it came to the presidency and Congress. The next presidential election would be a straight fight (albeit with a number of complications) between the Democrats and the Whigs.

As this polarization deepened, the Jeffersonian element among the Democrats came increasingly to the fore in the party. Van Buren had always had a clear picture in his mind as what he wanted the party to be—a coalition that closely echoed the states' rights Republican values of Thomas Jefferson. And even he now admitted that it had arrived where he wanted it to be. Jackson's cabinet, again shuffled, now contained, in his view, a full array of true Jeffersonians, replacing the more nationalist, probank, holdovers from earlier days. He was delighted. Jackson's main advisory body had now become, in contrast to earlier, as one historian has written, "Van Buren's cabinet."

The last stage in the final emergence of a coherent democracy behind Van Buren was the full integration of the voters into the emerging partisan structure. By the mid-1830s the sources of support for each party had become clearer than they had been in 1828, or 1832. There had been much sorting out of supporters and opponents since, thanks to the vigorous combat over the many battles of the past eight years. In the popular elections throughout the period, a variety of loyalties and hostilities shaped voter choice. The Democrats under Jackson had proven to be very strong among Southern voters in general, while, in the North, they drew support in the old Republican areas, as well as from those who were hostile to the Whigs' nationalist commitments. This voting pattern often had an ethnoreligious tinge to it as well. In many places, the Democrats did very well among non-Anglo-Saxon elements in the population, the Dutch in New York, and the Scotch-Irish in Pennsylvania and the Southwest, for example. Clearly, one element that attracted voters to the party was its anti–New England, non-Anglican, outsider aura. Given their backgrounds, both Jackson and Van Buren fit very well into this lineup.

Elsewhere, real differences over economic policy, and the existence of quite different perspectives about the economic future of the nation, divided voters. Jacksonians received ever increasing support from those still not integrated into the market revolution with its needs for banks, government-financed internal improvements, and a tariff policy designed to protect American products and markets. There were a great many stubborn agrarians, urban artisans, and shopkeepers, who continued to resist what they saw as large-scale, monopolistic institutions that restricted opportunities and misshaped economic life as well as the looseness of credit they championed, which posed such dangers to the unwary borrower. And they continued to fear, as they always had, following the Jeffersonian tradition, that any expansion of the federal government's power was always a threat to the individual liberty of the American people. They readily fell in with the rhetoric and policies of Jacksonianism.

Finally, despite their appeals to the people, the Democrats did not receive an overwhelming number of votes from the lower classes in society, certainly not enough to distinguish them all that much from the Whigs in this regard. Hostility among labor groups in New York City, and elsewhere, to what they saw as the Democrats' conservatism in socioeconomic matters had led to the creation of a Workingman's Party in the late 1820s and a basic split among the Democrats between its regular wing and a more radical group, subsequently called the Locofocos, a split which weakened the Jacksonians in a number of local elections.

At the same time, other urban workers, less well-off farmers, and others in rural areas, supported the Whigs instead of the Democrats. Whatever awareness existed among society's lower classes of their common needs, these people were also crisscrossed with a range of other attitudes, prejudices, hostilities, and alternative visions about the economic future, which were enough to overwhelm any specific class interest that may have existed in the minds of some. In contrast to those who clung to premarket agrarian Republicanism and who supported the Jacksonians as a result, others, similarly situated at the lower reaches of society, were caught up in the emerging market-dominant economy, believed that they benefited from its opportunities, or worked for those who were expanding as a result of it. Their attitudes, interests, and policy commitments led them to support the Whigs. They did not see the latter as an aristocratic party hostile to the needs of people such as themselves, whatever the Jacksonian rhetoric claimed. (And, it should be noted, the Whigs were slowly learning to engage in a populist rhetoric as well.)

Both parties had come a long way in firming up their appeal to different groups of voters. On the other hand, in the mid-1830s, to Van Buren's unhappiness, this evolution remained incomplete and often unpredictable. Full mobilization of the electorate had not yet been achieved despite the intense confrontations of the Jackson years. Voter turnout had moderately increased during his two campaigns for president but was still not impressive overall. (Just over 50 percent of those eligible to vote had cast ballots in the presidential election of 1832.) Moreover, despite the patterns of popular commitment that were increasingly discernible, many voters remained volatile, moving from one coalition to the other in successive elections as something attracted, or repelled, them for the moment. Others turned out, or did not come to the polls, in unpredictable fashion. They could not, therefore, be counted on to support one party, or the other, in dedicated, and regular, ways that party leaders could always count on. There was still a way to go for full satisfaction to arrive for Van Buren and his like-minded party-building colleagues.

THE ELECTION OF 1836

All of this political sorting out was the backdrop to the culmination of the fight for the presidential succession. That outcome was always clear. Despite all of the anger, assaults, and uncertainties of the ongoing political wars of Andrew Jackson's second administration, Van Buren moved inexorably forward toward the succession to Old Hickory. When the second Democratic national convention convened in Baltimore in May 1835, it unanimously nominated him for the office of president.

Unfortunately it followed that joyous moment by then engaging in a stiff fight over the vice presidential spot on the ticket. Jacksonians in the western states strongly supported Richard M. Johnson, a populist Kentuckian in the Jackson mold (a frontier soldier, he claimed to have killed the Indian chief Tecumseh back in 1813). He also had many followers in parts of the urban East where he had a reputation as a radical, pro-workingman, Democrat, who had fought to eliminate the much hated imprisonment for debt laws. There was a contest for the nomination, however, because many Democrats, led by party leaders in the South Atlantic states, loathed Johnson for his long-standing, continuing, and public liaison with a mulatto woman.

At first, Van Buren sought to find a party-unifying solution by seeking out some other candidate. (He and his New York colleagues initially favored Virginia's Rives for the post.) But they drew back in the face of Johnson's great popularity among so many party supporters. The convention ultimately nominated the Kentuckian by the required two-thirds margin after some grumbling and a little sleight of hand by its leaders. (A single delegate, the only one in attendance at the convention, was allowed to cast all of Tennesse's fifteen votes in the absence of the other delegates from that state.)

The convention also appointed a committee to draft a statement of party principles that, when presented, defended the necessary emergence of the Democratic Party and the practices associated with it, and then reviewed the attempts of the opposition to press down against the people's needs and expressed wishes. This platformlike document ended with strong praise of Van Buren as Jackson's successor, while underlining that the party's policies were the key to why one should vote in a particular way, whomever the individual candidate was who represented the party in a given election. If elected, the statement forcefully asserted, Jackson's designated successor would engage in what any Democratic candidate would do: the continuation of Old Hickory's crusade on behalf of popular rights and his defense of the people's liberties from their always overreaching domestic enemies.

As the campaign began, Van Buren was opposed by, in the words of one party supporter, "the combined fragments" of the Whigs, a coalition still having some difficulty in settling down into a full-blown, well-organized, and clearly defined opposition party. Despite the fierceness of their opposition to Jackson—and Van Buren—these partisan elements remained in uneasy alliance and were more unorganized than the Democrats. Their national Republican core, the Calhounites and other states' rights anti-Jacksonians, the Anti-Masons, and its other followers, all edgily abided one another in their common anger—to a point. The party's leaders decided, therefore, against holding a national convention in 1836 for fear of its great fragmenting potential on them.

In the absence of a national convention, and as a result of nominations put forward by state level meetings, the Whigs ran different candidates in different parts of the country, each of whom had particular appeal in the region in which he was nominated. They supported the Indian fighter and territorial governor, General William Henry Harrison, primarily in the northwestern states. The former close political associate, and friend, of Jackson, Tennessee's Hugh Lawson White, led the party ticket in the South, and Daniel Webster was offered to the voters in nationalist New England. Each, while attractive in his home region, had little following among party members elsewhere. Together, however, they posed a formidable problem for Van Buren in amassing an Electoral College majority.

Beyond their choice of candidates, the Whigs faced another conundrum. Given their differences and hesitancies, what policies and appeals could such a group run on? Jackson and Van Buren was their answer. Both the outgoing president's and the current Democratic candidate's reputations were much at issue during the campaign. The Whigs unstintingly focused on Jackson's excesses as president, and the threats they posed to the country if another Democrat with similar ideas succeeded him.

As the campaign got underway, for example, the stalwart Democratic Senator Thomas Hart Benton of Missouri led a campaign in the Senate ultimately successful, to expunge from that body's *Journal* the resolution of censure its Whig members had earlier passed against President Jackson. The Whigs opposed Benton's effort with as much ferocity as they were capable of and this issue, and the conflicts that lay behind it, was firmly enmeshed in the presidential campaign, providing the backdrop for an intense period of ideological assault and personal vilification.

As part of this assault they especially went after Jackson's handpicked successor, once more exposing his supposed iniquities. With Old Hickory gone from the scene, the Whigs argued, the American people could clearly see the coarsening of American political life caused by the Regency-type spoils system and other iniquitous policies that slaughtered Indians and destroyed the nation's financial system. Detailing their claims, the Whigs called Van Buren a mere caucus politician, skilled in wily maneuver, but otherwise of no statesmanlike distinction. Calhoun reminded voters of "the New York system of corruption & trickery." One Whig newspaper called Van Buren "a man of many offices without any deeds of public usefulness." Daniel Webster argued that such men as Van Buren and his ilk put "party above country."

The Whigs also arranged for the publication of a number of books that further advanced their characterization of Van Buren as a sly, disreputable, political manipulator. A widely circulated *roman à clef, The Partisan Leader*, written by the Virginia Calhounite Nathan Beverly Tucker, stressed the iniquities of partisan manipulation in American public life. Few could doubt who was being described in the book. At the same time, the Tennessee Whig congressman, David Crockett, about to go to Texas to die at the Alamo, published a similarly unflattering portrait of the vice president in which, among other sharp comments, Van Buren was compared to Jackson as being as "dung to a diamond."

Beyond the expressed negativism toward the partisan label and the hostility directed toward the individual who had created it, and wore it so arrogantly, the Whigs also turned the sectional screws as part of their anti–Van Buren strategy. Van Buren's recurring Southern problem, heretofore limited in impact, erupted in 1836. Once again the world of Southern oppositionist politics affected him even in the moment of the realization of his long–sought personal and political aspirations. No matter how much he tried to meet any and all criticism, tensions constantly exploded. "The excitement in the whole South is very great," a Democrat wrote as the campaign began. "The Whigs are endeavoring to bring it to bear on the presidential question."

Because both Van Buren and Hugh Lawson White were seen in the South as legitimate successors to Jackson, the Whigs tried to abase the former in the interests of the other. Could a Northern political leader, they repeatedly asked, particularly a noncommittal party politician always willing to compromise be trusted to protect the South's rights and interests—or would he give them away for some advantage to himself? From time to time, some Southerners had tried to push that question to the center of political affairs as the key defining element in their section's politics. The recent upsurge of antislavery abolitionist activity in parts of the North further fueled these attempts in 1836, as they raised questions about the extent, and intensity, of Northern animus against the South. "Vote for a Northern President from a free state," the editor of the *Richmond Whig* editorialized, "and when the test comes, he will support the abolitionists." Both the Calhounites, and the more orthodox Whigs, took up this theme with unremitting intensity. They believed that they had in it a winning issue against the much distrusted New York politician.

PRESIDENTIAL CANDIDATES DID NOT CAMPAIGN openly on their own behalf in this era. Surrogates, usually candidates for other offices, or other party spokesmen, appeared on Van Buren's behalf in public forums. Letter writing, on the other hand, was acceptable and expected. Since enough of an uproar among nervous Southern Democrats had been raised in what everyone believed was a race with a still uncertain outcome, Van Buren, and those who backed him in the slave states, responded to the Whigs' accusations by underscoring the Democratic candidate's long-established commitment to letting Southerners pursue their particular social and economic processes as they saw fit.

Van Buren issued increasingly powerful public commitments underlining his fidelity to Southern rights and asserting that he would not, as president, ever interfere with that section's social and economic arrangements. He strongly denounced abolitionism and his friends convened a public meeting in Albany to highlight his, and his party's, long-standing position against abolitionist agitation. Capping all of this, the candidate's colleagues gathered together his letters and other documents on the abolitionist issue, and published a pamphlet, "Opinions of Martin Van Buren . . . upon the Powers and Duties of Congress, in Reference to the Abolition of Slavery either in the Slave-Holding States or in the District of Columbia." It embodied all of the themes on the subject that he had pushed throughout his public life, and in which, he strongly averred, he continued to believe. Southerners had nothing to fear from him, Northerner or not. All of this seemed to work as much of the sectional agitation concerning his bona fides on these sensitive matters ebbed as the campaign progressed.

VAN BUREN ALSO TOOK ADVANTAGE of the many public letters that came in to him from political activists throughout the country to discuss what he forcefully argued were the real issues of the campaign.

These letters provided the occasion to lay out his and the Democrats' positions, and highlight the critical things that distinguished them from their opponents. The main matter for voters to consider continued to be, he argued again and again, as he always had, the ongoing pertinence of old party divisions and the dangers posed by the resurgence of Hamiltonian Federalism, especially the base intentions of its leaders to expand the power of the national government, unconstitutionally, into areas where it did not belong, doing so, always, on behalf of a small, privileged, elite group, within the nation. Such nationalizing-aristocratic commitments posed, as they had since the 1790s, an enormous threat to the way that people chose to go about their lives, and the fairness of the opportunities offered to them. Federalism-Whiggery needed to be exposed for what it was. That was the Democratic campaign's primary purpose, as Van Buren and his colleagues saw it, no matter how much their opponents sought to divert the people's attention elsewhere.

In all that he argued, he successfully belied the familiar canard against him that he always hid where he stood on the critical issues in the interests of protecting his electoral support. He remained a cautious politician, but not an uncommitted one. The debates between the parties had certainly sharpened understanding of where they and their candidates stood in 1836. Voters might not be told by Van Buren what exact level of tariff rates he would accept, for one example, but it was clear where he stood on that and on the other matters before them. Certainly, his state's rights, old Republican tone and arguments contrasted with his opponents' quite different positions on the policies that each argued for.

THERE WAS NO ONE ELECTION DAY IN 1836. As various state laws dictated, Americans went to the polls at different times, some in the early fall, most of them in early November. National turnout increased only slightly over 1832, despite the quickening of partisan polarization that had occurred in Jackson's second term. It reached just under 58 percent of the electorate (although it surged higher in a number of states where two-party competition had increased in intensity since 1832). Some new voters had entered the electoral pool since 1828, but a great many of them had still not been drawn into party warfare at the presidential level. (Voter turnout continued to be higher, often to a significant degree, in state and local elections in these years.)

Counting the ballots and reporting the popular vote took time in this highly decentralized nation with so many scattered polling stations. By mid-November, however, the outcome was clear. Van Buren won the presidency by a relatively narrow margin, his popular vote totals falling off substantially from Jackson's two comfortable victories, barely exceeding 50 percent of the nationwide total. He had about 30,000 more votes than his three opponents, while the number of Electoral College votes that he won fell from Jackson's 219 in 1832, to 170. The three Whig candidates garnered 113. (True to themselves, as always, South Carolina's leaders cast their state's electoral votes for none of the main candidates offered, but, rather, for the anti-Jackson, Southern states' righter, Willie P. Mangum of North Carolina.)

The fall-off in the Democratic vote nationally suggested that Van Buren was both less popular than his mentor had been and much affected electorally by the shaking down and clarifying of party lines that was under way, as well as by the coming together and expansion of a more united opposition, aided by the many defections from the original Jackson electorate. Overall, popular voting patterns had significantly shifted since 1832. Formerly overwhelmingly one-party states, some in New England favoring the national Republicans, and others, in the South, which had voted for Jackson by very large amounts, had moved toward much closer two-party competition in 1836.

Other election results were mixed for the Democrats. The new Congress remained in their hands while also reflecting the same tightening of party competition in various places that was evident in the presidential race. The Whigs gained some ground in the South, the Democrats elsewhere. Finally, resistance to Richard M. Johnson, which had most notably persisted among Virginia's Democrats, caused enough defections from him when the Electoral College met so that he did not receive the majority of the votes in that body needed to be elected vice president. Under the Constitution it was up to the Senate to determine his fate when it next met. It did so without much fuss, electing him to the post when it convened and counted the electoral ballots in early February 1837.

"WE ARE TO BE CURSED with Van Buren for President," New York's Whig leader, Thurlow Weed, wrote in late November. And so they were. The New Yorker had achieved his highest political ambitions at last. And the country appeared to be in very good hands—unless one was a Whig, a Southern contrarian, or some other opponent of the new president and his party colleagues. There was much to be said in his favor. Beyond his amiable and modest demeanor, and his widespread negative reputation, Van Buren was as well prepared as anyone for the tasks he was about to undertake given his long political career and his vast experience in the Washington cauldron since 1821. Furthermore, in addition to his political skills and constant close attention to detail, the new president had a strong sense of the direction in which he wanted to lead the country. The outstanding Democratic political leader of his day after Andrew Jackson, what could possibly stop him from enjoying four—or eight—years of further achievement in the cause of states' rights Jeffersonianism, whatever the ongoing recalcitrance of the always bitter, but so far futile, opposition, that faced him?

Of course, his frustrated political enemies had a very different view of his, and the nation's, future. None of them, neither Calhoun, nor Clay, nor Webster, nor any of their many Whig followers in Congress and in the states, were done with the despised politician about to move into the White House, whatever the exalted place he had reached, and the succession of victories that he had managed to win against them. Like that of the new president, the Whigs' political course also remained clear. They intended to bring him down as opportunity offered, with all of the force that they could muster in Congress, in the state legislatures, and at the polls.

Chapter Six

———○———

At the Summit

The Eighth President of the United States, 1837–1841

CHIEF JUSTICE TANEY swore the fifty-four-year-old Van Buren into office on the steps of the Capitol on March 4, 1837, with Andrew Jackson looking on. The new president and his predecessor cast sharply contrasting figures during the ceremony. The tall Jackson with his military bearing stood alongside and, to some observers, wholly dominated his shorter, less physically prepossessing successor. There was a great deal of cheering for the outgoing leader by the large partisan crowd in attendance. Nevertheless, whatever the physical contrasts and emotional currents present, there was no question whose day it was. Martin Van Buren had reached America's political heights.

Long financially secure, the new president continued to live as comfortably as he had during the many years of his move toward the national summit. A widower for almost twenty years, he had successfully raised his four sons, always keeping them emotionally and geographically close to him. He had many friends in New York and in Washington, political and otherwise. Beyond the masculine world that he inhabited, he had engaged in, some of his friends later recalled, occasional flirtations in the years since Hannah's death. But, if he had done so, they could not have been very serious. None had matured into a more permanent arrangement. He remained unattached. Personally reticent about himself and his immediate family though he was, he seemed to be a happy man as he looked out over the large crowd assembled to greet him and mark the departure of his predecessor and mentor.

Most of all, Van Buren entered the office of president at the top of his political form. By the time of his election he had lived in the nation's capital for almost fifteen years, and never in idleness. He had had a wide variety of experiences there, culminating in four years of on-the-job training—watching, and working with, his powerful predecessor. Van Buren knew and understood the office that he was entering, its relation to Congress, its range of power and responsibilities, and the workings of the American governing system more generally.

He was prepared in another way as well. In his previous career he had only occasionally been the initiator of very much in the way of specific policies. But he had been an intense guardian of an ideological faith, leading a tough and sustained battle against the threat of excessive national authority that emanated from the Federalists, both the old ones and those he saw as their current version in the Whig Party. That ideological sense remained strong in the new president. He was determined to be a devoted Jacksonian in office, dedicated to preserving and defending Old Hickory's policies and approach to governing America, as exemplars of the Jeffersonian commitment that was central to both of them.

This approach to governing did not need extensive further preparation or a great deal of scurrying to put together a legislative agenda in the time between Van Buren's election and his inauguration almost four months later. There was not, in his mind, all that much to do. The most pressing issues of the era had been confronted and dealt with during his predecessors's years as president. The hated and dangerous national bank was dead, Indian removal was in its last stages, the tariff issue remained dormant and under control, the American scene was prosperous and forward looking. Therefore, he believed that "the wisest course is to confine legislation to as few subjects as is consistent with the well being of a society & to leave as large a proportion of the affairs of man as is possible to their own management."

In summary, so far as Van Buren was concerned, as president his role was to keep the nation always on an even keel and firm in its present pathway. One historian has called his inaugural speech as president "essentially a charter for inaction." It was full of expressions of good feelings about the United States and its many triumphs, and arguments that those triumphs would continue if Americans held firm to the notions of repose, order, and Jeffersonian republicanism. He raised, as well, the one possible difficulty that the nation faced: the sectional tensions that had risen during the campaign, warning against their continuation in the public arena, and singling out, and condemning, abolitionism for its recent provocative activities seeking to overturn long-accepted notions. These fervent antislavery proponents were, he warned, engaged in just the kind of disorderly conduct that would hurt the nation and its future if they were not stifled and shut down. But, whatever the abolitionists' recent roiling of the political waters, they had made little headway, and he fully expected that they would now be quieted.

Establishing an Administration

Van Buren moved into his new home in early March, accompanied by his sons Abraham and Martin Junior, both of whom were to serve as their father's principal aides. Abraham, who resigned from the army to assist his father, was appointed Second Auditor of the Treasury Department, a post that had been held in recent years by whomever was the president's private secretary. Martin Junior ultimately was appointed to a clerkship in the Land Office for the same purpose. The president's other sons, John and Smith, returned to Albany after the inauguration, but remained in close touch with their father from there, especially keeping him abreast of the state political scene.

As in any new administration, there were teething problems due to the demands by those who sought personal rewards from the new president, and the dangers of party factionalism if the wrong appointments were made. Van Buren was able to finesse part of the problem. He left Jackson's cabinet largely in place: Secretary of State John Forsyth of Georgia, Levi Woodbury the treasury secretary from New Hampshire, the very able Amos Kendall still heading the Post Office Department, former Senator Mahlon Dickerson of New Jersey the secretary of the Navy, and Benjamin Butler

remaining as attorney general. All had been either previously supported by or their appointment acquiesced by Van Buren when he
was with Jackson. There was one change. Before he left office Jackson had appointed Secretary of War Lewis Cass to be minister to
France. Van Buren replaced him with Joel Poinsett of South Carolina, the leader of that state's Unionist, anti-Calhoun Democrats.

Several job-hungry political groups felt slighted by their failure
to get a cabinet post from the new president. Recognizing the inevitability of such disappointment, Van Buren found places for as
many of them as he could in foreign legations and in whatever other
positions were available. Since he was succeeding another Democratic administration, there were much less replacement of current
officeholders at lower levels beyond the cabinet than would otherwise have been the case, given the expectations of a partisan spoils
system. Such anger as was expressed by the disappointed was normal for the course, and Van Buren began his administration in relatively good political shape despite the unhappiness expressed by
some.

Part of the president's settling in involved less direct political
calculations. He found his new home larger than any that he had
ever previously lived in, with a staff headed by a housekeeper to
manage his domestic affairs. Van Buren had always been active socially and continued to be throughout his administration. He
hosted a great many dinners from 1837 on, and attended many
given by others: his own cabinet, foreign ambassadors, and members of Congress. He always included some of his political opponents in his invitations to dine at the White House. Both Henry
Clay and John Quincy Adams—but not Calhoun—came to dinner
soon after Van Buren became president. Beyond the social intercourse that he so enjoyed, the new president used such occasions
as a means of keeping tabs on the political currents across town on
Capitol Hill, and to take the opportunity to advance whatever he
had on his mind at a particular moment.

ONCE FULLY SETTLED IN, Van Buren established the practice of con-
sulting widely, seeking counsel from Democrats, both in Washington and in key states. From his retirement in the Hermitage Andrew

Jackson proferred advice and a great deal of encouragement, both of which Van Buren welcomed. In Washington, the president frequently used his cabinet as an advisory body. It met weekly at the White House, more often during times of crisis, with the individual members discussing what was before them. Van Buren listened to their views before he announced what his policy choices were to be. Such use of the cabinet as a collective body for policy discussions was not unusual before the days of heavy administrative burdens for the individual secretaries. And it conformed with Van Buren's long-established practice of hearing everyone out on the matters that came before them for their decision.

The new president would also have, at least in the beginning, a great deal of support in Congress. In the Senate, while Clay, Calhoun, Webster, and Hugh Lawson White were all ready to oppose whatever emanated from the president, the Democrats were in the majority. Van Buren could count on the support of a staunch group of Jacksonians led by such longtime colleagues and personal friends as Silas Wright, Thomas Hart Benton, Pennsylvania's James Buchanan, and Franklin Pierce, the leader of New Hampshire's Democrats, to defend and advance the administration's cause there. The House of Representatives was partisanly less secure since, in addition to the committed Whig and Democratic blocs, the chamber also contained a group unaligned with either party, and, therefore, unpredictable in its members' behavior in committee and on the floor. They could (and did), go either way on the issues before them. Still, when the House met, it reelected the staunch Jacksonian loyalist, James K. Polk, as its Speaker.

At one level, Van Buren got along with Congress during his administration much better than had Andrew Jackson despite the intense political atmosphere that remained the American norm from 1837 on. In contrast to his predecessor, for example, Van Buren never vetoed any act that the national legislature passed except to pocket veto a resolution about the papers of James Madison. It was quite a change from the early 1830s when the Jacksonians could not always command majorities in Congress, if not a true indication of the state of the nation's political temperature in the post-Jackson years.

PANIC AND RESPONSE

For, despite the bright beginning of his administration, Van Buren's four years in the White House were filled with wearing battles, primarily due to a national economic crisis that began almost immediately after he took office. By most historians' estimates, he was not a successful chief executive. The main reason for that evaluation lies in his inability to respond effectively to the sudden and unexpected downturn in the nation's fortunes, that is, to find a means, consistent with his ideological commitments, to improve the situation confronting him.

In his inaugural address, he had proclaimed that the United States presented "an aggregate of human prosperity surely not elsewhere to be found." The many elements making up the nation's market economy were at their full power when Van Buren entered the presidency. Enormous energy, unleashed by American cotton's increasing penetration of the English market, high prices for the goods shipped, the rush to purchase land in the West, and the easy availability of credit to do so, thanks to the growth in the number of local banks offering the loans that undergirded the boom, had fueled a period of great prosperity since the early 1830s.

Not everyone benefited from the good times. Both consumer prices and interest rates on bank loans rose sharply during the economic expansion. The inflationary pressures led to food riots in New York City just before Van Buren took office. There were other signs of distress elsewhere in the country. But these moments did not, at first, seem to undermine the fact that, by and large, the United States was in the middle of an unprecedented economic boom, one that clearly was being enjoyed by so many of its citizens.

The federal government also directly benefited from the extraordinary prosperity. It was able to pay off the national debt and then accumulate a significant surplus in its funds thanks to the great rise in customs receipts because of the nation's robust trade activity and from the sale of federally owned land. The extent of this accumulation prompted the passage by Congress in 1836, during Jackson's last months in office, of the Deposit Act, which gave part of the growing federal surplus to the individual states to use as they wished.

At the same time, the country's perhaps excessive boom conditions frightened a number of policy makers. The Jackson administration had grown concerned about what they saw as the speculative excesses under way, funded, in their view, by the availability of altogether too much easy credit. One of Old Hickory's last acts had been to issue the Specie Circular, an executive order mandating that all purchasers of federal land had to pay for it in precious metal, and not by the avalanche of paper currency circulated by private and state banks, as had been the practice. Since there was much less specie in circulation than there were paper banknotes, such currency restrictions clearly were aimed to cool off what the Jacksonians in command believed had become an overheated economy.

Democratic leaders did not believe that their restrictive monetary policies would hurt the nation. Quite the contrary. They were confident that these efforts would calm and stabilize a runaway economy. They were wrong. There had been severe financial shocks before 1837 but the one that now came down on the nation was the worst yet. It began overseas. English banks, whose loans were financing so much of America's economic development, were suddenly beset by some domestic problems of their own and, as a result, began to tighten their credit policies. Their tightening, in turn, set off a reaction that seriously affected the American banking community and its customers. The sale of Southern cotton to English mills fell significantly, and prices dropped accordingly, while high payments (in gold) due for land purchases, or to repay bank loans, remained payable as scheduled. Cotton brokerages began to fail as their outstanding loans came due, or were called in by hard-pressed bankers. In May 1837, New York's leading banks, affected by the drying up of British credit, suspended specie payments. They were no longer able to pay off their creditors in gold or silver as they were committed to do. As these large banks suspended their payments, smaller institutions followed suit. More disastrously, some of them found that their situation was too fragile for them to continue operations and had to close their doors to avoid insolvency.

Predictably, this banking debacle was followed by a more general economic slowdown as state governments and private investors were forced to pull back from financing ongoing enterprises such as canal and road construction, laying off thousands of workers in the process. At the same time, textile and shoe factories in the eastern states found their sales sharply declining and began to lay off many of their workers as well. In agricultural areas, commercial farmers found themselves seriously overextended. Since neither England nor the usual domestic markets were buying their products to the extent that they needed, prices for their goods continued to fall rapidly. In turn, these farmers could not keep up their payments on the land they worked, which they had often increased in extent during the boom years. They faced foreclosure as their local banks demanded the money due on their loans.

All of this, coming just after he became president, confronted Van Buren with a severe and quite unexpected set of problems. His first task was to formulate an appropriate government response to what he initially described to Jackson as "the dreadful state of the money market in New York." As the situation grew well beyond that, he called Congress into special session, to meet in September 1837, to consider ways of dealing with the growing national crisis.

When it met, the assembled representatives and senators learned that the president's response to the challenges before them was to follow the policy and ideological paths he had long marked out. His approach was extremely cautious—some claimed that they were naive and unhelpful. From the beginning he refused to accept that the hard money, antibank, policies of the Democrats since the early 1830s were at fault, despite such charges from both his political enemies and some members of the financial community. Rather, in focusing on the causes of the current downturn, he forcefully argued that the distressed financial community deserved little sympathy for their self-induced problems. The depression had been caused, Van Buren believed, by private greed and overspeculation—extravagant and excessive behavior that hurt normal economic processes. He particularly railed, as Democrats had for some time, against the too easy credit that had been extended by avaricious bankers for their own narrow purposes and without sufficient caution as to the effects their actions would have. Their selfish policies, not what

Jackson's government had done, were now ravaging the whole system.

More critically for his reputation and political future, in turning to what the federal government could do, his distrust of extensive national power in general was as clearly manifested as was his resistance to the banking frenzy swirling around him. Faced with what he would later call an "unusual derangement in the general operation of trade" as a result of the activities of overambitious entrepreneurs, he had no intention of changing the federal government's course or modifying his firmly held beliefs. Others might call them into question as the crisis deepened but not he. In fact, Van Buren believed that dealing with the crisis would become the test of his, and his party's, core ideology, the limited government notions of Jeffersonian-Jacksonian Republicanism.

"ALL COMMUNITIES ARE APT TO LOOK TO GOVERNMENT TOO MUCH"

To the increasingly beset president, the nation's political terrain remained as it had been since long before he entered office. Faced with a depression, he unflinchingly reaffirmed the virtues of the negative state and stuck to that policy throughout his presidency. His affirmation of this view, amid the cries of protest and groans of despair, is worth recalling directly. In his third annual message to Congress, in 1840, the president repeated what he had been saying since the beginning of the crisis, that

> those who look to the action of this Government for specific aid to the citizen to relieve embarassments arising from losses by revulsions in commerce and credit lose sight of the ends for which it was created and the powers with which it is clothed. . . .
>
> All communities are apt to look to government for too much. Even in our own country, where its powers and duties are so strictly limited, we are prone to do so, especially at periods of sudden embarassment and distress. But this ought not to be. The framers of our excellent Constitution and the people who approved it with calm and sagacious deliberation acted at the time

on a sounder principle. They wisely judged that the less government interferes with private pursuits the better for the general
prosperity.

Nothing could be plainer. Once again there was no trimming or
evasion on Van Buren's part—however inadequate his notions
might be in the current crisis—as his enemies claimed they were.
Nor was the statement unexpected given his long and pronounced
devotion to the ideas expressed. One historian refers to the "passiv-
ity" of his administration in its response to the disaster it faced.
That is an apt comment, especially in light of the activist behavior
of future American governments when faced with economic turmoil. But that was not quite the way Van Buren considered what he
was doing. His reaction to the depression revealed little that was
new in his thinking, but it did clarify and harden his long held commitments about economics and government authority. He clearly
established that he was in charge of his administration's policies,
and told everyone what they should expect would follow from that:
no deviation from the true path even when confronting an unexpected and most desperate national crisis.

Of course, he was not as rigid as he said he would be. The president would subsequently compromise and shift ground on some of
the specifics of his policies as opposition developed and conditions
changed. But such moves on his part were always limited, resting
within already demarcated boundaries, and they did not alter the
basic outlook or goals of his administration.

Whatever the particulars of his proposals, they always were
aimed at allowing the nation's economic system to right itself natu-
rally as he firmly believed it could be expected to do if it was purged
of the elements that distended and destroyed its normal operations.
Such conservative economic thinking proved unable to restore
national prosperity or improve the condition of those Americans
adversely affected by the downturn. Van Buren did not agree. His
unyielding commitment to his traditional ideology remained his
hallmark throughout the crisis.

NOT ALL OF THE ADMINISTRATION'S BEHAVIOR was passive during the economic crisis. Despite his well-established ideological

hesitancies, the president believed that the federal government had to attempt some initiatives. He and his advisers came up with a package of proposals designed to tide the country over the immediate crisis. They were, to be sure, limited in scope. First, the administration suspended the last payment of the federal money due to the states under the law passed in 1836 since there was no longer a government surplus to share. This was followed by the issuance of ten million dollars in treasury notes to increase the amount of money in circulation, and, finally, by the suspension of the required customs bonds payments by the nation's exporters in order to lighten their need to find the necessary money at a difficult moment for them. Each of these bills went through both Houses of Congress with relative ease, despite rude noises from the opposition challenging the president's limited notions about what he intended to do.

FIGHTING FOR THE INDEPENDENT TREASURY

The major proposal offered by the Van Buren administration was what came to be labeled the divorce bill, establishing an institution, the Independent Treasury, to receive the federal government's funds, thus separating the government from its reliance on the state banks for that purpose. The state-focused deposit bank experiment for the holding of federal revenues that had been initiated under Jackson, had failed. Many Democrats believed that the state banks had recklessly used federal money deposited in them to expand their loan and investment activities without adequate safeguards. Further, under the existing law once a deposit bank suspended specie payments on its debts, as so many of them had now done, the federal government could no longer place the money it collected in them. Some alternative site for those funds was necessary. To Van Buren, an independent depository, unconnected to the nation's banks, was a reasonable answer to the need.

Despite the administration's strong push on its behalf, however, the proposal proved to be quite difficult to get through Congress. Whatever the sense of emergency in 1837, and the president's well-honed skills in political maneuvering, the bill's introduction aroused furious opposition, and led to a prolonged and extremely difficult three-year battle before Congress finally passed the legislation very late in the administration.

Given the American political climate, the resistance offered to the proposal should not have been unexpected. As he developed his policy options in the emergency that he confronted, Van Buren encountered the kind of determined political resistance that he had long known from enemies convinced that his policies were dangerously wrong, and, therefore, eager to use the economic downturn to wound him, and bring him down, in the country's interest. In their view, it was the failure of Democratic policies, particularly the destructive Bank War, and the overcautious and too restrictive Specie Circular, that had stifled growth and led to the financial contraction and the ensuing national depression. Any additional Democratic policy making would only further devastate the economy.

Whigs were united, therefore, against Van Buren's proposal for the independent treasury, arguing, instead, for a return of a national bank as the best means to handle the finances of an increasingly complex, market-driven, credit-needing economy. Although some present-day economic historians (but not all) disagree with the Whig interpretation of the causes of the depression, the latter followed their own instincts and pushed such notions to their limits throughout the crisis.

At the same time, some members of Van Buren's own party joined the Whigs in opposition to the administration's proposals. There was a great deal of strain, and increasing disarray, among the president's original supporters as the economic crisis deepened. Democratic congressmen were feeling the heat of public opinion from their constituencies. As a result, party leaders had a difficult time maintaining unity behind Van Buren's proposals. In particular, there was among them an important bloc who supported state banks, and who argued that the Independent Treasury would severely, and unnecessarily, cripple those that were still functioning. These Democrats rarely, if ever, supported the president as the bill moved through the Senate and House. At the same time, some of the more ardent states' righters in the party looked beyond the economic exigencies of the moment and demonstrated wariness about the increase in central, particularly executive, power, over the states in banking policy. They, too, proved skittish about supporting the president when congressional roll call votes came to be taken on the divorce bill.

At the other end of the party's ideological spectrum, however, was another group who were hard money, antibank "radicals," Democrats who were extremely hostile to the credit system and what they saw as its destructive operations. While they supported the president, who, they believed, had moved closer to their position, they felt that they had to be extremely alert lest he turn back toward the easy credit people among them. In the middle of the party was a third group, the bulk of the party's members, led by Wright and Cambreleng on Capitol Hill, trying to etch out a policy that would keep the party together, but which increasingly leaned toward the antibank side on the issue—too much for some, not enough for others.

To Van Buren's consternation, some of his closest allies and earlier supporters, such as Virginia's Ritchie, and Edwin Croswell, the editor of the Albany *Argus*, long the Regency's mainstay, were at first hesitant about the president's financial policy. Their lukewarm acquiescence, or occasional unhappy disagreement, were the last things that Van Buren needed as he sought to forge a policy consistent with the nation's needs and his own views in a political arena of intense contention. His strategy through all of this was to work through his congressional lieutenants to get the necessary legislation enacted. Wright chaired the Senate Finance Committee and successfully shepherded the bill through that body against the strong opposition present.

In the House of Representatives, however, although his longtime New York colleague, Cambreleng, chaired the critical Ways and Means Committee which had charge of the divorce bill, the opposition proved to be strong enough to force postponement of its consideration in the special session in 1837. More seriously for the president, the proposal languished for two years thereafter, first because of the temporary recovery of the errant banks in 1838, which eased economic matters briefly, and because of the continued resistance to its passage under any conditions, a resistance that never gave way.

The economic bounceback, while welcome, was short-lived. Another serious downward plunge occurred beginning in October 1839, a plunge dramatically highlighted by the failure of the former Bank of the United States, now chartered as a state bank in Pennsylvania and still led by Nicholas Biddle. It now had to suspend specie payments and it never recovered. Beyond that, this time there was not another quick rebound by the nation's economy. The second downturn lasted into the early 1840s. Van Buren kept reminding Congress of the need for legislation to deal with the credit problem so as to prevent any further embarrassments of the kind that the nation was suffering. In reaction to these many reminders, constant pressure, and this new stage in the prolonged crisis, and despite the persistence of opposition to the scheme, both Houses finally passed the Independent Treasury bill in early 1840. Van Buren signed it into law on July 4, almost three years after its original introduction.

In all that he did, as he guided the bill through, the president was closely concerned to find a pathway through his party's divisions, adjusting and shifting the measure's provisions as it seemed appropriate to do so. Events kept moving him further and further from the position that he started with in 1837, and ever closer to the hard-money, anti–all banks wing of the Democratic Party. But that was where the center of gravity of his party more and more seemed to be settling as the crisis deepened and his stance was increasingly commensurate with that political reality. The state banks had failed in their tasks and, to the Democrats, a national bank was unthinkable. It was better for the republic's health, an increasing number of them them had come to believe, that a rigorous spartanism in economic behavior, especially in the credit system, should become, once more, the nation's norm.

Van Buren also revealed something about himself as a national, as well as a partisan, leader, as he worked his way through the economic morass that he confronted from 1837 on. He did not see himself as having to be a bold executive in the style of his immediate predecessor, even as the economy crumbled. He continued to have serious reservations about a too powerful presidency and too aggressive actions emanating from the White House. In what he did he preferred to work with the cabinet and in small conferences with important congressmen. Even in the face of stubborn resistance and the setback to his plans, he never made the financial issue the kind of rousing crusade in the public arena outside of Washington that Jackson had done so successfully over the national bank.

Despite his strong feelings that the bankers had operated in ways that were disastrous to the country, Van Buren could not bring himself to come out as a tribune of the people, seeking to mobilize the crowd against the malefactors on the scene with slashing oratory and dramatic actions. Clinging to old-fashioned notions about presidential propriety and power, he missed many opportunities to rouse support on behalf of his policy. He would neither shout nor intimidate. That was not his style, although in a number of his state papers he more and more revealed something of the draining frustration that he felt because of the persistent opposition to his policies.

WHILE ALL OF THIS ACTIVITY to shore up and revise the financial system was occurring there was, of course, little thought given in the White House—or elsewhere in the formal government apparatus—to any direct relief measures to help those individuals and families made destitute and desperate by the panic. Relief centers and soup kitchens were set up in many of the nation's large cities from 1837 onward where as many of those out of work and their families as could be accommodated were fed and sheltered. These were usually set up by private charities; occasionally they were supported by local government to some limited degree. The understandings of the period did not allow for any kind of federal intervention in such activities no matter what the extent of the need, or the limitations of private charities or state government budgets, hard hit by the depression. Certainly, although Van Buren saw examples of human suffering, and such relief activities, in New York City when he visited there, he never went beyond expressions of pity and concern. There was no room in his or most of his party colleagues' minds for anything more.

Finally, toward the end of his term, in his annual message to Congress, following in the style of the economic theories then current that he believed in, he called for restraint and "severe economy" by the federal government, that is, a retrenchment in its spending. "To keep the expenditures within reasonable bounds," he told Congress, "is a duty second only in importance to the preservation of our national character and the protection of our citizens in their civil and political rights." He followed through on his belief and saw to it that the federal budget was severely cut back, a policy that, contrary to his belief, further contracted the economy and led to even more layoffs in the workforce. Van Buren expected these layoffs to be temporary, and for the economy to recover its former steam as entrepreneurial confidence in government policies and restraints in the credit markets took hold. Despite calls for a much different, less conservative approach by the Whigs, and some in his own party (and by many economists since), such was his understanding and his hope.

ON THE BORDERS AND ELSEWHERE

The normal business of government continued throughout the protracted debates over the economy, as critical as they had proven to be. There were always other problems to resolve, administrative matters to deal with, unexpected difficulties of one kind or another arising and demanding attention. The volume of business that came into the White House often seemed daunting to Van Buren's two sons who handled the president's paperwork. Over time there were several cabinet changes. Secretary of the Navy Dickerson resigned in 1838. Van Buren first offered the post to his old friend from the British mission, Washington Irving. When he turned it down, it was accepted by another friend and writer of some renown, James Kirke Paulding, also from New York. Benjamin Butler and his family were unhappy in Washington and always eager to return home. Van Buren stayed their hand for a time but Butler also eventually resigned, in September 1838, to be replaced by the stalwart Tennessee Democratic Senator Felix Grundy. There were a number of further changes late in his administration with Grundy resigning to return to the Senate, and Amos Kendall leaving the Post Office.

Both were replaced, not unexpectedly, by experienced loyal Democrats, Henry Gilpin of Pennsylvania and John Niles of Connecticut.

One other personnel matter during his administration significantly roiled the waters for Van Buren. Confirming the long-standing suspicions of his potential for malfeascence, Samuel Swartwout, Jackson's choice as the Collector of the Port of New York, suddenly disappeared, taking with him, an audit revealed, over one and a quarter million dollars of customs duties collected on behalf of the national government. Van Buren had warned Jackson against appointing Swartwout ten years before. Old Hickory had not listened and now his successor faced the financial and political fallout from that appointment. Matters were not helped when Swartwout's successor, the able New York city lawyer and political activist, Jesse Hoyt, later also dipped into the till in a manner that was probably illegal, or, at least, unseemly, much to Van Buren's subsequent embarrassment.

MANY OF THESE SHUFFLES and frustrations over personnel were unavoidable, and part of the collection of matters that kept Van Buren—and every president—busy throughout his term even when major issues were not at the center of their concern. But there was a great deal of the latter as well. Difficult crises on the nation's borders kept reappearing throughout his presidency, adding further weight to the burdens that Van Buren carried. In Florida a protracted and inconclusive war against the Seminole Indians, which had been going on since Jackson's administration, kept much of the United States army fully occupied during his term without much in the way of results.

The seemingly endless war was extremely costly at a time of severe economic stringency for the government and, of course, politically irritating. As in the case of all matters that arose, the Whigs found much to assail in what they saw as the administration's expensive mishandling of this running sore and loudly let everyone know what their reservations were. There was little that the Democrats could effectively do in rebuttal—although they tried in their speeches and editorials. Despite some important military gains against the Seminoles during his term, the war kept going and would not end until after Van Buren had left office.

The war in Florida was a single aspect of the government's Indian policy as originally formulated during Jackson's presidency and readily accepted by his successor. During Van Buren's term the last stages of Indian removal from the southern areas east of the Mississippi were completed, unfortunately, in a particularly messy and highly destructive form. The army was in charge of the move. But it proved to be inadequately prepared to handle its responsibilities; certainly it had not gathered sufficient provisions for the length and hardships of the trip to the new Indian homeland. As a result, the tribal members who were forced to move suffered severely, and many of them died along the "trail of tears" to the area reserved for them across the Mississippi River.

Van Buren's role in these missteps was minimal except that he was in general charge of affairs and readily accepted the plans already in place. He could have been more attentive to what was going on but that was not the way he thought about governing. The policy's execution was in the hands of the War Department, and the president left Secretary Poinsett to the task. Stories appeared in the press, however, that recounted the extent of the Indians' extreme hardships, and their devastation along the route. The newspaper accounts provoked heated attacks on the government, first from humanitarian groups who had been fighting on the Indians' behalf for some time, and then by the Whigs, as always ready to challenge the administration and its policies in every way that could.

AT THE OTHER END OF THE NATION, the Canadian-American borderlands remained a source of great tension and twice exploded into confrontation and violence during Van Buren's presidency. A rebellion against British rule that began in Lower Canada in late 1837 attracted strong support from Americans living along the border in New York State and posed difficulties due to the number of Canadian refugees who used American soil as a base for raids into their homeland. "This frontier is in a state of commotion," a federal official sent to observe the situation wrote back to Washington. As the refugees and their American sympathizers increased their activities across the border, the British government responded strongly. There were exchanges of shots, some burning of American property by the British military, and a significant increase in demands from the area that the president use force against British rule in Canada.

At the same time, farther east, the long-simmering disagreement over the location of the border between Canada and Maine burst into open conflict as American settlers moved into disputed territory there and were resisted by British troops. The local authorities on both sides of the border—wherever it was—did not help matters by their hardheaded willingness to force confrontation and insist on compliance with their respective, contradictory, positions. As a result of the activities of the British authorities in the disputed territories, the bellicose Democratic governor of Maine, John Fairfield, called on the president for military support on behalf of American citizens attacked and imprisoned by strong-armed British officials.

Van Buren was having none of it. In both of these border disputes he sought, and ultimately found, negotiated solutions that largely calmed matters. Disturbed by the involvement of Americans in the Canadian rebellion, and the apparent support for them by New York Democratic politicians, he issued a neutrality proclamation in early 1838 banning any warlike acts by American citizens under threat of federal prosecution. At the same time he dispatched General Winfield Scott to the area to try to calm matters down. Congress also responded. Despite not unexpected bitter partisan recriminations, it passed a new neutrality law that defined the limits of the involvement by American citizens in foreign disputes. It also appropriated money to strengthen the nation's border defenses.

In spite of further threats and a great deal of bluster from those involved, Scott succeeded in his mission. The border between New York and Canada quieted down, although a number of incidents continued to occur there until the end of the administration. It also left behind, in the "highly excited state of feeling on the northern frontier," as Van Buren described it to Congress, a great deal of frustration, and much anger, among many of the Americans living along the border. All of it provided much raw material for a subsequent political backlash against the president and his party.

WHILE ALL OF THIS WAS OCCURRING on New York's borders, the Maine boundary crisis also angrily bubbled along. Governor Fairfield had mobilized the state militia to confront the British in the disputed territory. Van Buren and the British minister in Washington agreed between themselves that they would not let matters decay any further but, rather, seek a peaceful solution to the crisis. The president called on Winfield Scott once more, sending him to Maine in early 1839 to calm matters, if he could. Despite the belligerent huffing and puffing by many citizens of the state, Scott was again successful, and the whole matter was moved into the dip-lomatic arena, to be finally resolved in 1842 by the Webster-Ashburton Treaty. Here, again, Van Buren's prudence and tactical skills helped defuse a crisis that had attained significant force for a time. Here, too, however, a potential political backlash against him was left simmering along the Maine frontier because of the continued disgruntlement among many citizens of the state.

Finally, there was the continuing matter of Texas on the nation's southwest border. In his last annual message to Congress in 1837, Andrew Jackson had called attention to the Texas revolution against Mexico and the complications that it posed for U.S. relations with its southern neighbor. The Texans were pushing hard, first, to have their independent status formally recognized by the United States, but only, second, as a preliminary to being annexed. Either course would provoke a confrontation with Mexico at a moment when relations between the two countries were, as usual, particularly tense over a number of long-standing issues. There also existed much wrangling between some Northerners and Southerners over the acquisition of what many considered to be an inevitable slave area, thus expanding the institution beyond its present boundaries. Although Jackson favored bringing Texas into the Union, he held back from pushing for it in deference to such complications. Just before he left office, as the result of congressional prodding, he did move part of the way by officially extending American recognition to the recently established Texas republic.

When Van Buren became president, the pressure to move the Texas matter further along increased as the new republic's agent in Washington pushed very hard among the political classes for immediate annexation, stirring up some congressmen and newspaper editors on the republic's behalf. In particular, several important Southern congressmen came out publicly in support of Texas being brought into the Union most promptly. But Van Buren moved slowly and carefully as he dealt with the issue. Much of the campaign for annexation was occurring in the summer and fall of 1837 as he was first confronting the economic crisis. A number of historians suggest that he was particularly concerned that any moves in Texas's direction would lead to a harsh sectional confrontation between the North and the South. Although such differences between the regions were expressed at the time, often strongly, it may be premature, and an exaggeration, to stress them too much in the presidential decisional calculus at this point. There were plenty of reasons, tied up both in the state of Mexican-American relations and with the other problems that he was dealing with for Van Buren to proceed slowly and warily.

Whatever the reasons, during the remainder of 1837 and into the next year, Van Buren, working with Senator James Buchanan, who chaired the Senate's Foreign Relations Committee, helped move the outstanding differences with Mexico toward peaceful resolution, suggesting that they be submitted to arbitration by a third party. He also made it clear, very early, publicly and privately, that there would be no annexation of Texas by the United States at this juncture. Although some pressure, and a great deal of grumbling about the matter, continued in various quarters, thereafter, for the moment the issue faded from immediate political consciousness although it would subsequently rise again to bedevil Van Buren after he had left office.

PERSISTENT POLITICAL CONFRONTATION

During the first two very difficult years of his tenure, Van Buren stayed close to Washington. In the summer of 1838 he took a trip, with members of his family and Secretary of War and Mrs. Poinsett, through western Virginia to White Sulphur Springs. At other moments he managed to enjoy some leisure time in places close to the national capital such as Georgetown, or in nearby Virginia retreats. He did not return to his home state until the summer of 1839, when he visited New York City, and then went on to Albany and Kinderhook, where he had recently purchased a house on a large plot of land. He spent some time in Saratoga Springs, and then traveled through the western parts of the state. Each time that he went off on these excursions Whig newspapers described him, not unexpectedly, given the way that they always characterized him, as not resting so much as engaging in backroom political activities for his own benefit.

And when he returned to the White House after each trip away, he found no lessening in the amount of business, large and small, that demanded his attention. During his term, whatever his inclinations to go slow, some piece of legislation, or some need for the government to act, was pressed on him for decision. Several times, for example, he urged Congress to liberalize the public land laws, first, by reducing the price charged by the federal government, and, second, by extending an important benefit to the actual settlers on the public domain by allowing them to have first claim when new lands were put up for sale—the so-called right of preemption.

He also made an effort on behalf of some the nation's wage earners. Even before the economic downturn, there had been calls by leaders of the nation's fledgling labor movement to reduce the length of the workweek. Van Buren responded during the depression—perhaps as a means of increasing employment opportunities for those out of work. By executive order, he put into place a ten-hour working day for federal employees on the government's many public works construction projects. It was quite a liberal move for its time. In most commercial enterprises, the normal workday in that era usually was from twelve to fourteen hours.

In such matters, and in others as well, political uproar, or at least strong opposition, not unexpectedly, followed each of his initiatives. By now he was fully accustomed to being accused of giving in to some pressure group, or engaging in an electoral ploy solely for his own advantage. Chopping away at him in this manner continued right to the end of his term, culminating in one final partisan uproar. The difficulties along the Canadian border and in Florida had indicated to members of the cabinet that some attention had to be paid to America's military strength and efficiency. In particular, Secretary of War Poinsett suggested legislation to increase the size and improve the professionalization of the army, including rationalizing the nation's rather diffused and incoherent state-centered militia system. Poinsett suggested that the militia be brought under federal direction for training so as to provide for its effective use by the national government when emergencies occurred.

The first part of the secretary's proposals passed through Congress. The army was enlarged, and some gingerly directed steps were taken toward improved professionalization. The second, dealing with the state militia, ran into a political storm as charges of executive usurpation, that is, unacceptable federal control over the militia, roused both Whigs and states' rights advocates against Poinsett's proposals. In the face of the storm, Van Buren backed away from the legislation and nothing further was done except to indicate, once more, the depth of the political passions that could be aroused around specific issues and, in this case, the symbolism and threat of an allegedly too-powerful presidency.

TENSIONS OVER SLAVERY had been apparent in some of the debates over Texas policy. A number of South Carolina's congressmen added to those by bringing up various perceived threats to slavery during the already angry debates underway over the Independent Treasury bill. Clearly such matters continued to play a role in the sensitivities and political consciousness of some Southerners despite the attempts by other political leaders there to damp matters down. At the same time, abolitionists in the North increased their campaign against the institution and the domestic slave trade during the Van Buren administration, largely through intense propaganda activities. They issued a great many pamphlets, and extensively petitioned Congress, calling for a number of things to be done to rein in what they saw as an evil blot on the United States. Despite a resolution, originally passed by the House of Representatives during Jackson's presidency, not to receive such petitions—the infamous Gag Rule, John Quincy Adams, now a congressman from

Massachusetts, insisted that they should be received in that chamber. The ancient right of petition could not be violated, he strongly argued, even against the abolitionists, and even if the president, seeking to hold his southern political flank, wanted it to be.

Each of Adams's attempts to change the House's rule in the late 1830s was met with outraged resistance, and the existing restrictive rule against receiving the offending petitions remained in place. But the need to face the issue over and over at the beginning of each new session of Congress rubbed everyone's wounds raw. Van Buren, as always, tried to stay out of what was occurring on Capitol Hill, but several times he lashed out against abolitionism in official messages and made it very clear, as he always had done, that, in his view, slavery was a matter for the individual states to handle as each of them wished. To him, it was not the national government's business.

As if he needed anything more, Van Buren's usual non-involvement tactics and occasionally expressed antiabolitionist viewpoint, were challenged by the *Amistad* case in 1839, when a ship of that name, originally sailing from Africa, but now out of Havana, Cuba, filled with Africans destined for a southern landing, and then being forced into slavery, was seized by an uprising of its human cargo. They ultimately brought it into port in New London, Connecticut. From there, the fate of the people on board rested in the court system as abolitionists brought a number of cases, claims, and counterclaims, seeking the Africans' freedom, all of which kept the matter bubbling for some time.

From the first, the federal judiciary was involved in the matter and that demanded involvement, as well, by the attorney general, and his superior, the president. In the circumstances, Van Buren took, not unexpectedly, a very legalistic—and pro-Southern—approach to the matter, with his administration pointing to the nation's treaty obligations that dictated that the Africans be returned to Spanish authorities in Cuba. Beyond that, the president insisted that it was a matter for the courts to resolve, which they ultimately did by ordering that the Africans be returned to their homeland, not to Cuba, a decision that went against the administration's legal beliefs, public arguments, and decided wishes.

Despite the intervention of John Quincy Adams before the Supreme Court on behalf of the Africans, the length of the proceedings, and the bitter abolitionist assaults on the way that the administration handled the matter, the *Amistad* case did not arouse as much general interest in the political arena as it might have. Many Americans were concerned. Many more were not. Nevertheless, it was still another reminder to Van Buren, if he needed it, that the president's role in any matter that came up was always going to be on people's minds, and destined to be politically charged, and a potential threat to his political situation, as a result.

"BEYOND THOSE LIMITS I SHALL NEVER PASS"

Life in Washington had not been all unhappy turmoil for the much beset president. To his delight, Van Buren's family continued to thrive. During his presidency his oldest son, Abraham, who had just turned thirty, married Angelica Singleton, the daughter of a prosperous South Carolina planter. After their European honeymoon, the couple moved into the White House where the new Mrs. Van Buren served as the president's hostess for the last two years of his term. At the same time, his free-spirited second son, "Prince" John, who had once danced with England's Princess Victoria, and who had earned a deserved reputation as an often unrestrained playboy, at last showed signs of settling down. He courted and, in 1841, would marry Elizabeth Vanderpoel, who came from a Kinderhook family. After their wedding they remained in Albany where John's legal and political careers continued to prosper. Van Buren's other two sons remained close, as well, dividing their time between New York and Washington.

But ever pressing political realities always clouded the happiness of the president's personal life. The warfare that erupted over every move that the president made, on the borders and in Washington, only underscored how uneasy these years were, despite Van Buren's original hopes for a calm period in office. Elected triumphantly in 1836 as the follower of, and successor to, Andrew Jackson, he had very much wanted the tumult of Old Hickory's years in office to settle down so that he and the nation would serenely bask in the economic prosperity of the time. He should have known better, given his own experiences over the past decade, and his belief that intense political divisions were normal, and always to be expected, in the robust but fractious nation that he now led.

As a leader he had shown definite traits that reflected that previous experience and the way that he preferred to do things. Occasionally he suggested, as he wrote in his autobiography about another matter, that he "acted the part of listener rather than of a contestant." This was rarely, if ever, completely true. As policy maker and activist, once drawn in by the Panic and the other matters that had filled up his days, he had remained true to his Jacksonian commitment in domestic affairs, the ideals that were central to his political being, and had demonstrated his abilities as a tactful, careful, diplomatic leader. He was fully involved in the policies and actions of his administration, leading, prodding, and, while always listening to the advice of his associates, deciding for himself on the course that the government would follow. He believed that such actions were an appropriate way to approach his duties as president—even if he set a different example from his mentor, the self-proclaimed crusader and tribune of the people, Jackson.

In any event, it had been an exceptionally tumulous four years for Van Buren and his supporters. "No President," Senator Thomas Hart Benton later summed up, "ever had a more difficult time." The president and those around him undoubtedly concurred. But, despite being hounded and bloodied by the force of the opposition to everything that they had attempted to accomplish, they also believed that they had done well given the problems thrust upon them by forces that were, they argued, outside of their control. Peace had been preserved despite many provocations, potentially divisive domestic confrontations had been avoided, and, at last, Congress had passed legislation that would, they strongly believed, lead to the stabilizing of the economy, not only in a most effective way, but also in a manner consonant with the Republican tradition.

In his inaugural address, referring to the rigorous limitations on national power that he found in the Constitution, Van Buren had told his audience that he agreed with them, and "beyond those limits I shall never pass." He tried to live up to that promise and believed that he had done so. He had kept the Jeffersonian faith. His ideas had come through intact into the last year of his term, whatever his, and their, political scars, due to the ever present, determined, and wrong-headed, resistance of the Federalist-minded politicians in Congress and elsewhere. He had, in short, as the Democrats saw it, ruled the country reasonably well.

That was one way of reading the situation, and a reassuring one to the president. There were other ways of doing so, both then and later—ways that stressed the inadequacies of his policies, and the weakness of his governing efforts, during the economic crisis. Who was right? The always politically sensitive and astute Van Buren knew that the final reckoning as to the course he had pursued since 1837 would only come, as always, from the assessment of his tenure by the voters, first, in the many elections that occurred in the states throughout his term, in the contests for seats in Congress in 1838 and 1839, and then culminating in the most critical contest of all, his own campaign for reelection to a second term in 1840 at the head of his party and, as always, of the Jeffersonian-Jacksonian Republican cause. Those frequent elections had never been far from his mind as he worked away in the White House throughout the busy and contentious times that had followed his inauguration.

Chapter Seven

———————O———————

"The People Could Not Be *Rallied* for Van Buren"

AS BOTH PARTIES gathered their forces for the upcoming presidential campaign, they were nearing the end of a critical period of political evolution. The fallout from all that had occurred since Van Buren became president continued the sorting out and refinement of the nation's party lines that had been underway for a decade. Both Whigs and Democrats had continued to mature into clear ideological opposites—disciplined armies made up of different groups of supporters perpetually at war with one another. Each still harbored some inconsistent elements in its ranks. But these had grown fewer, and less distracting to each party's main message, as the years had passed.

Beyond the two dominant coalitions at the top of the political world, there still were a number of activists who, while deeply involved in the policy arguments of the day, refused to subsume themselves completely within either of the major parties. Calhoun and his followers had never considered themselves Whigs, for example. Rather, since the early 1830s, they had believed themselves to be in a necessary, but temporary, alliance with the Clay-Webster coalition against the dangerous excesses of Jacksonianism during the nullification and bank wars, and then, again, in 1836, and afterwards, against Jackson's designated successor.

At the same time, the restlessness of many in the Democratic Party over the Independent Treasury culminated in a serious and unrepairable rift within its ranks. A number of influential Jacksonians

137

who had supported Old Hickory, and then his successor's run for the presidency, left a party that they believed had now moved too far toward radicalism on issues of banking and the needs of commercial enterprise. These defectors, labeled Conservatives, once free of their former partisan alliance, also articulated an antiparty stance, and thought of themselves as an independent political force having policy differences with both the Whigs and the Democrats. To Van Buren's chagrin, these party defectors included some influential leaders from his home state, among them United States Senator Nathaniel Tallmadge, as well as other long-standing friends of his from elsewhere, most particularly, William Cabell Rives of Virginia, once a close ally and confidant of the president.

THE FINAL SHAPE OF THE PARTY SYSTEM

Both of these blocs remained at the edge of affairs as two of the few groups not yet finding a comfortable ideological resting place in the hardening partisan structure. Each had some votes and influence in Congress and in parts of the electorate. Both, therefore, had an ability to keep their concerns alive on the public stage. The question in the late 1830s was could they do so effectively outside of the party system? Whatever the inclinations of either bloc, the answer was no, and each became, during the last part of Van Buren's presidency, more firmly than ever part of the two major coalitions controlling the political arena. To the president's delight, Calhoun and his bloc of Southern contrarians began to cooperate with the Democrats during the Independent Treasury debates in Congress.

Although Calhoun moved cautiously, and his followers in Congress could not always be counted on by the administration, warmer personal relations between the longtime antagonists developed as well. The South Carolina leader and Van Buren began to meet, both politically and socially, for the first time in almost a decade. The signs were clear and positive. By 1839, Calhoun indicated that he and his followers supported the president's reelection. They argued that Van Buren had, whatever his earlier deficiencies, now proven himself to be fully committed to the states' rights position that the

South Carolinians championed. This remarkable turnaround from past events provided an important addition to Democratic strength, not only in Calhaun's home state, but in other parts of the South as well.

The Whigs, in their turn, won the support of most of the Conservatives. The latter's anger against the administration's, and the Democratic Party's, increasing hard-money stance drew them closer to the probanking Whigs toward the end of Van Buren's term. The Whigs also gained significant additions to their ranks from among the numerous Anti-Masons still active on the scene. The latter had maintained an independent political presence since the mid-1820s in Pennsylvania, western New York, Ohio, and a number of New England states, although many of them had supported the Whigs in national elections. In the middle and late 1830s, the movement's leaders, such as Thurlow Weed and William H. Seward in New York, and Thaddeus Stevens in Pennsylvania, moved into the ranks of the Clay-Webster forces, bringing with them a large number of much appreciated voters.

As a result of these countermovements, while there still were political incongruities remaining in the two emerging partisan line-ups, some states' rights Southerners among the nationalist Whigs, for example, as the 1830s came to an end, both parties had become more coherent in their membership, outlook, and public advocacy. Furthermore, the durability of alliances and allegiances among political leaders, and their supporters, that now settled in, would remain a dominant facet of the nation's solidifying political architecture for a decade and more.

One outcome of this process was the final clarification of the Democrats' policy stance. By late in Van Buren's term, the party was showing, in its views of economic policy, a more anticapitalist and radical face than it had earlier articulated, one that even more sharply distanced it from the Whigs on these issues. While Van Buren was certainly no radical in comparison to some of the urban workers' movements and hard-money forces abroad in various places, such as New York's "Locofoco" Democrats, his views on the dangers of profligate banking, in his words "a force which the boldest might fear," had now brought him and the more radical blocs together ideologically. As the Washington *Globe* noted in 1838, "there never existed so thorough a separation and so exact a delineation and opposition of the two parties, as at this moment." Democratic spokesmen argued that this was all to the good. Ideological clarity and unity, Van Buren and his colleagues believed, would help them maintain their electoral power against their adversaries, not only in the immediate future, but for a long time to come.

The "Tornado"

The American election cycle was, as always, a busy one in the late 1830s, beginning with the closely watched state legislative contests in New York in 1837, which took place after the onset of the financial panic. Such indicator elections told political leaders a great deal about how things were going among the voters and what was likely to happen in the next set of confrontations. Van Buren had always engaged in sophisticated, for the time, electoral analysis, seeking information each year from local Democratic leaders, and putting together what he learned, to get a sense of New York's voters as another election approached.

But others had learned to follow his lead. Whig Party activists were now also seeking out and utilizing the same kind of information that the Albany Regency had always gone after. Interrogating local party leaders, Whig leaders, like their opponents, keyed on the critical questions: Who did, or did not, come to the polls? What attracted, or repelled, them once they got there? What was the distribution of the vote between the parties, especially compared to previous contests? How could the results be summed up? What did they mean for the future? Such analyses were particularly cogent as the parties entered their new era of increasingly well-organized unity and policy coherence. Unfortunately, the evidence collected did not always present as sharp a picture of the political landscape as the leaders wanted, especially in a mercurial period of the shaking down of voter commitments. Whatever their hopes, no one yet knew what would be the ultimate electoral results of the political winnowing of the past decade.

The answer came quickly enough and it was not to Van Buren's advantage. The first signs of trouble appeared in the fall elections of 1837. In New York State these contests were an unexpected disaster for the Democrats. The Whigs won a large majority in the state assembly, taking an extraordinary 121 of the 148 seats there while also winning almost all of the state senate seats fought in that year. The rejuvenated Whig Party in the state, under the command of its shrewd leaders, Weed and Seward, had learned how to deal effectively with the problems of management and mobilization necessary to win modern elections. To his chagrin, they had adapted Van Buren's techniques, all with very good effect for themselves and their party.

This "New York tornado" as Van Buren labeled it, was repeated elsewhere as seven other states that had supported the president in 1836 went for the Whigs in their local elections a year later. The combination of potent economic issues mobilized against them, and the Whig maturing as an organization, was too much for the Democrats in the dark days of 1837. Yet there was always hope among the Van Burenites that these disasters at the polls were only temporary. Since the revival of national political conflict in the twenties, the Democrats had done extremely well in presidential races. They believed that their occasional losses in other contests were largely due to temporary aberrations (the depression) or their own careless missteps, which were correctible. Their dominance of American politics would continue if they pulled themselves together and mounted the kind of campaign among the people of which they were capable, and which they had done so successfully over the past decade.

Election prospects did, in fact, improve for them after the 1837 setbacks. Despite Seward's stunning election as governor of New York in 1838 over William Marcy, and other Whig gains there, including the loss of his congressional seat by Van Buren's close associate, Churchill Cambreleng, other state and congressional elections went better for the Democrats in that year of some economic recovery. While the overall results were mixed, the voters indicated, once again, to the president's relief, that many of them still had a strong commitment to the Democratic Party that would, he believed, remain powerful and decisive.

A year later the positive signs continued. Van Buren was buoyed by a number of Democratic victories in 1839 in local elections in such key states as Virginia and Tennessee, where James K. Polk was elected governor, and by the reduction of earlier Whig majorities in other important places, including New York. Whatever the extent of recent losses, the indicators of the voting returns seemed more and more positive for the Democrats. At the same time, beyond the cold calculation of the numbers, party observers noted other signs of their continued strength. When Van Buren returned to New York for the first time in almost three years early in the summer of 1839, for example, he was greeted everywhere by stirring receptions from large and enthusiastic crowds, popular outpourings that raised his and his colleagues' spirits immensely. Democratic strategists concluded that the enthusiasm manifested everywhere the president went, from New York City to the western reaches of the state, was a most positive sign for the future.

"MATTY VAN IS A USED UP MAN": THE ELECTION OF 1840

Van Buren was, therefore, confident of his prospects as the year 1840 began. The key to success in his reelection campaign lay, as always, in the Democratic Party paying meticulous attention to its organization at every level, in getting its traditional message out, exposing the Whigs for what they were, and what they threatened to do—this was to be one more contest between "the democracy and the aristocracy"—and then ensuring, to the fullest extent that they could, that the party's loyal supporters all went to the polls on election day.

But it was not to be. Van Buren had never before faced what lay in store for him in 1840. The Whig leaders had learned their lesson well since their loss to him four years before. They believed that they had their best opportunity ever to overthrow Jacksonianism, now embodied in Old Hickory's acolyte. They outgeneralled Van Buren and his associates from the outset with a surprising explosion of energy in a well-organized, rousing, often vicious, populist crusade against the sitting president.

The Whig assault in 1840 began with their unexpected choice of a presidential candidate. After much maneuvering before and during their national convention, which was held in December 1839, Whig leaders convinced the delegates to forsake their party's ideological leader, Henry Clay, who expected to be nominated once again, and turn, instead, to someone whom they believed had attractive—and winning—qualities without Clay's negative political baggage. (Clay was anathema to the Anti-Masons, and to many antislavery northern Whigs. He certainly would not attract enough Democrats to make an impact, and his appeal to new voters was, at best, uncertain.)

Instead, the party's choice was a war hero akin to Jackson, William Henry Harrison. He had won military glory when he defeated the Indians and their British allies at the Battles of Tippecanoe in 1811 and at the Thames in 1813. He had also proven to be a surprisingly popular vote getter as one of the three Whig presidential candidates in 1836. To appease the states' rights Southerners in their party, the convention nominated the former Virginia senator, and one time Jacksonian, John Tyler, for vice president. The combination was summed up, and celebrated, in the Whigs' memorable slogan, "Tippecanoe, and Tyler, Too."

The party members also demonstrated how much more sophisticated they had become in their organizational commitments and practices. They were everywhere in their onslaught: organizing local campaign committees in every state, holding unparalleled numbers of mass rallies that noisily filled the air with what was at issue, mobilizing Tippecanoe clubs to march through the streets howling for their hero, and establishing campaign newspapers that put out their message everywhere.

Veterans of Harrison's military campaigns came forward to be cheered; a young Horace Greeley edited the *Log Cabin*, a highly successful, and widely distributed, campaign newspaper. The Whigs involved women in their campaign in ways that went far beyond the usual norms of American society. They attended, and participated in, Whig election rallies, helping to organize them and, most provocatively in this male-oriented political society, speaking at some of them as well. In another departure from tradition,

Harrison spoke at rallies and celebrations near his home in a way that no previous presidential candidate had done.

All of these activities made their contribution to rousing the voters to join the crusade in the fall, and getting them to the polls to vote Whig when election day arrived. Many of the more traditional Whigs were uncomfortable with what they now had to do to bring the masses to their side, activities that they had severely criticized in earlier times. But they were persuaded to follow the course anyway, with surprising and effective consequences.

To an extent, much of what the Whig organizers and spokesmen put forward in this "hurrah" campaign was deceptive hoopla, eliciting, as a result, a great deal of scorn and outrage from their opponents. Democrats claimed that the Whigs were more noisy than informative in their appeals, concentrating their energies on raising the roof rather than educating the electorate as to their plans. But both sides understood that there was much more going on than what later generations only remembered as the campaign's "mindless pageantry." In addition to thorough organization, and an attractive candidate rousingly presented, the Whigs strongly articulated some familiar themes in order to undermine their rivals. Hell raising and frivolity could, and here did, rest on substantive, politically potent, foundations.

What the Whigs wanted to do—and successfully accomplished—was to raise, and plant firmly in public consciousness, all of the negatives associated with Van Buren from his past career, and add to them his abject failure as the country's leader in a time of crisis. Although their national convention did not issue a party platform, fearing splits among their members over the specific details of proposals, beneath the hoopla the theme of the Whig campaign was always crystal clear. First, they put forward, once more, the old idea of the partisan abuse of the republican political system due to the manipulative wiles of party hacks trying to be statesmen, that is, Van Buren, his associates, and the whole system of political management associated with them. So far as the president was concerned, "he never originated anything to benefit his country," they argued. "He never fought to secure her glory; he has done nothing but plot to elevate himself."

The recently revealed corruption in the New York Customs House and the spoils system, more generally, were also grist for the Whig call for the reform of government, and its return to its true republican roots. Such financial irregularities, and the appointment of the unqualified to office, were now endemic in the system that Van Buren had helped establish and so forcefully championed. The Democrats, they thundered, had become a new, arrogant, aristocracy, hostile, like the old, to the people's needs and wishes. What the Whigs pushed was a well-worn characterization of those associated with the rise of the party system, advancing their own cause with their particular rhetoric. The historian Major Wilson accurately refers to "the antiparty pieties of the furiously partisan Whigs" in 1840.

Whig campaign speeches, editorials, and pamphlets, approached the issue of antirepublicanism and aristocracy in another way as well. They renewed their long-standing charge of executive tyranny against the Democrats, reminding everyone of the grave danger to the Republic from a too powerful, "monarchial," president, bent on amassing too much power to himself and then using it to engage in unconstitutional behavior. Such evil ambitions had once been embodied in Jackson—"King Andrew" in Whig iconography. But the threat of monarchy, Whigs argued, was not dead. All that anyone had to do was consider the behavior the current inhabitant of the White House. In such matters as the Independent Treasury and militia reform bills, Van Buren and his associates had infamously continued along the party's long-standing pathway designed to increase, unconstitutionally, the president's span of control at the expense of proper local authority.

"MARTIN VAN RUIN"

Beyond the ever present sins of the Democratic Party and its leader, the majority of the Whigs' campaign rhetoric focused on the condition of the American nation. Party spokesmen rang every change on the economic depression that they could, not only lamenting the nation's sad state, and the people's intense suffering, but, most especially, the indifference of the president and his party in the face of the disaster. In particular, the Whigs took advantage of an opening offered to them by Democratic editorialists' dismissal of Harrison as a simple, naive, and somewhat doddering country bumpkin, unfit to be president, to dramatize the policy failures and blind arrogance of Van Buren and his party. Their "Log Cabin and hard cider" campaign, with its potent symbols of good republican values and behavior, took on especially clear meaning in the prevailing depressed economic situation.

Whig egalitarian rhetoric filled the air throughout the campaign. party spokesmen emphasized the contrast between their own man and the despised president in terms that people could particularly understand in this year of economic crisis. In 1840 the Democrats became the elitists and anti-American claque of aristocrats. Whigs hurrahed for the poor and deprived and portrayed their candidate not as idle and overly innocent, but, rather, as simple, honest and hardworking, while the high-living Van Buren remained ensconced in the lushly furnished palace on Pennsylvania Avenue. This was, as Henry Clay said to a Whig rally, "a contest between the log cabin and the palace, between hard cider and champagne." None of their rallies was complete without a log cabin and barrels of hard cider in evidence to remind everyone of the political and policy differences in play.

In fact, if it mattered, the "simple" Harrison was a Virginia aristocrat who had never lived in a log cabin. But such precision did not count for anything in 1840. The portrayal offered of Van Buren fit into two emerging images that were growing into standard electoral fare—both embodied by Harrison: On the one hand, the plain-living, honest farmer who, through his own efforts, had pulled himself up from his beginnings, and, on the other, the heroic figure who had served his country with distinction, and who was now summoned by the people, once again, to clean up the Democrats' mismanagement of the national economy. The contrast with the sitting president was, the Whigs argued, a profound one—once again skating over the fact that it was Van Buren, not Harrison, who had emerged from society's lower reaches and who, although never a soldier, had gathered a wide range of useful political experience, and demonstrated much civic ability, as he had risen through the ranks.

A major centerpiece of these anti–Van Buren efforts was a speech in the House of Representative by the Pennsylvania Whig congressman, Charles Ogle. "On The Regal Splendor of the Presidential Palace," full of exaggeration though it was, starkly dramatized what was at stake: how much Van Buren had lost touch with the American people and their condition, spending the money of "poor farmers" and "poor laborers" to enhance his own life style in Washington. Reprinted as a campaign pamphlet and widely distributed by the Whig organization, Ogle's speech was a spectacular assault on a dandyish, clueless, and uncaring president, more interested in "the trappings of royalty" that he brought into his residence and the "foolish displays of splendor" of his aristocratic way of life, than in the dismaying condition of the American people during his time in office. Every change on his overextravagent high living as a "lavish spendthrift" of public monies in the face of economic despair, was rung by delighted Whig orators, editors, and pamphlet writers.

The point was clear. It was necessary to remove "Martin Van Ruin" from office or the country would continue to suffer from his misguided policies and his antirepublican, antipopular beliefs and behavior. The president was a "used up man," and there was someone better at hand ready to serve the people in his place. In contrast to Van Buren's demonstrated failure as president, the Whigs would restore prosperity through vigorous government action. Harrison may have been sixty-seven years old, but he and his party associates were in tune with the people's needs, and would vigorously look to meet them once in office. Only they could, given what had happened during the past four years. The American people's choice, therefore, was clear-cut as the election approached, enunciated in the title of another of the Whigs' telling pamphlets, "Harrison and Prosperity or Van Buren and Ruin."

"IT IS INEXPEDIENT AND DANGEROUS TO EXERCISE DOUBTFUL CONSTITUTIONAL POWERS"

Van Buren was not politically idle as the Whigs shaped their savage campaign against him. He and his associates had long been considering what they needed to do to win once again, given all that had occurred within the party and in the nation since 1837. They had a great deal to think about. At the outset, for one, despite the Democrats' desire to concentrate on other things, sectional irritations continued to lurk around the edge of affairs and pose problems for the president. To meet the continued anger of some Southerners, Andrew Jackson demanded that Van Buren replace Vice President Johnson on the ticket in 1840 with someone more respectable, such as former House Speaker James K. Polk. But Van Buren did not want to rock the boat at this juncture. He believed that the restive Southerners would go for the Democratic ticket despite Johnson's foibles, and he wanted to retain the strength in the West and among Eastern workers that he believed the vice president brought to the cause. But the situation was ticklish and its electoral impact remained problematic in parts of the South as the campaign began.

THE DEMOCRATIC NATIONAL CONVENTION met in Baltimore in early May. Rousingly renominating Van Buren without controversy, it left, by the design of its leaders, the vice presidential spot on the ticket vacant in order to reduce the tensions that Johnson provoked among them. The delegates announced, instead, that party members in each state were free to make their own choice for that office as they saw fit. It was an awkward strategy and it was not clear what such choice might lead to. Fortunately, so far as Van Buren saw it, a number of potential challengers to Johnson dropped out as the campaign got underway, and he remained the party's sole visible candidate for the vice presidency.

The nominating formalities attended to, and possible electoral weaknesses addressed as best they could be, the Democrats quickly established that they were ceding nothing to their opponents. In contrast to Harrison's active campaigning, Van Buren's role in the effort to reelect him was unexceptional; that is, it conformed to the expectations of the time. He remained in Washington as the campaign opened, living a quiet, dignified life in the White House, following his usual routine as the nation's chief executive despite the clamor around him, meeting with his cabinet, and other government officials, and being personally unobtrusive in his party's electioneering efforts throughout the months leading up to election day.

But, of course, he was never uninvolved in what he had always engaged in with zest and ability. Despite his public noninvolvement, his experienced hand was on everything that occurred in the race, if always quietly and out of sight. He considered strategic matters as they came up, consulted with supporters, and contributed to the formation of campaign strategy. Surrogates for the president, party leaders, and officeholders throughout the country stumped for votes on his behalf. Early in 1840, Andrew Jackson journeyed to New Orleans to celebrate the twenty-fifth anniversary of his great victory over the British. Many saw, and some condemned, his trip as an attempt to stir up voters for Van Buren whatever the nonpartisan claims made for the journey. Elsewhere, Silas Wright took the lead in speaking extensively on behalf of the president in New York, James Buchanan followed a similar course in Pennsylvania, as did Polk and Felix Grundy in Tennessee. Other Democratic leaders did the same in Van Buren's cause in their own states.

During the campaign the Democrats relied on all of their other well-honed skills at mobilization as well. In addition to the many speakers out on the hustings, they unleashed an extremely partisan press on their candidates' behalf. Amos Kendall left Van Buren's cabinet to edit the party's national campaign newspaper, the *Extra Globe*. In New York, Democrats established *The Rough Hewer* as a campaign newspaper to supplement the *Argus*. These, and other party newspapers, along with thousands of pamphlets and a number of campaign biographies written especially for the occasion, were widely distributed by Democratic Associations and Committees of Vigilence, who, once more, closely organized matters at the local level on behalf of their party and its candidates.

Federal employees, such as census takers, postal employees, and custom house clerks, among others, most of them loyal Democrats, distributed campaign documents and worked to mobilize large rallies for the cause and, on election day, get people to the polls and then carefully watch the vote counting. Many of these partisan employees were also expected to contribute a portion of their salaries to the party. Vigorous nationwide campaigns such as this were becoming quite costly: printing bills, the travel costs for visiting speakers, and the supply of food and drink at campaign rallies, all had to be covered. (The Whigs did quite well in this matter, drawing on their own partisan state employees, as well as calling on some bankers, and other commercially involved citizens, for the financial support that they needed.)

BEYOND ALL OF THIS DEMOCRATIC SCHEMING AND ACTIVITY was a substantial message. The party's, and Van Buren's, conception of the political arena, of what was at stake in the election, and how the Democrats would retain control, remained as it always had been. The Whigs had made him the center of their campaign. In contrast, the Democrats did not. Their publications made little mention of the party's presidential candidate, nor did the Democrats discuss him directly during the campaign. That was not because they thought he was unpopular and a drag on the ticket. Rather, at the center of all of their activities and expressions was, as always in the party's litany, "measures, not men." What the Democrats primarily campaigned on was not the attractiveness of either candidate, but on their claim of the superiority—and rightness—of their creed. Van Buren and his party were more determined than ever to defend their vision of the negative state, and the continued danger to the people of Federalist aristocratic particularism. Policies, right ones, and wrong ones, were at stake, not whether one was supposedly a plain-living farmer or not.

They reacted to the specific Whig assault, therefore, in familiar, simple, and coherent ways, beginning at the national convention that issued the nation's first major party platform, forcefully articulating their ideological outlook. It focused on what Democrats argued were the relevant issues, especially the differences between themselves and their opponents. All of their strict construction ideas, and the specific themes by which the Jacksonians had defined themselves for more than a decade, were once more laid out before the voters: Their opposition to spending federal money for internal improvements, their hostility to protective tariffs, to a national bank, and to the federal assumption of state debts. Beside being economically destructive, all of these specific policies, which fostered additional power at the national level, would, they continued to argue, inevitably lead to authoritarian, not popular, rule in the Republic. In contrast, their candidates, once in office, would always carry out the Democracy's core policy commitments, "to foster and perpetuate those great principles of constitutional liberty," that is, "that the federal government is one of limited powers . . . [and that] it is inexpedient and dangerous to exercise doubtful constitutional powers."

The platform set the tone for the party's campaign. Democratic spokesmen went after Harrison, vigorously exposing his many inadequacies and pretensions. The Van Burenites' primary focus was always on what Tippecanoe stood for, that is, on his, and his party's, ideological deceptions. The general was a front for the resurgence of the unacceptable, failed, and dangerous policies of the past. If he was chosen by a deluded electorate, the latter would quickly discover that behind the uproar on his behalf, Harrison, himself, as one Democratic editor wrote, was "avowedly a Federalist." He favored a high tariff, a national bank, unconstitutional expenditures for internal improvements, and all the rest of the frightening Federalist "heresies" against the Constitution, which, looming as they did at the very center of the Whigs' purpose, threatened so many Americans because of their excessive claims for national power.

In the same breath, Democrats acknowledged, and underlined, the fact that their very different commitments had not shifted since 1837 despite the depression. There was no reason to modify them. Rather, as constitutional truisms, they had become, quite properly, frozen into permanence. They were the only notions that the American nation could live by and preserve all the things that it stood for, and its people cherished. The choice before everyone that fall was, therefore, clear, whatever was being hidden by the "Federalist" campaign hoopla against the president.

"WE ARE FULL OF HOPE," Van Buren wrote to Andrew Jackson in early September as the campaign got underway, "although the struggle outstrips incomparably anything that has gone before it in point of profligacy on the part of the opposition." His own course was clear, whatever the Whig shenanigans. He continued an earlier practice of responding by letter to inquiries about his policies from groups of citizens, refuting in them the Whig attacks on him.

Others alerted the Democrats in various places to the work they had before them, often offering precise details as to what they should do. He wanted organization and discipline, not drama. He was less publicly dismayed by what the Whigs were doing than angry at their lies about him and pretenses about themselves. Those had to be repeatedly exposed.

There was nothing surprising in Van Buren's activities in 1840. Once more, he demonstrated that the familiar charge of noncommitalism, and the persistent characterization of him as too adaptable ideologically in electoral situations, were both misplaced. He was fully with his surrogate campaigners, and the party's platform, in their relentless reiteration, and reinforcement of the main themes that defined the Van Buren democracy. He knew where he stood on the policy issues of the day, he believed that he understood the nature of the opposition, and he believed that, once aroused by the Democratic campaign, the voters would surely be with him on the matters before them. In his mind, they could not do otherwise.

THE DIFFICULTIES THAT VAN BUREN had previously had with the skittish Southerners in proving his commitments as a Northern man not to interfere with slavery, were not as noticeable in 1840 as they had been four years before. To be sure, some sectional tensions erupted during the campaign—as they always did. The antislavery agitation of the late 1830s in parts of the North had led to the formation of the Liberty Party by some of its leaders to contest the presidential election, with a predictable, anxious, and angry reaction from Southerners. But, despite their commitment and their enthusiasm, the Liberty Party did not seem to pose much of an electoral threat to the Democrats. The former's core vote, such as it was, was small, and largely lay among Whig-leaning groups. (The Liberty candidate, James Birney, was to win only about 7,000 votes for president, about one-third of one percent of the national total, most of them in the Whig country of western New York.)

More to the point, by then, Van Buren and his party associates believed that they had successfully dealt with the issue. Like everything else that they said that year, the Democrats relied in this area on their established commitments, and the policies that flowed from them. The party's long-standing, persistent, defense of localism was the key. In their national platform, they reminded the Southerners (and others) that Congress "had no power under the constitution to interfere with or control the damestic institutions of the several states." Those states, they continued, "are the sole and proper judges of everything appertaining to their own affairs." Such arguments and approaches, whose meaning was clear to the intended audience, had brought the Democrats much popular support in the past. They were expected to do once again as the nation went to the polls.

"A MISTAKE IN THE PUBLIC MIND": VAN BUREN GOES UNDER

The American political community had grown used to fervent and vicious political confrontation. But national politics had never experienced anything like the campaign of 1840. A giant carnival of rallies, marches, and oratory sharply marked a massive Whig attempt to mobilize all of those who were discontented with the state of the nation. And, on election day, it worked against the similar, but insufficient countermeasures of the Van Burenites. The founding father of systematic political organization and popular mobilization behind specific causes and sharply etched symbols was outmatched and ultimately crushed at the polls by the Whigs' "hurrah" efforts.

Turnout for the presidential election reached unparalleled nationwide levels in 1840. The mobilization of new voters had been going on steadily throughout the 1830s as the two parties developed their skills at organization and their ability to articulate clear, coherent appeals. Still, in the last two presidential races, only an average of about 56 percent of those eligible to vote had done so. In 1836 about one and a half million voters had turned out. Four years later, almost two and a half million, over 80 percent of those who could legally vote, surged to the polls in an unprecedented display of popular mobilization and commitment. (In New York State, almost 92 percent of those eligible to do so voted for president.) It was a powerful movement forward for the American political system, one that began an era of very high turnout in presidential, and other, elections as voter involvement continued to intensify, and the mechanisms of popular mobilization were honed to ever higher degrees of efficiency on behalf of both major parties.

When the many votes that had been cast were counted, the results stunned the incumbent president and his optimistic colleagues. A majority of the electorate had responded to the Whig message as that party's leaders had wanted them to do. The closely watched October state elections went against the Democrats. There were substantial Whig majorities in such key states as Ohio, Indiana, and Georgia. A month later, the results confirmed October's dire omens for Van Buren. The popular vote totals were close—the president received 47 percent of the total cast nationally. He actually won more popular votes this time than he had gotten in 1836. Some of the states that he lost were closely competitive between the parties. With only a few slight shifts of voter sentiment in them they could have gone the other way into his column.

But none of those considerations, no matter how appealing to his and his party's search for an optimistic perspective, did him any good. The main point was that the final result was decisive. Despite the relatively close popular vote, Van Buren was swamped in the Electoral College. Harrison won popular majorities, and all of the electors, in nineteen of the twenty-six states with 234 electoral votes, including New York's 42, to the president's seven states and 60 electors. Van Buren won Virginia and four other Southern states, but only New Hampshire and Illinois in the North and Northwest. And the Whigs would comfortably control both houses of Congress—for the first time alongside a president of their own party. After twelve years of Jacksonianism—and Van Burenism—Whiggery commanded the nation.

Van Buren believed that his defeat stemmed from "the instrumentalities and debaucheries of a political Saturnalia in which reason and justice had been derided." Some of his fellow Democrats, including Andrew Jackson, believed that, in addition to the deceptions, outrageous practices, and lies, of the Whigs, there had also been a great deal of anti-Democratic fraud at the polls, repeat voters, others imported from one state to another as the case demanded, vote buying, and the rest of a range of similar illegal practices. Francis P. Blair, who had performed yeoman service on Van Buren's behalf as editor of the Washington *Globe*, spoke for many Democrats when, after the election, he referred to "the most enormous injustice and corruption in the canvass and fraud at the polls ever witnessed in any country."

But, if such practices existed to the degree believed by the losers, they were not an adequate explanation for Van Buren's defeat. Both sides engaged in some fraudulent practices, and made outsized appeals to passion and drama. The outcome of the presidential election stemmed from more than "corruption in the canvass and fraud at the polls," however. Van Buren lost because the issues and the times were overwhelmingly against him, and because the Whigs took full advantage of the opportunity offered to them by the nation's unhappy travails since 1837. "The people could not be rallied for Van Buren" was the final lamentation of one Democrat. That was because, in the eyes of too many Americans, there was good reason for them not to vote for this president's reelection.

To be sure, most voters read the partisan appeals in 1840 through the lens of their own experience and heritage, as well as how each of them viewed their current situation and prospects. Many of them retained their strong faith in the Democrats and Van Buren; others reasserted their equally imbedded Whig commitments. Such voter continuities were based, as always, on each person's economic interest, pertinent social, ethnic, and religious, loyalties, and long-standing support of one or the other party. These people were each coalition's core voters—their base.

Other voters, however, read the current political scene differently and, because of that, severely damaged Van Buren. In some parts of northern New York and Maine there were negative reactions against the president for his unacceptable nonaggressive policy toward England during the Canadian border controversies. Defections from the Democrats because of the draining battles over financial policies, and the angry Southern resistance to Richard Mentor Johnson, also hurt the ticket. But, more critical than such 216 localized reactions, were two other elements that severely compromised Van Buren's chances: The Whig mobilization of their core popular vote to a degree previously not accomplished, and, most of all, the powerful pro-Whig impact of the economic collapse on some Democrats and many uncommitted voters.

Van Buren's problems were twofold: First, his principles, no matter how deeply rooted in the Jeffersonian tradition, and how fervently held by his supporters as the proper American creed, no longer seemed adequate to many Americans. The economic situation in the country underscored his policy failures, and he, himself, seemed to have little to offer except his determination to stick to the same course that his government had followed since the Democrats took office. At the same time, the Whigs had found a clear, consistent, well-organized, and well-articulated means of bringing his weaknesses and failures out in the most dramatic, overwhelming, and persuasive ways. What was left to cause people to continue to support him? Democratic arguments about resurgent Federalism, or in favor of traditional Jacksonian policies and approaches to governing, even in the face of a deep crisis, were overwhelmed by the reality of an unprecedented economic collapse and the Van Buren administration's failure, in its wake, to do much about it beyond mouthing timeworn truisms about the virtues of limited government responsibility.

Perhaps he and his colleagues relied too much on what now appeared to be stale notions of what was at stake—Democratic spokesmen could not forbear from continuing to label Harrison, even after his victory, as "the standard bearer of the Federal and Abolition parties"—at a time when other things seemed more crucial to the electorate. Many of the voters who had been less involved in previous elections, or who now came to the national polls for the first time, made it clear that the Whig appeal against the president's ideological and behavioral failures had fully penetrated into their consciousness. Van Buren's solid Jeffersonian dogma, and anti-Federalist articulation, did not work in 1840—to his surprise and electoral destruction.

CODA

Van Buren was, not unexpectedly, saddened and deflated by his defeat and, more than that, outraged by what had occurred. He later referred to his loss as "a mistake in the public mind." He could not understand that it was his policies—or lack of them—that had brought him down. For all of his political acuity, he could not believe that a Whig victory was possible. Therefore, since the Democrats were America's popular party, they could only have been beaten by the kinds of misrepresentation and fraud that the Whigs so extensively and artfully engaged in in 1840. That provided grounds for optimism despite the result. He was confident, therefore, that the party of Andrew Jackson would soon return to power on the back of their unimpeached policy commitments. A month after the election he sent his last annual message to Congress, containing a review of his administration as well as one more clear affirmation of what the Democrats stood for. There were no surprises in the message. How could there be? He remained unbowed, at least in the public arena where he had always worked so effectively.

After that there were only the few months remaining before the Harrison administration came to Washington. In his last days in office, over the winter of 1840–1841, Van Buren maintained an upbeat and genial public face to the nation. One visitor in mid-February described him as "gracious . . . fat and jolly," even in the aftermath of defeat. There were still official matters to be dealt with, which he continued to do as he always had, with—as ever—constant controversy erupting between the parties when he did so. Senator Clay tried, and failed, to have the Independent Treasury law repealed in the last days of the Twenty-sixth Congress, creating one more partisan confrontation over financial policy. Again, when Van Buren made a final appointment to the Supreme Court in the very last moments of his administration, due to the unexpected death of a sitting justice, the Whigs, not unnaturally, strongly resisted. Clay attempted to delay a vote on the nomination so that the incoming Harrison administration, only days away from assuming control of the government, could name the new member of the Court. His efforts failed. The Democratic majority in the Senate held together and confirmed the president's appointee, Peter V. Daniel of Virginia, just before it, and the president, left office at the beginning of March.

These final days were not only taken up with politics and governing for the defeated president. He continued to carry on a vigorous and nonpartisan social life as had always been his habit. When General Harrison arrived in Washington and, as custom dictated, called on the president, Van Buren went out of his way to be gracious and welcoming, even breaking precedent by calling, accompanied by his cabinet, on the new president at Harrison's hotel and then entertaining the president-elect at dinner at the White House. In one last gesture of his civility he offered to move out of the president's house before he was required to do so if Harrison desired to move in early. Tippecanoe did not so desire.

On inauguration day, Van Buren was not in sight amid the massive public celebration of the Whig triumph that filled Washington's streets with one last "hurrah" for their successful candidates. The practice had been that defeated incumbents, that is, the Adams family in 1801 and 1829, did not attend their successor's inauguration, and Van Buren did not—although there is some evidence that he was willing to do so if asked by the incoming president. But he was not invited to the swearing in ceremony at the Capitol or the celebrations that followed. It was not his day to be seen, and he spent it in his temporary quarters in the house of his last attorney-general, Henry Gilpin.

His term had ended, not, certainly, as he had wanted it to, but, he believed, with a reasonable amount of dignity displayed in its final moments by the outgoing administration. It was time, in Van Buren's mind, to move on. He had no intention of remaining in Washington City now that he had been so decisively rejected, and no longer had any official duties there. A few days after Harrison's swearing in, the ex-president called on his successor one more time to pay his respects preparatory to his own departure. A few days after that, in the second week of March, he left the capital, after almost twenty years in residence there, and, accompanied, as always, by members of his family, began the long journey back to his home state.

Chapter Eight

The Partisan Leader at Bay, 1841–1847

VAN BUREN WAS FIFTY-EIGHT YEARS OLD and in good health when he left Washington and returned to the Hudson valley. He had continued to gain weight and lose hair during his presidency. But whatever the signs of his aging, he remained vigorous and eager to get on with his life. Arriving in New York City in the third week of March 1841 to a large and enthusiastic, if rainy, reception from loyal supporters, he broke his journey there, spending several weeks with his close friend and colleague, Benjamin F. Butler, in the latter's house in lower Manhattan. While in the city he bought furniture for his new residence, attended the round of dinners inevitably offered in his honor, and enjoyed some of the many opera and stage performances that New York offered. Rested and refreshed, Van Buren resumed his journey in early May, traveling up the Hudson River by boat, reaching his home village of Kinderhook just over two months after leaving the presidency. His fellow townspeople welcomed him back with another warm reception.

The ex-president's course seemed well set as he arrived. The property that he had purchased just south of his native village in 1839 was to be his new and final home. The former Van Ness estate consisted of 50 acres and a house that was, when he bought it, a relatively large and comfortable one built in the Dutch colonial style characteristic of the region. Van Buren had purchased an additional 150 acres of farmland and orchards to add to his new estate, naming the whole Lindenwald, after the stand of trees lining the entrance to the property. He spent his early weeks there putting everything in order, receiving the furnishings he had purchased in New York City, guiding the work being done to renovate the house and improve the property, and becoming, once more, part of the scenery of his village.

ONCE HE HAD SETTLED IN, his life at Lindenwald displayed Van Buren's outwardly social being, his personal warmth, and his always strong commitment to his expanding family. Whatever was going on in the inner depths of the ex-president's soul because of his defeat, his public face in Kinderhook seemed untroubled and always filled with goodwill. His sons were all with him for a time after his return before Abraham and his wife, Angelica, who had lost a newborn child the year before and was again pregnant, returned to her father's home in South Carolina. (They would come back to Kinderhook on a regular basis and live in a cottage close by Van Buren's home.) John was in Albany with his new wife pursuing both his law and political interests, and the youngest, Smith Thompson, was also living there after he, too, married in that spring of the family's return to New York. All of them visited Lindenwald frequently. Only Martin Junior, who was always on the edge of poor health, now lived regularly at home with his father.

Van Buren entered his new life as a retired country squire with apparent enthusiasm. He followed a vigorous regimen, managing a household staff of six, and supervising the workings of his property by a hired manager. He could be found most days touring the place and demonstrating his interest in the ordinary activities of a working farm. In the evening there was excellent food to be enjoyed, and often spirited conversation with neighbors, or guests from farther afield, or quiet reading in his library on the ground floor—all of the trappings of a contented gentleman enjoying his later years. He was already beginning to think about the rebuilding and expansion of his home that would ultimately transform it into a much larger and more ornate residence. In all that he was doing life seemed good, if very different from what he had been engaged in for so long. He soon boasted of the success of his farm in providing not only produce for his own table, but also a surplus for sale in the local markets.

THE RETURN TO POLITICS

Although elderly by the standards of the time, Van Buren's appearence of being in gentlemanly retirement was deceptive. At first, to be sure, he largely stayed out of view. He was in a new situation that took some getting used to. Since 1812 he had held office steadily and had never been out of the public eye. His plans and objectives had always received important notice and had often borne fruit. Now he was on the sidelines as he been only once before since entering the national stage, very briefly, after his rejection by the Senate in 1831.

But he was never committed to remaining at home and only tending his crops. He and his friends did not believe that his political career was over. The presidential election of 1844 was already on the horizon and very much on their minds. Van Buren would be sixty-two years old in 1844. Only Jackson and Harrison had been older when they had run for the presidency. This did not bother him or his many supporters. Whatever his age, and although recently defeated, they considered him still to be the leader of the Democratic Party nationally, and, as such, an important political player with much more to accomplish before he ended his career.

Van Buren largely followed a policy of political reticence in 1841–1842 even as his partisans remained active on his behalf and others sought to ferret out his intentions. Before very long, however, he returned to public consciousness as he began to travel away from Kinderhook including making visits to old friends beyond New York State. All of these trips were widely reported, and speculated about, in both Democratic and Whig newspapers. His most ambitious foray was a five-month tour of the southern and western states beginning in early 1842. During it he visited both Andrew Jackson at the Hermitage in Tennessee, and then Henry Clay at the latter's estate, Ashland, in Lexington, Kentucky. Two such stops; even if he claimed that he was only visiting old friends, provoked, in many people's eyes, notions of very heavy political activity underway. There was endless rumination, in particular, in both friendly and other newspapers, about what was discussed when he visited Clay and stayed with him for four or five days.

Sometime after Van Buren returned to New York, he determined to seek renomination by his party, fully expecting to avenge
his 1840 defeat. When he made the final decision to run again is
not certain. There was constant pressure, from the first, coming
from Democratic meetings in various states, some of which called
for his renomination for president as early as 1841. In a public letter in that year, the ex-president seemed to indicate, in his usual
cautious style, his availability for renomination if the party wished
him to lead it once again. The omens were certainly favorable at
several levels. Jackson strongly supported him for another run. (Old
Hickory also, as he had done once before, pushed his fellow Tennessean, James K. Polk, for the vice presidential nomination on a
Van Buren ticket.) By many calculations, there remained a potent
Democratic electoral majority in the nation waiting to be reenergized and mobilized. In fact the party came surging back from its
1840 debacle to do well in the state and congressional off-year elections of the next two years. All of the signs for 1844—and for Van
Buren's return—appeared to be quite positive.

RIFT IN THE DEMOCRACY

But his political pathway after 1841 turned out to be different
from what he and his friends expected it to be. Van Buren's defeat
in 1840 materially affected the dynamics of his party as well as
those of his own career. In the minds of many Democrats the ex-
president was not a desirable choice for renomination. Whatever
the range of his current support, they thought that he carried too
much political baggage that militated against his running again.
They argued that he had irredeemably lost his way politically in
1837, and subsequently fallen too far in public esteem. As a result,
while the succession after Jackson had been clear, and had benefited Van Buren, now, in the eyes of a number of powerful and ambitious Democrats, control of the party was up for grabs. Several of
them, in Congress and in the states, began actively considering a
run at the presidential nomination themselves, using the alleged
electoral deficiencies of an elderly and defeated candidate as the

focal point of their resistance to Van Buren continuing on as the dominant force in the party and becoming its inevitable nominee.

At the same time, Van Buren's long-standing ideological problems with various party groups also adversely affected him. At both the national and state levels, the condition of the democracy after its stunning defeat in 1840 opened up previously papered-over fault lines and induced a search for new policy initiatives as well as for fresher candidates. Some party leaders more openly expressed their frustrations over the Democrats' policy limitations and magnified the importance of the differences separating them from one another. Given what many of them saw as the ex-president's unyielding stance on most matters, and his resistance to any change in his accustomed ways of thinking, the rise of new issues and new takes on older policies brought out enough anti–Van Buren sentiment in the national party to be noticeable and potentially a threat to him.

The condition of New York State's Democratic Party also caused Van Buren a great deal of worry in the early 1840s. There, too, his traditional, rather austere, republicanism no longer seemed adequate to many Democrats in his home state. To them, the development needs of New York demanded more robust government involvement than the party had usually been committed to under Van Buren's leadership. Pushing their views aggressively in party councils in the late 1830s, they were as resolutely opposed by others who remained as committed, as they had always been, to the ex-president's version of the Jeffersonian vision. The splits among New York State's Democratic leaders as a result of these ideological differences, first, over banking policy, and, beyond that, toward the market commercialism that was becoming so prevalent in the nation, left, in their wake, many serious strains, much anger, and a clear potential for further heated confrontation within party councils.

These state party splits grew worse after Van Buren left the presidency and returned to New York. In the early 1840s the development-minded Democrats in the legislature did not hesitate to support increased state spending for a wide array of canal and other internal improvement building projects. They did so even though these enterprises originated in the administration of the new Whig governor,

William Henry Seward. The more traditional Van Buren Democrats in the state were appalled by the behavior of their supposed party colleagues toward their enemies on such issues and made their feelings known in the sharpest terms. The strong differences between the two blocs erupted at every party meeting held in New York even as the state democracy began to point toward 1844. The differences became serious enough to lead, as well, to the Van Buren group establishing a new newspaper, the Albany *Atlas*, to represent their views, since the long-established *Argus* now usually spoke on behalf of the ex-president's party enemies in the state.

Van Buren and his closest supporters strongly disagreed with those, both in New York and elsewhere, who suggested that he was a weakened candidate, well past his prime both ideologically and chronologically. And, despite the case being offered against him, and the signs of growing opposition to his renomination, the Van Burenites retained the initiative. They remained the party's dominant force, both nationally and at the state level. Key party leaders throughout the nation indicated their continuing loyalty to Van Buren throughout 1843 and into 1844. As they did so, the renewed recognition of his leadership role was sharply underscored, and his renomination in the latter year seemed to be more probable than not. "Many a man who now pouts his lips and hesitates and sneers," his friend George Bancroft wrote to him in mid-1843, will ultimately "make huzza for Van Buren." He would surely have the opportunity, his friends confidentially believed, for one more electoral challenge to the Whigs' extreme and unacceptable policy heresies.

THE "MONGREL ADMINISTRATION"

But it was not to be. Instead, Van Buren reaped the whirlwind of all of the negative, or skeptical, feelings about him, and the persistent internal disagreements among Democrats concerning the party's future. His political role and ambitions came apart, not all at once, but clearly so as the political scene heated up. At first, the Harrison-Tyler administration provided many reasons for Democratic optimism about their return to national power. The Whigs

quickly fell into disarray after their triumph in 1840. Harrison unexpectedly died after a month in office and chaos subsequently
reigned in administration ranks. The nationalist Henry Clay, and
the new president, the states' rights champion, John Tyler, battled
over the significant policy differences between them, differences
that their party had ignored earlier in their determination to beat
Van Buren. As a result, by mid-1841, the national political scene
was in spectacular disarray. Tyler vetoed a number of basic Whig
proposals on the national bank, and other matters, that Clay had
guided through Congress. Party reaction to the president, "His Accidency," in their bitter parlance, was thunderous, and fervently
hostile to him. Relations became so polarized by the actions of both
sides that a Clay-dominated party congressional caucus formally
read Tyler out of the Whig Party in September 1841.

Matters seemed to be looking very much to the Democrats' and
Van Buren's advantage. But that proved to be an illusion—at least
for the former president. His movement toward a triumphant
renomination at the upcoming national convention became entan-
gled with the resurgent presidential ambitions of two of his old foes:
the beleagured Tyler, and a revitalized John C. Calhoun. Both men,
the Virginia states' righter and the South Carolina nullifier, were
well experienced in the Southern contrarian tradition that was always so skeptical of national political parties, and highly suspicious
of Northern political leaders. They now used that tradition for their
own political advantage.

Despite his political ostracism, President Tyler continued to
nurse hopes for his election in 1844 and began to seek ways to
carve out a place for himself in the political spectrum that would
bring him victory. For a while he looked for friends among the Democrats as way to rebuild his hopes—after all, they all favored states'
rights over excessive national power. His moves in this direction included an offer to Van Buren, sounded out through Silas Wright, to
appoint him to the Supreme Court, presumably in order to get the
ex-president out of the way. That went nowhere—Wright made it
clear to Tyler's emissary that Van Buren would not be interested—
but it was an indication of the president's intense ambitions.
"His Accidency" then offered the position to Wright—with the

same negative results. Other Democrats were similarly unforth-coming to the president's overtures.

Tyler's Democratic option having made so little headway, the president turned elsewhere for support. With both the Whigs and Van Burenites opposed to him, he saw a chance for himself only if he could break the powerful hold that the two major parties main-tained on the political scene. He focused, therefore, on forging sup-port behind an issue that he hoped would bring together dissident Democrats, his own corps of states' rights Whigs, and the bulk of Southern political leaders, regardless of party, in support of his can-didacy in 1844.

At the same time, John C. Calhoun reentered the fray seek-ing to find a way to at last be elected president. Not unexpect-edly he looked South, especially focusing on the old issue of free trade and Northern tariff oppression of his section. He picked up some support from free trade advocates outside of the South, es-pecially after the Whigs passed a new, higher tariff in 1842 that the Calhounites suggested was another unacceptable threat to their prosperity. As they mobilized on behalf of the South Car-olinian, Calhoun's supporters also reopened attacks on Van Bu-ren for his long-standing efforts to find a middle way on the ques-tion of tariff protection that would, they insisted, as they had ten years and more before, hurt Southern interests just as much as the Whig efforts in this area.

All of the toing and froing of this president making made little headway in 1842–1843 despite it having some success in roiling the political waters and challenging any complacency existing in Van Buren's camp. Tyler was increasingly written off by both Whigs and Democrats. His supporters, his "corporal's guard," as they were de-risively dubbed, were too few to mount an effective effort on his behalf. The Calhoun boomlet also began to ebb as his circle of sup-porters did not expand in numbers as much as hoped—or was needed for him to get anywhere. At the same time state Democratic conventions continued to declare their support for Van Buren's renomination. By January 1844, twelve of the eighteen state party conventions that had met had come out for him as their choice in 1844, and four of the other six were noncommital as to who the nominee should be, choosing neither to support him, nor to back any other candidate against him.

Everything seemed to be falling into place to ensure his renomination. Van Buren's lead in the delegate count, and in newspaper and leadership support, looked so promising that other potential Democratic challengers to him began to rethink their position. Once again, the force of party loyalty, and the imperatives of staying together against their common enemy, all that Van Buren had always stressed to his fellow Democrats, were working effectively on his behalf as the time for the party's national convention approached. Originally set for November 1843, it was rescheduled to May 1844, primarily at the urging of Democrats opposed to Van Buren, presumably to give them more time to mobilize their forces against him. Van Buren agreed to the delay in order to keep things calm within party ranks and provide no occasion for further divisive complaints from other Democratic blocs. He was confident that he had nothing to lose by being forthcoming to his opponents.

Nevertheless, all of the rumblings, including the brief but intense excitement about the tariff, indicated the unwavering desire in some quarters to find a way to bring Van Buren down. While their force had ebbed, those opposed to him had not become inactive. They, however, needed a spark, some means of changing the political trajectory that favored Van Buren as 1843 ended. They found it in an unexpected corner of the American political universe as Calhoun and Tyler came together. When they did, American politics—and Van Buren's place in them—were never the same again.

It began when the always politically restless South Carolina maverick wandered off the Democratic reservation once again. In early 1844, Calhoun unexpectedly accepted an offer from the president to enter his cabinet as secretary of state. He and the outcast president, now joined together in what one Van Buren supporter referred to, disdainfully, as "the mongrel administration," entered into machinations that got them and their personal ambitions nowhere politically, but which did bring down Van Buren with stunning force.

Most Democrats expected to fight the upcoming election on the traditional issues that had divided the Whig and Democratic

Parties for the past twenty years. Clay's aggressively pushed legislative program in 1841 indicated that the mainstream Whigs were still deeply committed to an expansive use of federal government power to promote economic development. Tyler's vetoes had forestalled Clay's plans for the moment. But with the Kentuckian almost certain to be his party's presidential candidate in 1844, the future direction of Whig policy was clear. Against that, Van Buren intended to once again make the Jeffersonian-Jacksonian argument for limited government, the safeguarding of individual liberties, local control in domestic affairs, and against the exercise of such government power as the Whigs always sought to deploy. On these old issues Democratic leaders believed that Van Buren's chances for reelection were excellent.

TEXAS FEVER

The slavery issue had weaved in and out of American politics throughout Van Buren's national career. In particular, the angry rhetorical expressions of the Southern sectionalists rose and fell as various dangers and irritants appeared to threaten what they held dear. Such passions had had, from time to time, in John Ashworth's words, "a temporary muddying effect upon the political parties," dividing Northern and Southern wings from one another on some emblematic issue. But sectional tensions had not, so far, crystallized into a formidable force able to affect the way that the national parties argued and behaved. Martin Van Buren's democracy had been strong throughout the Union and had sustained itself by always stressing a national, not a sectional, perspective. Tyler and Calhoun's sudden preemptive strike about Texas now threatened all that Van Buren had so carefully constructed.

The Republic of Texas remained on the edge of American public consciousness in the early 1840s. Agitation for its annexation to the United States had been brimming on the fringes of affairs ever since first, Jackson, and then Van Buren had refused to take it up during their administrations. Texas leaders pushed hard in Washington in the early 1840s, proannexation popular rallies had met, prominent political leaders had come out in its favor, and the Tyler administration had been carrying on secret negotiations to achieve a coming together of the United States and the independent republic. Tyler, and then Calhoun as secretary of state, increased the range and intensity of the government's involvement by publicly adopting the annexation cause as their own.

Tyler believed that the issue had much potential to rescue his ambitions. So did Calhoun for himself. When he entered the cabinet in the spring of 1844, he forcefully embraced the Texas annexation cause and gave it a provocative twist that caused an uproar. The question of acquiring Texas always contained several dimensions. To begin with, many Americans (most especially Democrats) in the areas immediately adjacent to it, as well as in other parts of the growing Mississippi valley, and in centers of Democratic Party strength in many parts of the Union, favored the republic's annexation. They believed that the absorption of the rich lands of east Texas were a natural and inevitable next step forward in America's continental growth. What was clear as the issue unfolded, whatever its roots in presidential politics, was the strong revival among the Democratic Party faithful of the old Jeffersonian impulse in favor of the nation's continued landed expansion.

Intensifying the proannexationists' concern was their belief that the British government was engaged in anti-American mischief in Texas that directly threatened the nation's interests. Whether true or not, it significantly added to the strong case among many Americans, always suspicious of the once mother country's ambitions in North America, that something now had to be done and quickly to forestall Britain's imperialist meddling. Tyler moved to meet their wishes, noting that he was doing so after a decade in which the pleas of Texas representatives in Washington to join the Union had been ignored by those in power allegedly fearful of the impact of the issue, both domestically, and on Mexican-American relations. Unfortunately, in Tyler's view, they had let their fears overcome the clear needs of the nation.

THE SECOND DIMENSION of the annexation issue was the presence of slavery in Texas and the resistance of some Northerners—not only abolitionists—to adding any additional slave territory to the United States. But Calhoun was having none of their opposition. In his public arguments, especially in a letter that he wrote as secretary of state to Richard Pakenham, the British minister to the United States, he deliberately stressed this aspect of the matter. Instead of focusing on the expansionist urge, or the threat of a British presence there, he fused Texas and the defense of slavery, emphasizing that the United States primarily wanted to acquire the territory as a means of protecting the South's peculiar institution from the powerful external abolitionist threats that, he argued, were gathering on the horizon. Calhoun saw this approach as a shrewd, probably last ditch, means of forcing Southern Whigs and Southern Democrats to join together behind him on behalf of the preservation of their threatened, slavery-dominated society. And, of course, Calhoun's sectionalist tactic was aimed right at Van Buren's political heart.

Van Buren's relationship with his Southern supporters and his attitudes about slaveholding were critical to what now happened to him. His long-standing Southern problem, the actively promoted suspicions about his loyalty to the section's interests, the personal dislike of some Southerners toward him personally, and the hesitations of others about his political wiles and motives, had all persisted throughout his national career despite his repeated efforts to assure and reassure the jumpy, skeptical, and unfriendly among them.

When Texas was brought forward and Calhoun forcefully underlined its sectional dimension, the ever alert New Yorker saw, and tried to avoid, the trap being set. In what followed he thought matters through as a politician, one determined to keep his road to the White House as calm and as uncluttered as possible. His position on expansion, in general, and Texas, in particular, had never been central to his concerns. He had been loath to take Texas annexation up when, during his presidency, the republic's minister in Washington had tried to arouse support for annexation among congressmen and other important opinion makers.

His caution on the issue had stemmed from several traditional motives that he considered critical. First, his natural prudence, both generally and in foreign affairs, as he had demonstrated while engaged in active diplomacy, caused him to hesitate, given the consequences of annexation for Mexican-American relations. Second, he was certainly aware of both the proslavery and antislavery sensitivities of Democratic voters, and did not want unnecessary irritation stirred up. He had prepared to fight the upcoming election on more traditional policy grounds and not on this. Texas would provoke howls from antislavery groups, and might negatively affect Democrats in some closely competitive districts in Ohio and New York.

Yet, while New York and other Northern Democrats occasionally felt antislavery pressure from some of their constituents, they had managed to contain it until now. Most Northern Democrats continued to accept their party's, the South's, and Van Buren's longstanding position that slavery was a local matter not to be interfered with by outsiders. In the case of Texas their indifference about the subject, and commitment to a hands-off policy about it, led many of them to ignore slavery's presence and to be agreeable to other explanations for supporting annexation. They particularly fell in behind the notion that bringing Texas into the Union was necessary for the safety of the nation; that is, it was the key to protecting New Orleans and the Mississippi from the British and their persistent anti-American intrigues in the Southwest.

Still, the potential for unnecessary uproar over expansion was real. The Whigs certainly intended to oppose it, and that might give them new life and energy, and a weapon against Van Buren in parts of the North. What did he need to do? Missouri's senior senator, Thomas Hart Benton, still one of the most loyal of Jacksonians, and a strong supporter of Van Buren, took the lead in seeking to rally Democrats by denouncing what was afoot in the Tyler-Calhoun machinations, and urging the party's traditional caution on the matter. Coming from a slave state himself his arguments against Texas annexation at this juncture had force. On the other hand, although he was a powerful and highly direct assailant of the enemies of the democracy, he was also still too much of an individualist to carry his full weight in party councils, especially among other Southerners. What neither he nor Van Buren saw was the way that the issue was becoming a critical defining one in his party and, therefore, highly useful to the ex-president's enemies. To many Democrats, the time for Texas to enter the Union had arrived. They believed that further delay served no purpose. Van Buren did not agree and that proved to be his undoing.

A "FATAL LETTER" TO WILLIAM HAMMET

All of the political elements at play after 1841 now came to the fore as the presidential campaign season came into view. Each of the matters held against Van Buren probably contributed to what occurred, although it is impossible to sort them out and rank them with much precision. The upcoming election was likely to be close. He carried a great deal of negative political weight from his presidency and his defeat in 1840. The question that many Democrats asked was: should the party chance their fortunes with a rejected elderly man as their candidate, especially in light of the new issue of expansion that seemed to be sweeping so much before it? The Texas issue gave force and direction to a long-standing accumulation of anti–Van Buren positions and outlooks, and, most of all, coalesced and dramatized the opposition to him as a shopworn and unattractive candidate who had not kept up with the desires and needs of his countrymen.

Van Buren moved to clear the air so far as his intentions were concerned. He had received many letters seeking, often demanding, to know his position on the Texas matter. He used, as his occasion to confront such pressure, one of the letters of inquiry he had received from William Hammet, a Mississippi congressman and delegate to the forthcoming national convention. In his response, he tried to lay out the issue as he saw it. As always, Van Buren thought that a middle ground was possible between the immediate annexationists being urged on by Calhoun and Tyler, and the ouright rejectionists in the Whig camp. Unsurprisingly, he reiterated earlier warnings against the immediate annexation of Texas as being premature because of the likelihood that it would have a disruptive impact on Mexican-American relations. He did not oppose

Texas joining the Union at some later point when such disruptive consequences were no longer a threat, or when the American people were consulted about it, and a majority of them indicated that they were clearly in its favor. In short, he argued, not right now, but eventually: Texas annexation was possible if certain conditions were dealt with first.

Silas Wright thought that Van Buren's Hammet letter succeeded in laying out the middle course that he sought. But the ex-president's stance gave his opponents a potent weapon against him. He had not said anything really new about his own position. But he did drive a wedge between himself and the large body of more and more excited proannexation Democrats, North, South, East, and West. It did not help that at the same moment that Van Buren's letter was published, the likely Whig presidential candidate, Henry Clay, also issued a letter from Raleigh, North Carolina, opposing Texas annexation now and for a long time into the future.

To many who wished to think so, the timing of the two letters smelled of manipulative collusion between two old politicians against the country's interests. That was not true. Such collusion had not happened despite the heavy-breathing suspicions of the conspiratorially minded. More to the point, perhaps, suddenly the leading presidential candidates of both major parties were shutting off what many Americans vocally demanded—no delays, no complications, no resistance to the immediate annexation of Texas. In addition to proexpansion Democrats in the western states, volatile Southern Democrats, going through what the historian William Freehling has labeled a "sense of crisis" over Texas, demanded more than Van Buren gave them in the Hammet letter. Any further delay in bringing Texas into the Union was intolerable. Immediate annexation was the only possible policy that made sense to these Southerners in the current dangerous situation, and the only one they would accept. As one of them told Van Buren's friend and designated campaign biographer, George Bancroft, "Texas must immediately become American or [it] will soon be British."

Such sentiments fueled the great uproar against the former president that followed his Hammet letter. That uproar was, to be sure, largely organized by his enemies within the party for their own purposes. But their involvement could not hide the fact that the opposition went beyond the obvious anti–Van Buren haters to include the core of the Democratic Party and its beliefs about the virtues of further territorial expansion. Van Buren was caught in a force that had grown beyond his usual ability to confront and handle difficulties in a deft and effective manner. Most ominously, as a result of his position, the democracy seemed to be in danger of coming apart over his candidacy. He was repeatedly told that angry annexationists might bolt the party if he was its nominee for president. Van Buren, who was always sensitive to the power of the voters, and always eager to shape his party's story to make it as compelling and as attractive as he could, one that resonated with the electorate's needs, demands, hopes, and prejudices, had made a serious misstep on the Texas issue so far as his own position was concerned.

He might remain strong among many committed Democrats in the party's traditional wing, both leaders and the rank and file. But in states in the West and South where there were closely competitive electoral situations, it was clear that the anger raised by Van Buren's position on Texas could severely hurt the party. He knew that, and others among his friends had cautioned against doing anything that would tip the balance against him. The Hammet letter did just that. Among the blows that he suffered in its aftermath, one of the sharpest came from his longtime colleague in building and maintaining the national democracy, Thomas Ritchie, still the leader of the party in his home state. Under severe pressure from fellow Virginia Democrats, Ritchie told Van Buren that "I am compelled to come to the conclusion that we cannot carry Virginia for you."

But even worse was to occur. What Van Buren had not expected was the way that the very old and failing, but still inflexible and fiery, Andrew Jackson, intervened in the widening dispute among the Democrats. In a public letter, which he actually had written the year before but was now made public, Old Hickory stated that, in his judgement, there was an immediate need for the United States to annex Texas in order to forestall British designs there. As a result, Jackson continued, in a subsequent colloquy after the publication of Van Buren's position, his friend should step aside for the good of the party and the nation. Van Buren's "fatal letter" to Hammet ruled the New Yorker off the current political scene, he believed, whatever the still strong pull of their close, long-standing, relationship. If he did not withdraw, the party was in great electoral danger.

WHY DID VAN BUREN take the public position that he took against Texas, a position that fatally wounded him among so many Democrats? Certainly part of the reason was his belief that the issue would not become as important as it did. If he and Clay had discussed the matter while Van Buren had visited the Whig leader in 1842, which his enemies claimed that they had done, they may have simply understood between them that neither was going to raise the expansion into Texas matter. Now that it had been raised, Van Buren hoped to damp it down. He wanted no difficulties, either from Mexico, or from those seeking to manipulate the issue to hurt him. The letter may have seemed the best way out—caution, close analysis, and, as he saw it, no foreclosure of anyone's hopes, just delay in meeting them.

Whatever his motives were in writing it, the letter had worked differently from Van Buren's expectations. He was particularly shaken, both personally and politically, by Jackson's expressed Texas ardor and resulting advice to the party and to himself, and by Ritchie's unexpected reservations as well. Nevertheless, despite these two very sharp blows against him, Van Buren did not give up hope that he could bring the Democrats back together behind him and his candidacy. Calhoun and Tyler had poisoned the well, but the former president still thought that he could count on the power of party commitments to carry him through. Everything that he believed, and had long taught, about the necessity for internal party harmony remained cogent and could be expected to work in his favor *once the Democratic nomination was his.* His shaky colleagues would all fall into line as the election approached. None of them wanted a Whig victory in November.

"THE REANNEXATION OF TEXAS, THE REOCCUPATION OF OREGON"

But Van Buren's followers soon realized that the nomination was not yet securely his and that, more ominously, there was seepage underway in some of the places where he had been strong. Jackson had helped to legitimize the resistance of loyal Democrats to his renomination. Many more of them than even the most pessimistic Van Burenite had expected had become convinced that he should not be the party's standard bearer in 1844. They believed that too much that was politically vital to them would be lost if he was.

If so, the question became, who should take his place? Among the various other candidate who had been named by those party meetings that had not supported Van Buren, Lewis Cass of Michigan stood out for the breadth of his support, especially in the western states. Cass and Van Buren had been colleagues together in the Jackson administration. Since then, Cass had made a strong reputation for himself as an avid expansionist. James K. Polk also began to emerge as a possibility as well. Van Buren, following Jackson's urgings, had communicated with the Tennessean earlier, as did some of his friends, about the vice presidency, and both the Van Burenites and Polk and his closest colleagues thought that the former Speaker of the House was going to be named to the second place on the Democratic ticket. But some of Polk's allies in Tennessee quietly began to consider other possible options if Van Buren was sidetracked by the uproar that had been raised against him.

THE CLIMAX OF ALL OF THIS intense public and behind the scenes battling came at the Democratic national convention which opened in Baltimore in May 1844. Van Buren enjoyed a commanding lead in the delegate count; in fact he had a majority of the votes as the convention began. But he was cleverly outmanuevered by the forces arrayed against him, who proved to be well organized behind the leadership of Senator Robert J. Walker of Mississsippi, and ready to strike. There were 266 accredited voting delegates, 146 of whom, a majority, were committed to vote for Van Buren, at least on the first ballot. In the crowded confusion on the opening day of the meeting, the opposition forces were able to seize control, amid much disorder, and force through a reassertion of the party rule that had been used in past conventions (at those times in order to bolster Van Buren) that the successful nominee had to win two-thirds of the delegate

count, not just a simple majority of those voting. The Van Burenites strongly opposed the rule but, significantly, were unable to
marshal their full delegate majority on his behalf when the vote
was taken.

On the first nominating ballot Van Buren received the 146
votes committed to him, about 55 percent of the total cast. But,
then, the long months of secret, and not so secret, maneuvers
against him began to bear fruit. As Walker's forces aggressively
pushed against him, many of the delegates committed to Van Buren made it clear that, as they saw it, their votes for him on the first
ballot had fulfilled their obligation, and they could, and would,
move to other candidates on subsequent roll calls. They did, and as
a result, Van Buren's totals on successive ballots slipped significantly while Cass's numbers increased. It became quite obvious
that the Democratic Party leader could never receive the necessary
two-thirds of the vote in the convention.

Benjamin Butler commanded the Van Buren forces in Baltimore, while in Washington Silas Wright maintained contact with
other Democrats as the convention drama unfolded. Both had been
aware of the growing anti–Van Buren sentiment as it was expressed
among Democratic officeholders and editors in Washington. But
they continued to believe that the opposition could be overcome at
the convention. When it was not, Van Buren's colleagues were
thunderstruck, appalled, and deeply angry, but finally realistic
about their situation.

They began, however reluctantly, to look elsewhere for another
candidate, determined to defeat those who were bringing Van Buren down—led, as they saw it, by the all too ambitious Lewis Cass.
At first, the spotlight turned to Silas Wright. In fact, Van Buren's
close ally might have been nominated in place of his fellow New
Yorker if he had been willing to allow his name to go forward. But
he forcefully refused to be considered. Suddenly, James K. Polk
took on a different focus. The apparent vice president designate, a
committed Jacksonian in the Van Buren style, who had always been
close to the latter, and who was also an ardent expansionist on the
Texas issue, became a compromise choice as the newly proclaimed
"Young Hickory" of his party.

On the ninth ballot Butler emotionally withdrew Van Buren's name and threw New York's support to Polk. Virginia followed, and then the rest of the very excited convention fell into line. The Polk partisans, who had been shrewdly waiting for this break, moved fast to shore up their friendship with Van Buren by offering Silas Wright the vice presidential nomination. But the latter quickly turned it down as he had the chance to be nominated for the presidency. He made it very clear to the party's leaders that his refusal was because of his loyalty to his senior colleague and leader, and in protest against what the convention had done to the ex-president.

NEWS OF THE "GRIEVOUS WRONG" that he had suffered hit Van Buren very hard. Being denied the nomination was the second sharp political blow he had received, beginning with his 1840 defeat. The long curve upward in his political career had abruptly halted. He had every reason to withdraw and wash his hands of all further political activity. He had occasionally expressed his irritation about the Southern hesitancies and suspicions about him. What was happening now went far beyond any of that. Still, whatever his anger against those Democrats who had opposed his renomination, indifference or withdrawal was never his way. Whatever his personal anguish, the party in convention had made its choice. The platform was full of expansionist sentiments calling for "the reannexation of Texas and the reoccupation of Oregon." But it also included advocacy of the traditional Democratic policies that Van Buren had long championed. As he saw it, he and his closest colleagues had no option, given their deeply ingrained notions of party discipline, commitment, and loyalty, but to support the candidate chosen. They understood that political parties were always factionalized at the top. They sustained themselves by their ability to maintain the loyal support of their voters despite such factional differences. All groups should, and usually did, reconcile themselves to the way that the internal party maneuvering turned out once the election campaign began and everyone's focus returned to the important differences *between* the parties instead of concentrating on those *within* each party.

Such was the position of Van Buren and his supporters in the Spring of 1844. The defeated ex-president acted as he believed that

it was his reponsibility to do. To his credit (in his and his supporters' eyes), he did not sulk in his tent but, rather, effectively worked
on behalf of the democracy's duly nominated presidential candidate. And, despite their feelings, so did his followers. There was
good reason for them to do so. Besides his being a seasoned, loyal
Jacksonian, Polk had not been involved in the furious machinations
that had brought the ex-president down. As John A. Dix, one of Van
Buren's close associates, wrote after the convention, "If we could
not have Mr. Van Buren, certainly they could not do so well as to
give us Mr. Polk."

Leading his loyal troops from Lindenwald, Van Buren did what
he could, in his usual vigorous political style, to elect the Polk ticket
and to restore the Democrats to their rightful place at the head of
the government. The Van Buren wing of the party was fully mobilized and intensely active as the campaign developed. Being as fully
engaged as they were, they won the accolades of other Democrats
for their efforts. "Wright & Van Buren have behaved nobly," one
wrote to Polk after the election. Polk agreed, writing to George Bancroft that Van Buren's "magnanimous and zealous support of the
nominations . . . is characteristic of the man, and places me under
lasting obligations to him."

Beyond the surface acquiescence there was, however, a certain
amount of heart burning. Obviously, relations between Polk and
Van Buren's supporters were edgy from the beginning. The empha-
sis of the Polk partisans on territorial expansion issues during the
campaign did not help matters. In addition to such differences over
priorities, the sense among Van Buren's friends of Polk being beholden to them grew stronger as the campaign developed. It was
made constantly clear to Polk how important Silas Wright's run for
the governorship of New York was for the Democrats' success in
what promised to be a very close contest. Polk did win New York
State in November but the margin by which Wright won the governorship was greater than that garnered by the new president.
Wright's coattails made a difference in a crucial, and very close,
state for the president-elect, confirming that the Van Buren wing,
certainly in the eyes of its members, still counted for something in
American politics.

"NEW YORK IS, I FEAR, BETRAYED":
THE POLK FIASCO

Polk was to be president. The Democratic majority, however thin, had been restored at the national level. Van Buren celebrated the triumph of his party—and New York's key role in bringing about the victory—as he would, and he meant it, whatever his personal unhappiness. But then everything began to come apart for him as he was forced into the most bitter political period of his life. He believed that his wishes in regard to the cabinet's makeup, and other presidential appointments, would get the kind of favorable response from the incoming administration that they deserved. As he saw it, Van Buren brought some political power to the table over such matters. Certainly, his long service, his position, and his support for Polk gave him the right not only to be listened to, but to be heeded.

The president-elect received letters of advice from Van Buren and seemed receptive to what he read. He consulted with the latter's friends, and indicated his willingness to give the New Yorkers their due, specifically one of the two top cabinet positions, either the State or Treasury departments. Van Buren was "well satisfied," as he wrote to an ally, "that the P. elect goes to Washington with the most upright intentions" toward himself and his allies.

But his optimism was premature. As time passed between the election and Polk's inauguration, the whole matter of the high-level appointments fell into extraordinary confusion between Polk's headquarters in Nashville, then Washington, as the president-elect traveled there, and the Hudson valley, as signals were misunderstood, and other political pressures, not the least bit friendly to Van Buren, began to affect "Young Hickory." Finally, Polk's impatience, and lack of sureness as the matters were dealt with, led him to do things that horrified the Van Burenites. The episode ended in a rather bitter exchange in the White House between Van Buren's son, Smith, who had been sent to Washington with a letter for Polk, and the new president. The result was much ill will, and a great deal of affronted pride, in Kinderhook.

Polk's original cabinet list, which he had brought with him from Tennessee, certainly recognized the Van Buren wing's claims. But, as it was finally constituted, the cabinet was nowhere near what the ex-president and his friends expected. Nor was it, in any way, compatible with their interests or notions of what was appropriate. Van Buren had recommended his close associates, Butler, and Azariah Flagg, for the two highest cabinet positions, and then proved willing to have Butler serve as secretary of war instead, although that office was not considered quite as prestigeous as either the state or treasury departments.

When Polk finally acted, however, none of the New York's leading Van Burenites were appointed. Instead, the new president named William L. Marcy, once a close colleague of the former president, but now the leader of New York State's anti–Van Buren Democrats, as secretary of war, the only leader from the Empire State in the higher reaches of the new administration. And the ardent expansionist, Mississippi's Robert J. Walker, who had played a major role among the anti–Van Buren forces at the national convention, became Polk's secretary of the treasury. The two top cabinet positions were to be held by enemies, not friends. It was a stunning reversal.

Van Buren made his disappointment and frustration clear to the new president but to little avail. The best that can be said for Polk in 1845 and later, as he constructed his administration, was how grievously uninformed he was about New York politics, or how indifferent he seemed to be about the serious rifts there, how petulent he became as he dealt with the intractable factional divisions endlessly brought before him, and how little he appreciated how much he should court the still formidable Van Buren. The new president did offer his defeated rival the ministry to Great Britain, a post which was turned down with alacrity. (Van Buren was not even Polk's first choice for London. He originally considered giving it to Calhoun.)

Certainly, the London offer did not compensate for the blows the new president had rained on his predecessor as party leader. "New York is, I fear, betrayed," was a not untypical comment among the reeling Van Burenites when the cabinet was announced. Polk had done a great "injury" to the real Democrats of the state. Nor did matters end there. Polk's appointment policies beyond the cabinet level continued to roil the waters of national, and New York, party factionalism throughout his presidency. Among other actions Polk replaced Van Buren's close supporter, Frank Blair, as editor of the administration newspaper in Washington in favor of a new party organ edited by Van Buren's erstwhile close ally, the defector, Thomas Ritchie of Virginia.

While the president did try to make some lukewarm amends by offering other appointments to the Van Buren group, that effort did not go very far, and probably worsened the situation between them. What the administration offered to the Van Burenites the latter considered to be too little and too late. Nor did Polk's bestowal of a number of patronage places on some New Yorkers close to the former president begin to address the issues of party balance among different blocs, and the direction of future policies, that Van Buren believed were at the core of his dispute with the new president and the unprovoked assault by the latter on him and his associates.

On the other hand, unprovoked or not, Polk had his reasons for the decisions that he took. He did not deliberately set out to embarrass, or ill use, the former president. He was too experienced a politician not to want to hold his party together. But he never could find an acceptable way to accomplish that, given his own limitations and all of the other elements that were in play as he constructed his administration. His actions were perhaps devious, as the Van Burenites came to believe; they certainly were hasty, and foolish. But one additional critical thing shines out: Van Buren, in the eyes of the new administration, was much less of a force to be reckoned with than was thought by the New Yorker and his supporters. To the Polk democracy, now riding as high as one could get in American politics, Old Kinderhook's day was clearly done.

THE MARTYRDOM OF SILAS WRIGHT

The hostile feelings established in 1844 and 1845 did not subsequently diminish. Van Buren never visited Washington during Polk's term. It was just as well that he did not. The president's men repeatedly underlined their feelings over the next four years, keeping

Van Buren and his supporters at arm's length throughout. John Van Buren did visit the capital on behalf of his father but reported back that he found Polk to be distant and unforthcoming. To be sure, the administration proceeded to reinvigorate the traditional Democratic agenda. Texas entered the Union, albeit accompanied by a war with Mexico, and the president moved ahead on behalf of long-favored Democratic policies. The administration reinstituted the Independent Treasury that the Whigs had killed in 1841, and passed a new, lower, tariff in 1846. Polk also vetoed a congressional attempt to expand federal support for internal improvements construction, and had, finally, added Oregon and California to the Union. It was quite an imposing executive and legislative record, one fully in keeping with the tenets of Jacksonian democracy.

But the Van Burenite anger against Polk was not assuaged by such achievements. Whatever the surface politeness may have been—it was often strained—beneath the surface at Lindenwald and elsewhere, where Van Buren was still considered to be important, ill will only increased as his and his friends' sense of betrayal grew ever stronger from 1845 onward. They did not disagree with Polk's achievements. They welcomed them when they were congruent with their own principles. What Van Buren and his supporters argued was that the president had also taken too many actions that hurt the party internally and that gave the wrong Democrats—those not always faithful, in their view, to the party's cherished traditions—too much authority.

Van Buren always believed that he, and those with whom he was allied, represented the true principles of the Jacksonian Democratic Party while their party opponents did not, certainly not with the same intensity and commitment. He also believed that his long efforts to work with the Southerners in his party, to be sensitive to their particular concerns, and to accept their perpetual crankiness in the interest of party unity and larger national purposes, embodied the way that all Democrats always had to act so as to balance out their internal differences and maintain and advance their common cause as Jacksonians.

Unfortunately and unforgivingly, the Van Burenites believed that their sensitivity to Southern interests had not been balanced by any reciprocal recognition of the interests of other Democrats. Instead, the Polk-encouraged Southern Democrats had overreached on their own behalf, and ignored what remained necessary to keep the national coalition working together. Van Buren and his supporters, therefore, more and more came to believe that for themselves, and for the soul of the Democratic Party as they understood it, they had to confront the Polk problem directly. Despite the administration's Jacksonian policy commitments, the New Yorkers believed that unless they were part of the power group directing party affairs, it would lose its way under the leadership of those now in command. They saw themselves, and their ideas, being driven toward political oblivion unless the tide running against them could be reversed, the real democracy reestablished in the party's councils, and the president brought to see the errors of his ways. The question was how to do these things?

Some Northern Democrats outside of Van Buren's immediate circle were coming to agree with the latter about the Polk administration's behavior. Certain of its policies, in particular the compromise of the Oregon boundary below the 54°40' line demanded by many expansionists, and the provoking of a war with Mexico, as the Van Burenites had predicted would happen, led to much hostility among normal party loyalists and a sense that the decisions being made by a Democratic administration no longer adequately reflected consideration of the needs of the different groups in the party. They agreed with the defeated Van Buren that Polk had rent the democracy, largely to favor certain of its elements, most especially, its Southern wing. They, too, believed that it had to be reclaimed and rebuilt on the basis of comity and reciprocity among its different factions in pursuit of a common cause.

Their chance to face up to the president came in August 1846. In reaction to Polk's missteps, Van Buren Democrats, and other party members from the northern states, joined some Whigs in introducing and supporting the Wilmot Proviso as an amendment to an appropriations bill desired by the administration. The proviso would prohibit slavery in any territory acquired by the United States as a result of the war with Mexico—an acquisition that everyone expected to come about when a treaty of peace was signed. Whatever its antislavery roots, and those were clear, the proviso was also a direct and resounding slap against those Southerners, Polk Democrats and Calhounites both, who had brought Van Buren down by arousing a sectional issue against him, and who then ignored and betrayed him and his colleagues. The proviso's supporters believed that they had acted in the interest of maintaining the true balances and proper direction of Jacksonian democracy.

Although the Wilmot Proviso did not pass both houses of Congress, then or later, it garnered more support among northern Democrats in 1846 than administration leaders expected. As a result, it became a significant mark of the split in the democracy, and a signal that its future would be beset by continued conflict as the different blocs battled for control of the party each claimed as its own.

Van Buren never specifically laid out in detail how he actually viewed the Wilmot Proviso when it was first proposed. But, whatever he thought about the antislavery substance of the proposal, to him it was something that incorporated an attitude, a framework, that he supported about the nature of American policy, the proper behavior of the Democratic Party, and a way that Polk and his followers could be led to understand their missteps. If he was now behaving, as his adversaries claimed, as a factionalist, a position that he had always previously denounced, he believed that it had become necessary—albeit only temporarily—given the way that Polk had split the party. The Wilmot Proviso was not a full declaration of war against the president, but it certainly reflected a powerful response to a conflict that Tyler and Calhoun had started, and that Polk had benefited from, at the ex-president's—and he would add—both the party's and the country's expense as well.

AND THEN SILAS WRIGHT lost his reelection bid and died within a year. Van Buren's close friend and second in command had served out his two-year term as governor of New York and then reluctantly agreed to run for reelection in 1846 in order to help his party once again, as he had done to such critical effect in 1844. He told Van Buren that he had not enjoyed being governor, or living in Albany, and had hoped that he would not to have to seek the office again. But he did, out of his deep sense of party loyalty, and, in his second try for that position, he lost. Wright's popular support sagged in some of the Hudson River counties where an intense "antirent" uprising against onerous and obsolescent land laws had culminated in riots, violence, and the death of a deputy sheriff. Governor Wright took a hard law-and-order stand against the people involved, even in the face of strong popular support for the antirent leaders. That stance hurt him at the polls that November in the affected counties. (It also probably did not help Wright's chances that John Van Buren served as one of the prosecutors of the arrested antirent agitators when they came to trial.)

In addition to these state problems, 1846 was a Whig year more generally, not only in New York. They made electoral gains in several key states. But, to many observers, most especially among those around Van Buren, such reasons were not as cogent as were the acts of party betrayal that they saw emanating from Washington and other places where Polk directed matters. The causes of Wright's defeat were clear to his New York friends. It had happened, they believed, because of the refusal of many anti–Van Buren New York Democrats to vote for the party's candidate. These defectors were the same Democrats President Polk had rewarded in 1845 and since, at the expense of the true Jacksonians of the state. The administration—"Polk, Marcy, Cass, and their treacherous crew"—had countenanced such acts, even at the cost of losing a Democratic governorship in a pivotal state. Wright, himself, believed that he would have won "if all the divisions of our party supported the ticket truly and faithfully." But the anti–Van Buren Democrats had not, and the Van Burenites, once again, found much reason to be outraged, and to intensify their denunciations of their party enemies.

Matters only grew worse. Wright returned to his farm in Canton and happily resumed his vigorous country life. He and Van Buren kept in touch in the first half of 1847 as they always had, trying to work out their strategy for the upcoming presidential and gubernatorial races that were due in 1848. Some of his colleagues began to push the idea that Wright should stand for the presidency then. Whatever his feelings about that, the suggestion rapidly took off and grew in power among a wide range of New York Democrats, and among party members in other states, as well. (Polk had earlier committed himself to serving only one term.) In the months after his gubernatorial defeat Wright was becoming the new hope of the Van Buren Democrats, the one who would lead them back to their proper place within party councils, and lead the nation back to true Jacksonian leadership.

But it was not to be. Once a hard drinker, and not always in the best of health, Wright suddenly suffered a stroke in August 1847, and died the next day at the age of fifty-two. With him went any remaining willingness among the grieving Van Buren-ites to keep still and accept their political fate. They believed that Wright had died, indirectly perhaps, but clearly, at the hands of the Polk administration. It had betrayed him, and the true de-mocracy, during the gubernatorial election for its own purposes, and cut the heart out of him as a result. Van Buren and his allies believed that they no longer owed the president, or those associ-ated with him, anything—except the most bitter anger and re-lentless distrust. Their urgent need, now, was to find a way to bring their enemies down and then restore their party to its true pathway. The direction that they took to meet their passionate determination to thwart their party opponents astounded, and then profoundly shook, the American political universe.

Chapter Nine

---○---

"The Most Fallen Man I Have Ever Known"
The Party Leader Becomes a Political Rebel—For a Time, 1848–1852

As Van Buren considered his political options after Silas Wright's death he was, for the first time in many years, alone at home in Kinderhook. His family had scattered more than in earlier times. His oldest, son Abraham, his closest aide over the past ten years, had returned to the army at the outbreak of "Mr. Polk's War," and was now serving with his father's longtime friend, Winfield Scott, in Mexico. Both John and Smith had moved to New York City and established law practices there. Martin Junior, for the moment in better health, was in Washington where he kept his father abreast of what was going on in the last days of the Polk administration. Although they were in constant touch with each other, the elder Van Buren very much missed his sons' presence in his everyday life.

At the same time, family tragedies also formed a larger part of the texture of the lives of the Van Burens than anyone would have wished. Two of his sons lost their young wives prematurely. John's wife, Elizabeth, died in 1844, after only three years of marriage. Smith Van Buren's wife, who had given birth to three children, died at the end of 1849, also after only a brief time together. Not surprisingly, the intense grief caused by these losses lasted a long time. Ultimately, however, Van Buren found some compensation amid these tragedies. Along with Angelica's two sons, and John's daughter, Smith's children now became an important part of their grandfather's life in retirement at Lindenwald. All of them visited him often, usually for extended periods.

BARNBURNING

Amid the travails of his personal life and his loneliness, the ex-president's political activities remained an important, perhaps a necessary, part of his being into the late 1840s. Van Buren's inclinations at this point in his life seemed to be that he would not again serve as the head of an army on the march. He kept insisting to correspondents that he had retired from active politics. He was no longer willing to participate directly in the public arena, and he would no longer be a candidate for office. In his place, his closest associates, such as Benjamin Butler, were expected to take over direction of the Van Burenite forces and regain their place in national party councils. At the state level, his son John had become an increasingly important political player, among other things becoming New York's attorney general in 1845. Many among the Van Buren group now looked to him for leadership—albeit with the expectation that his father was involved in such, as well, however indirectly.

And the elder Van Buren was involved, if largely from his study at his home, as counselor and strategist to his allies. The letters to and from Lindenwald, and the many visits of Democratic politicians to discuss matters with him, along with the rest of the constant restless activities underway in Van Burenite councils, indicated that, whatever the public face of matters, he had not lost his zest for political involvement, or his intense commitment to restore his party to the command of his allies—the democracy's Jacksonian core. There would be no acceptance of what had happened to them since 1844.

How could the Democratic Party regain its Jeffersonian-Jacksonian essence? To begin with, the Van Burenites had to first recapture the initiative in New York State, and then be recognized by the national party as the legitimate representatives of the Empire State's democracy. The extremely bitter and complex intricacies of state politics had, by late 1847, created an unbelievably divisive atmosphere in the Empire State, adding a great deal to the existing schisms between the Van Burenites and their party opponents. The Van Buren group had, for some time, been labeled Barnburners, either because they were intent on purifying the rat-infested party, or, alternatively, because they were willing to burn down the barn (party) to destroy their enemies. Whatever the origins of their name, the Barnburners were convinced—it was their guiding star throughout—that all of their opponents'—now labeled Hunkers—energies were directed toward diluting, or eliminating, the basic Jacksonian policies that had distinguished the democracy in the state and that had been personified by Silas Wright and those who stood with him—and who now mourned him. The Hunkers had originated in the bitter state battles over banking and internal improvements in the late 1830s, taking positions that were anathema to the Van Buren wing and contrary, in the latter's view, to the party's traditional positions. It was an old battle but a still potent one in the mid-1840s as other issues, such as territorial expansion and the containment of slavery were added to the mix. There was no peace among New York's Democrats, nor could there be after Wright's unexpected death.

It was amid this debilitating fragmentation that the Wilmot Proviso took on critical defining importance among the New York Democrats. To be sure, from the beginning some of the Barnburners had been quite hostile to the extension of slavery. But there had always been a range of opinions about how far to push their hostility, and a general sense among most of them that they should be cautious about it. Now, in the summer and fall of 1847, the proviso was moved to the center of affairs as a necessary goal to be achieved given what had happened to the party, and the country, under Polk's leadership. New York Congressman Preston King, from Silas Wright's old district along the Canadian border, reintroduced the proviso into the national House of Representatives and, along with other Northern Democrats, pushed it vigorously against the equally stiff resistance of Polk and his congressional allies.

Whatever their priorities might be, whether to highlight the close ties between the Hunkers and the Southern-dominated Polk administration, or out of genuine antislavery feeling, or, most likely, out of some combination of both, the Barnburners also pushed hard for the adoption of a resolution, similar in tone and content to the Wilmot Proviso, to be included in the state party platform that was to be adopted at the upcoming Democratic convention meeting in Syracuse scheduled in September 1847, just after Wright's death.

But the Hunkers controlled the state party apparatus and were unyielding toward their enemies. Backed by the patronage of the Polk administration, they thoroughly dominated the state convention. They refused to adopt the Wilmot Proviso, ignored the Barnburners' policy demands on other issues, and placed their own people on the Democratic electoral ticket, dismissing whatever claims that the Barnburners had to some of the positions. Among other casualties, the Hunkers denied John Van Buren the party's renomination for the office of attorney general.

Once more the Barnburners found themselves roughly handled by their party opponents. In such a situation, were there limits to their loyalty to those now dominating the state democracy? The Van Buren of earlier days would have said that there were few, or no, such limits. He had always unceasingly sought to calm and short-circuit internal party divisions, let alone permit such to lead to Democratic fragmentation. But that was at an earlier, and very different, moment. Matters had changed significantly since then, as he saw it, and extreme remedies were now called for.

It would be a mistake to see his subsequent actions as hypocritical, and contrary to his past preaching and behavior. He may have been determined to have his revenge on those in his party who had turned on him. He would not have been the fully formed human being that he was if urges to get back at his enemies did not comprise some part of his personal makeup. But, whatever the force of such emotions, he remained too much of a shrewd calculator of political situations to let such personal resentments dictate his pathway now. Given the events of 1844–1845, he believed that the Barnburners' commitment to the Democratic organization had limits if the party's leaders were no longer true to its basic ideals. And, to Van Buren, they were not. The Hunkers were not acting to further traditional Democratic policies, but, rather, were distorting and changing them in unacceptable ways. At the same time, the Hunker leadership was determined to keep party control in its own hands, no matter how much its members' behavior debased Jacksonianism. In such a situation, Van Buren was driven by what he saw as the need to recapture the party that he had created, to bring it back to its original moorings, and to reassert both its core ideas, and the way that its leaders had to operate if the democracy was to remain viable, and its purposes accomplished. The party had lost those qualities in 1844 and 1845. It was time to get them back.

The New York Democracy split asunder in 1847. The Barnburners angrily walked out of the state convention, reiterating, as they left, their determination to regain control of the Jacksonian movement in the state. From then on, there were separate state party committees, and separate local organizations throughout New York, each of them carrying on a war against one another, as well as against the Whigs. It cost the party dearly in the state elections in November 1847, which the Whigs won relatively easily, and boded very ill for the following year's critical contests when both the presidency and the governor's office would be at stake, unless some way could quickly be found to restore Democratic unity in the nation's largest state.

Confronting the National Democracy

The Barnburner protest against the Hunkers and their supporters in Washington was taking on an inexorable quality that ultimately led them in a completely unexpected direction: formal separation from the national democracy in the presidential election. Matters went slowly at first as different political leaders tried to sort matters out in their minds. Martin Van Buren tried to restrain his son John and Benjamin Butler from moving too fast. Whatever his warnings, however, events kept moving along one particular pathway—and the elder Van Buren increasingly became part of it.

Soon after the angry party split at Syracuse, Van Buren left Lindenwald for an extended stay in New York City that lasted throughout the winter of 1847–1848. During his residence there he committed himself fully to his colleagues' vigorous search for justice for their cause. He wrote a long document that came to be labeled, by both friends and enemies, as the "Barnburner Manifesto." It was edited, and in some places revised and extended, by John Van Buren, with the help of another rising Barnburner star, Samuel J. Tilden, who had been friendly with the older Van Buren for some time. It was finally publicly issued in April 1848 as the "Address of the Democratic Members of the Legislature of the State of New York."

It may have been the most scholarly document that Van Buren had written to this point in his career. The "Address" began with a long examination of the Barnburners' claims to be recognized as the regular Democratic Party of New York. All of the party's rules, precedents, and practices supported their claims, he argued, despite their opponents' hold over the state organization. Beyond that, Van Buren explored, in great detail, the legal and constitutional precedents that persuasively demonstrated the power that Congress had over the territories, including the right to exclude slavery from them. He analyzed, and quoted from, a range of sources going back to the Constitutional Convention in 1787, including a number of Supreme Court decisions that had been rendered since. The gist of his message was that not only did Congress have the right to restrict slavery in federal territory if it wished to, it had done so in the past, and it should now exercise that power once more. In a section that remained as he originally wrote it, Van Buren was as direct and as plainspoken as anyone could be in public discourse. "No resident of a free state would, we think," he argued,

> venture to claim that the establishment of slavery at this day in territories of the United States where it does not now exist, would be either wise or expedient. Not even the allurments of the Presidency could, we hope, induce an adhesion to a heresy so revolting.

He backed up the constitutional arguments, and the strong anti-slavery extension tone of the whole, with an equally strong message exalting the necessary dominance of free labor in the new territories to the exclusion of African slavery. The implanting of slave labor in these areas would be destructive to the nation's interests, and undoubtedly provoke social unrest, as free labor would resist going into places where they would find themselves working alongside African slaves. The territories should, in his view, remain white. Such racial impulses were hardly new among the Jacksonians of Van Buren's generation. Their enduring, and often expressed, commitment to a white republic was as profound as any other aspect of their outlook. Van Buren certainly shared in that perspective and always had done so.

The "Barnburner Manifesto" was the opening gun in the Van Burenite bloc's offensive to regain control of their party and return it to its correct course and regular practices. They continued their assault by next demanding that the national party, at its nominating convention in May 1848, recognize the Van Buren group as the true and only democracy from the state of New York. In the jousting with their state party enemies the Barnburners continued to carefully observe all of the democracy's well-established rules for calling meetings and selecting delegates. As the Barnburners saw it. the Hunkers, in contrast, had not done so. Rather, they had illegally manipulated the process at various points, allowing them to seize control of the Democratic apparatus in the state. The Barnburner delegation had the legal right, therefore, Van Buren insisted, in a letter laying out the strategy that they should follow, to be deemed the only regular Democrats of the state and to occupy the state's seats in the upcoming official meeting of the entire party.

When the Barnburner delegation arrived in Baltimore to present their demands, they found two things that greatly offended them and that threatened what they believed was their due as loyal, not to say mistreated, Democrats. First, it was clear that their *bête noire* of 1844, the unacceptable Lewis Cass, was most likely to be the Democratic presidential nominee on an anti–Wilmot Proviso platform. Second, they found that party leaders, after some unfriendly hemming and hawing about their claims, would not meet their demands. In the interest of preserving unity, they offered only to split the difference by seating both Barnburner and Hunker delegations, with each casting half of the state's vote.

This supposed compromise was unacceptable to the Barnburners. Their position was clear. They were the only real Democrats of their state. Their opponents had no legitimate claim to be recognized, let alone honored, by the national party, whatever the political calculations involved. If the Baltimore Convention now favored the Hunkers by accepting them instead of the Barnburners, or on an equal footing with the latter, despite their policy and organizational transgressions, then it, too, was behaving corruptly. It was doing so for only one reason: to placate, or submit to, the demands of the party wreckers and unprincipled men calling themselves Democrats—those who had destroyed Silas Wright. No true Democrat could accept that. When the Baltimore meeting did not agree to deal with the Barnburners on their terms, the latter concluded that the party had irrevocably lost its claim to represent the Jeffersonian-Jacksonian tradition. The Van Buren group, therefore, was obliged, in the view of its leaders, to act now in a different manner, rather than staying in Baltimore and participating under conditions that they believed were destructive of all the positive things that the party had once represented. They left Baltimore, once more in anger and frustration.

FREE SOIL

BUT DID THIS MEAN BOLTING THE PARTY in a presidential election year? That was the new, unexpected, and formerly unthinkable dimension of what now occurred. The political reaction against slavery's expansion had grown much larger than that of the Barnburners alone, and it was accompanied by an increasing determination by many antislavery activists to challenge the old parties in the upcoming election. Many believed that establishing a third party was the only way to accomplish their purpose. That, of course, raised troubling questions in Kinderhook. Van Buren was certainly not, at first, willing to desert his own creation in a national election. He hesitated at each of the junctures that followed, as his son and others moved down the path leading toward revolt. But as the split deepened, and other options were closed off, the momentum of events propelled the elder statesman-leader of the Barnburners toward the unthinkable. He could not acquiesce in the party's choices and direction in the Polk era, nor the way that the party in New York State was now operating. The Polk men, and the Hunker leaders, had gone too far in their pandering to the out-of-control Southern wing, and had not restored the internal conditions within the party that Van Buren deemed to be imperative as the only way to ensure its future.

He may not have wanted to bolt, or again be a presidential candidate, but events outraced his wishes. At a Barnburner meeting at Utica in June, soon after the Baltimore convention, the participants, joined by some antislavery Whigs, pushed further than ever. They nominated him for the presidency as an independent candidate on a Wilmot Proviso platform. An earlier biographer of Van Buren has written that "for a man who had made party discipline the keystone of his political career, the Utica nomination was almost a physical blow." If it was, it was the first of several. The Utica convention's action was followed, in August, by his nomination by the much larger Buffalo convention of the newly formed Free Soil Party—a nomination by a third party that he accepted, whatever his deep reluctance, many qualms, and previous arguments and behavior.

VAN BUREN'S INVOLVEMENT in the Free Soil movement caused shock and consternation among most people caught up in American politics, including, in particular, some longtime opponents of the extension of slavery. The latter, who had been in the forefront of mobilizing the Free Soil movement in 1848, at first found the Barnburner leader's role to be completely out of character, likely to be destructive of their cause, and outrageous in its affront to their deeply held commitment against slavery. Van Buren's career and his reputation stood in the way of their believing that he was now genuinely opposed to the extension of slavery, whatever he said in response to the Free Soil nomination. Of all of the places one expected the ex-president to locate himself politically, the head of an antislavery extension third party, most activists would agree, was the least likely.

Such antislavery critics had history on their side. No matter what his personal outlook may have been, Van Buren had always

publicly seen slavery as a political matter. He had never demonstrated opposition to it as an all-important institution in certain
parts of the United States. His record on the matter had clearly
been one of the conventional mid-nineteenth-century Democratic
politician that he was. Slavery existed. It was constitutional. Southerners, with whom he had to work for the Democratic cause, were
extremely sensitive about it. Therefore, they were to be reassured,
and any issues raised about it were not to be allowed to grow large
enough to be divisive within the party.

Given that well-established record, how could true antislavery
activists work with him now? A debate raged among them for a
time, with a number of their leaders insisting that, whatever their
qualms, this was too good an opportunity to pass by—even with Van
Buren as their national standard bearer. They had too much to gain.
In the end, in spite of their persisting reservations and the ongoing
hostility of some, most antislavery leaders accepted him after the
Buffalo meeting had acted. Others came around, in their turn, as
the campaign developed. Whatever he had once been, Van Buren
was now at the head of a movement that they believed in, and fully
supported, whatever their feelings about the candidate heading
their national ticket.

Democrats were similarly astounded at what was happening
and even more appalled and furious. To many of them, Van Buren
was not only occupying strange but also the most tainted ground
imaginable. He had become, as James K. Polk wrote, "the most
fallen man I have ever known." A loyal party editor referred to him,
not uncharacteristically, as "the Kinderhook Iscariot himself." The
Polk administration reacted angrily to the challenge. Those Barnburners who still held federal office, including Benjamin Butler,
United States attorney in New York City, were removed and replaced by Hunkers. This may have been intended to teach a
pointed lesson to the dissidents, but the removals neither calmed
the political waters nor improved relations among the warring party
groups.

Perhaps Van Buren was the despicable things that his enemy,
the president and the latter's allies, called him. But there was
much more to his behavior than they suggested. There is no ques-

tion of his resentment against the now-dominant groups within the party that were clustering around Lewis Cass. There is also no doubt that he was a reluctant candidate, as an individual of a certain age, and one forced to be the leader of a third party against his old organization. But beyond the obvious, there were other impulses in play. For one, had he left the party or had the party left him? Van Buren continued to believe that the latter was the case and that the Polk-Hunker-Cass-et al.'s defection from the true democracy of Andrew Jackson justified his 1848 strategy and behavior, however stunning they were. Whatever the ex-president's long devotion to his own creation, and his cautious approach to risky enterprises, he believed that the extraordinary situation that they were now in demanded sharp and dramatic action. He had come to think, along with his closest associates, that no other way was possible once they had been shut out of the Baltimore convention in the way that they had been.

STILL, THE VAN BURENITES WERE NOT VERY COMFORTABLE as they entered the campaign. Too many of their newfound allies had been their traditional enemies for too long. They found themselves joined together with many northern "Conscience Whigs," and recent members of the antislavery Liberty Party, extraordinary companions with which to share an election campaign. The Free Soil Party's vice presidential nominee was Charles Francis Adams, the son of Van Buren's once bitter enemy. There were also things in the Free Soil platform with which the Barnburners strongly disagreed. All of this were heavy burdens for them to carry, whatever the provocation. Benjamin Butler's son wrote, long afterward, that he did not think, for these reasons, that Van Buren's "heart was in" the movement that he now led.

Nevertheless, he was the Free Soil candidate and, whatever his inner feelings, he worked to mobilize his allies as a united bloc to carry on their campaign. In particular, he and his lieutenants kept emphasizing to their fellow Barnburners that their joint efforts with their former enemies held out the promise of accomplishing the necessary reorientation of the Democratic Party back to its true commitments. At the same time, in his public statements in response to the Free Soil organization and his own nomination, Van Buren repeatedly argued that all of the Free Soilers had much in common ideologically. None of them threatened slavery in those states where it constitutionally existed. As to allowing slavery to expand into territory now free of it, they were as one in opposing it. He argued, as he had before, that the Southerners were overreaching, ignoring long precedent stretching back to the Northwest Ordinance of 1787, and they had to be stopped by Congress enacting a law like the Wilmot Proviso. As he had constantly argued, it had the power to do so, whatever the South's denial of that claim, as it also did to abolish slavery in the District of Columbia.

As they settled down and found the will to work together, the Free Soilers carried on a spirited campaign fully consonant with the usual style and energy levels of the major parties. They put up candidates for a number of offices throughout the North, including several governorships and seats in Congress. Beyond the nominations, the whole paraphernalia of the normal electoral activity of the major parties— speakers, mass rallies, intensely argued pamphlets, and sharply worded newspaper editorials—formed the structure of their vigorous challenge to the established partisan network. Van Buren and his newfound allies pushed hard the notion that there was no other course to follow. As one of their pamphlets put it, both the Democratic and Whig candidates, Cass and Zachary Taylor, one a "Northern man with Southern principles," the other "a Southern man with Southern principles," were "utterly unworthy [of] the suffrage of a free people."

In keeping with tradition, Van Buren did not, himself, actively campaign. Once again, he engaged in extensive letter writing, either making suggestions to his associates, or responding to requests from interested citizens for his opinions, including one asking him to deny rumors that he was a slaveholder and an infidel. (He wrote back denying both charges.) There was no lack of surrogates to speak on his behalf. Both Benjamin Butler and, particularly, John Van Buren energetically led the coalition's fight throughout the fall campaign. John made a large number of speeches promoting the cause in New York and elsewhere. Others, both Democrats and Whigs, joined in the crusade against slavery's extension as well, covering most of the northern states with their advocacy.

The Van Burens were too politically astute to believe that victory was possible. In 1848, most Democratic Party leaders, including such Van Buren loyalists as Thomas Hart Benton, supported Cass and their traditional party organization. Most northern Whig leaders, including the strong antislavery extension advocate, William Seward, and the party's leader in Illinois, Abraham Lincoln, supported Zachary Taylor. The Free Soilers also fully understood that the compelling force of party loyalty, which Van Buren had done so much to nurture among the voters, would keep most of them in their accustomed party ranks on election day. Nevertheless, whatever their party's electoral limitations, they hoped to accomplish much, even in defeat, accomplishments that would restore the democracy to its rightful values and behavior.

THE OVERALL RESULT OF THEIR EFFORTS in November was not as substantial as some of the most optimistic among them had hoped. Van Buren won no electoral votes, receiving just under 300,000 popular votes nationally for president, about 10 percent of those cast in 1848. (It was a total, to be sure, that was better than any antislavery movement had previously garnered in a presidential race.) He did attract a noticeable number of votes in parts of New England, finishing second in Massachusetts and Vermont, and in Ohio and Michigan. His best result, in the number of popular votes he received, was at home in New York where he ran ahead of Cass winning about half of his nationwide tally there, largely from traditional Democratic voters. In so doing, he ensured that Taylor won the state from his Democratic opponent.

AFTER THE REBELLION

Van Buren seemed satisfied by the result, given his realistic assessment of the limits of what he could hope to accomplish. The Barnburners had delivered a stinging blow to their longtime former allies and, in his optimistic view, taught them an important lesson. Whatever their totals were, the Free Soil efforts in a very close election had made a major contribution to the defeat of Cass, his objectionable Hunker Democratic supporters, and the unacceptable and despised heresies of Polkism. "How soon," Francis P. Blair wrote to Van Buren after the election, "Mr. Polk's perfidy has its retribution." The Democratic Party needed the Van Buren wing. He still led a powerful political army.

But, what now? If Van Buren's motives had been, as he claimed, to restore the democracy to its first principles, with he and his colleagues as a crucial element in the party, there was much still to be accomplished. The New York Hunkers, and Polk's allies elsewhere, had not given up. They remained bitter, extremely hostile, and unyielding to the Barnburner–Free Soil faction that had caused such mischief. The war continued. And the future leadership and center of gravity of the defeated party remained unclear, even as Polk prepared to leave office in early 1849.

Most of all, did the Free Soilers intend to continue as a third party? Some of the movement's leaders wanted it to, and kept its flame burning bright. To them, the issues that they championed remained politically relevant. Retaining their separate identity, some of the Free Soilers temporarily allied themselves with antislavery blocs in one or another of the major parties at the state level in the year or so after 1848, in order to advance their cause by electing candidates who were acceptable to them. As a result, a number of Free Soilers were elected to the United States Senate by coalition votes in 1849 and 1850.

Despite these victories, the party's support began to drop off significantly. In particular, a strong feeling developed among many of the Democrats who had revolted with Van Buren in 1848 that, having accomplished much of their purpose in Cass's defeat, and in the humiliation of those who had brought Van Buren down four years before, it was time to return to their natural political home. Maintaining a separate organization, or engaging in temporary, cross-party coalition activity in these brighter circumstances for them, was not Van Buren's position, nor that of most of the other New York Barnburners who had come with him into the Free Soil ranks in the presidential race.

Ultimately, they deeply believed, and kept reiterating to one another, that only the Democratic Party could accomplish what the

country needed. Under Polk there had been reason for them to revolt. Such was no longer the case. And there were good, traditional,
reasons not to maintain their commitment to the Free Soil Party. As
Van Buren afterwards wrote about the 1848 election, again using
quite familiar words, the result of that contest had been "the eleva-
tion of an old-school Federalist to the Presidency, and the administration of the Federal Government upon the long exploded principles of Federalism." Whether true or not, he continued to think in
his usual categories and believe in their relevance.

Such an outcome had to be prevented from happening again.
Alone, the Barnburners realized that neither of the Democratic
Party's warring factions could win elections, each could only prevent the advancement of the other. It was clear that party unity,
based on its traditional ideological foundations, was essential—as it
had always been—for the advancement of Jeffersonian-Jacksonian
policies, and to defend against continuing Whig attempts to re-
shape the American system in an unacceptable manner. Soon after
leaving the presidency, a worn-down James K. Polk died unexpectedly, rounding out a dark era for Van Buren, and symbolically marking its end. Why not, one Barnburner wrote to a Hunker leader,
now "let *by gones* be *by gones?*"

THE TERRITORIAL-SLAVERY ISSUE remained unresolved as the Whigs
took over the national government for the second time when Taylor
became president, and it remained a major barrier in 1849 to any
return to the traditional politics that Van Buren had always championed. Fortunately, so far as the Democrats were concerned, Congress did find a formula (not including the Wilmot Proviso) to settle the continuing deep fissures over the western territories
acquired from Mexico. Henry Clay, back in the Senate, and his
young Democratic colleague, Stephen A. Douglas of Illinois, successfully worked out a set of compromise proposals on the territorial issue and other sectional concerns.

Their Compromise of 1850 was controversial. Until his death
in mid-1850, after only a year and a half in office, President Taylor
adamantly resisted its provisions. Both extreme Southern sectionalists and Northern Free Soilers lashed out against it for giving too

much away to the other section. Calhoun, also back in the Senate, let out one last blast on behalf of sectionalism and slavery, by assaulting the proposals. (Like Taylor, he, too, died in 1850, in the midst of the congressional deliberations.)

But, despite the rumblings from the extremes, the leaders of the two parties, including the new president, the veteran New York Whig, Millard Fillmore, accepted the compromise proposals as a way out of their recent troubles, a way that would allow them, as one congressman said, "to return to the business of the nation," that is, the traditional battles between Jacksonians and their opponents over financial matters, the economy, and the proper role of government in domestic affairs, generally.

Van Buren and most of his fellow party rebels agreed with this view despite their hesitancies about a number of provisions in the 1850 settlement. Reunion seemed to be the logical thing to do, to forge once again, if possible, the kind of cooperation among all Democrats in New York, and between the party's Northern and Southern wings, as once had been the norm. That cooperation had been to good purpose for the nation, and it could be again. Tentative feelers between the New York factions, led by John Van Buren for the Barnburners, and Horatio Seymour of the Hunkers, were made as early as 1849, and were partially successful despite the hostility that remained high among many in both groups. A group of Hunkers, led by William Marcy and Seymour, labeled the "Softs," agreed with their erstwhile Barnburner enemies that continuing their split would only lead to further electoral defeats and disaster for all that they believed in. The Softs, therefore, determined to make peace with the Van Buren bloc, if not with great friendliness, certainly with a sense of political realism about the need for unity. Further meetings were held by the two factions' leaders, resulting in the patching up of their differences, at least to a point, followed by the official remelding of their separate organizations, and, then, their cooperation in state elections.

Democratic reunion was incomplete, however. The negotiations were accompanied by a sharp and angry split among the Hunkers. The still intransigent "Hards" among them rejected any coming together with the defectors to Free Soil. They held out, and even offered separate tickets of their own in elections into the early 1850s. The result was, at best, therefore, only partial in its effect, continued internal conflict, and some further electoral defeats in New York. But, at least, the Barnburners were, once more, firmly lodged in their natural political home.

Van Buren was not in the forefront of these moves toward party reconciliation, but he certainly favored them. Throughout the period of intraparty courtship and negotiation, he continued to offer counsel and strategic advice to his Barnburner sons and their allies, arguing persuasively that the culmination of this renewed purpose lay in shaping and supporting the regular Democratic ticket in 1852. Before the party's national convention in that year, he, and they, decided, however hesitant some of them continued to be, to fall in behind the candidacy of their state's favorite son, William Marcy, for the presidential nomination as the best of the candidates offered to the party in that year.

At the national convention, once more in Baltimore, the scene of their previous humiliations in 1844 and 1848, Marcy lost out. But the Van Burenites found it easy to accept the nomination of another dark horse, Franklin Pierce, New Hampshire's long-standing Jacksonian party leader, and, to the Barnburners, an acceptable representative of the party's commitments and traditions. Martin Van Buren's public letter of endorsement of Pierce, written to a meeting of the Tammany Hall Democracy, announced the firmness of the party reunion, although it was his only overt political activity in 1852. Most of the other Barnburners returned to the party with him and worked on behalf of the national ticket. It was like old times, capped by Pierce's success at the polls that November against another Whig general, Winfield Scott, and a much reduced Free Soil Party. The Democrats, largely reunited, had returned to national political dominance where they so fervently believed that they belonged.

As they rebuilt the unity of the Democratic Party, neither Van Buren nor the men around him saw, as others would later, that all that had happened in the political arena since the onset of the

Texas controversy in 1844, was the prelude, the first steps, into an era of the most bitter and destructive sectional conflict. Rather, in their minds, all that had occurred between 1844 and 1848 was a dismaying diversion from first principles and ultimate purposes. But now, to their relief, that unfortunate eruption had ended. In the early 1850s, they saw the disruptive sectionalists of the past few years in full retreat in both North and South. Free Soilism was fading as an important political force. Jacksonians and Whigs, somewhat scarred in the aftermath of the bitter confrontations of 1848–1850, but bringing their traditional battles with them, had returned to a central: place in American politics, a position where they had always rightfully belonged. As many of them continued to believe, whatever the anger, agitation, and turmoil of the past half decade, nothing basic in the nation's politics had really changed. Given what Van Buren had always argued about the dynamics of the American political arena, how could any of them think otherwise?

Chapter Ten

═══════════════○═══════════════

Political Afterlife,
1852–1862

THE ACTIVITIES THAT LED to Democratic Party reunion, climaxing in the election of 1852, all but closed out Martin Van Buren's long career at the center of American politics. Political matters would no longer form the essence of his life as they had for so long. He continued to read the partisan press regularly, and write to, and chat with, friends about public events. But after Pierce's victory he moved into a political afterlife, remaining quietly at his home, tending to his property and personal affairs, and learning how to live in permanent retirement.

GENTLEMAN FARMER IN REPOSE

His sons were also in political withdrawal. John, previously the most active of them in the public arena, turned his attention once more to his law practice in New York City. He occasionally made political speeches, but, like his father, having settled back into the Democratic Party, he contented himself, largely from the sidelines, in hoping for the best, that is, the Jeffersonian-Jacksonian movement's everlasting dominance of the nation's political affairs. Van Buren's other sons, always less involved in the cut and thrust of partisan electoral politics than John, joined the elder Van Buren in his new life. Abraham and Angelica continued to spend part of the year at her father's plantation in South Carolina, and the rest of the time in Kinderhook. Since 1849, Smith and his family, at his father's invitation, had become permanent residents of Lindenwald. Growing closer than ever to his youngest son, Van Buren decided to will the estate to Smith, believing that he was the most enthusiastic of his sons in his commitment to rural life.

At the urging of Smith, the elder Van Buren hesitently agreed to the extensive renovation of Lindenwald under the direction of a noted architect, Richard Upjohn. The results were both spectacular, and briefly unsettling, to the house's owner. The old Hudson valley–style mansion was rebuilt in the currently modish Italianate fashion favored by Upjohn, complete with a tower at one end. The house was greatly increased in size, ornateness, and its physical comforts. Van Buren, who had grumbled about the cost of its reconstruction, and the inconvenience it caused him as work proceeded, settled back into it, uneasily at first, ultimately with a great deal of pleasure.

As he had before, when retired to Lindenwald in the early 1840s, Van Buren spent his time horseback riding around his land, fishing in the creeks on the estate, surveying his crops, enjoying his grandchildren, dining well, and frequently entertaining neighbors and political friends in the evenings. (Henry Clay was among the first to be invited to the rebuilt mansion.) On those quiet days when no visitors were present, he passed the time reading and writing to old friends and colleagues. Although his interest in its condition remained high, he left the running of the farm to Smith.

THE DISINTEGRATION OF THE
AMERICAN POLITICAL ORDER

Whatever his personal sorrows, occasional physical infirmities, and determination to withdraw from public life, this time for good, Van Buren was never entirely politically inactive even in his advanced old age. From time to time he was approached by someone seeking his perspective about events in Washington or Albany. From his comfortable study in his rebuilt mansion he wrote many letters to his political allies from times past such as Thomas Hart Benton,

Francis P. Blair, Henry Gilpin, Benjamin Butler, and Azariah Flagg, sharing his opinions with them, and receiving theirs in return. He occasionally responded, as well, to others, less famous or important, with his usual combination of caution about actions to be taken, and more clarity about his point of view than many were willing to credit.

He remained critically aware of the intense tumult that had risen to dominate American political life after 1852. Despite the Democrats' successful reunion behind their traditional policy commitments, and the nature of government power—matters that had originated in the Jacksonian era, and which had then been subsequently finely honed by Van Buren—the restored peace and unity did not last. They were sharply challenged by the political revolution of the 1850s. That seismic event began as an anti-immigrant uproar against both of the old parties, and then was powerfully fueled by the reopening of the territorial conflict between the North and the South. The uproar became widespread, and potent enough to cause chaos in the major parties, and then recast the party system from its traditional national moorings into a much more sectionalized construction.

A loyal Democrat, then and always, Van Buren was not happy—but did not say so publicly—with Senator Stephen A. Douglas's Kansas-Nebraska bill in 1854, which was the main cause of the extraordinary popular furor—really an uprising—in the north, and the powerful assault on the Jacksonian party that followed. He "mourned over its adoption," considering it wrongheaded in both its purpose and the procedures involved to settling whether slavery would be legal in a federal territory formerly closed to it. He thought it to be imprudent in its potential and, in his mind, dangerous to the Union's serenity, as it proved to be. Reopening closed, and highly sensitive, wounds was never his way of doing business.

Given his unstinting party loyalty, so resurgent since 1848, Van Buren also deprecated the rise of the sectionalist Republican Party after 1854, and looked with great alarm and foreboding as the democracy ripped itself apart into sectional pieces in the late 1850s over the same issues that had roiled it so severely a decade earlier. Some of his Barnburner allies, Preston King for one, joined the

Republican Party in response to what they considered the same kind of Southern aggression that had derailed Van Buren in 1844, and humiliated him thereafter. Some observers hoped that the ex-president might do the same, given his Free Soil commitments in the late 1840s. There was even an approach to him by the New York Republican leader, Edwin D. Morgan (through his old ally, Francis P. Blair), asking whether Van Buren would be a delegate to, and perhaps even preside over, the upcoming Republican convention of 1856.

That suggestion was a serious misreading of where the ex-president stood politically, then and forever. If his political instincts had ever been to challenge and overthrow the prevailing truths of politics, they had now been thoroughly tamed and remained so. He had not changed his mind about party loyalty, and which of the major parties represented what he considered to be the best of American values and interests. His loyalty even led, eventually, to his accepting Douglas's Kansas-Nebraska Act as reasonable policy for the territories if its intent and terms were carried out in ways that were fair to all of those involved in settling the area. That was up to the newly elected president, the veteran Jacksonian, and Van Buren's longtime party colleague from Pennsylvania, James Buchanan.

But the aged, often indecisive, and much pressured president flubbed the opportunity. The act's purpose, to domesticate the slavery issue by allowing a local dimension to predominate in its settlement, was not carried out as Van Buren hoped. The consequences of that, and all else that was happening in politics after 1854, were increasingly gloomy as the retired president viewed the scene. He realized that no one had, as yet, found an effective political solution to the issue of slavery in the territories. And that failure was a great waste. To him, the core issues facing the American people remained as they always had been: the best means of keeping an always fractious Union together, and the reenergized need to forestall the new Federalist onslaught embodied in the rapidly growing Republican Party.

His deep and abiding faith in the Democratic Party led him to hope that it would find a way, even now, to restore itself into the kind of dominant national political force that it once had been and that the United States still needed it to be. His hopes and outlook had never faltered in their basic commitments, and those would not change even as conditions on the national landscape were so dramatically transformed. He had made his political choices long before. After that, there was, in his mind, little further to discuss.

LAST SPARKS

As the years of Van Buren's retirement passed, he continued to make the rounds of the spas and resort hotels of upstate New York, and to visit New York City from time to time, as he always had done. Early in his leisure years, out of necessity, he made his most ambitious foray away from home. Worried by his son Martin's continued frail health, he followed medical advice that he take him to see doctors in Europe. In the spring of 1853, therefore, he traveled once more to the Old World after more than twenty years, for an extended stay. Leaving his son under doctors' care, primarily in London, he moved on to Ireland, then to France and, once again, to Holland, where he delighted in speaking Dutch to the political and social leaders that he met there. Continuing on, he had a brief reunion with members of his family in Switzerland and then, after an extensive and vigorous round of sightseeing, formal and informal dinners, parties, and meetings with many of the great political personalities of the continent, he settled down comfortably in Italy, near Naples, for an extended stay.

There, not totally unexpectedly, he was suddenly summoned back to Paris to be with his ailing son who had come over from London. Things had degenerated rapidly for his son after a brief optimistic period as a result of his treatment. Increasingly unresponsive to the ministrations that he was receiving, his health was in rapid decline. Van Buren's third son died in March 1855 in the French capital, at the age of forty, of the wasting tuberculosis that had plagued him for so long. The elder Van Buren was once again faced with having to deal with personal sorrow of the most stunning kind.

Overcoming his grief was not any easier than it had been at previous such times when his wife and two daughters-in-law had died. While in Italy, before Martin's death, he had returned to a diversion that may have helped him now. For some time past he had turned his well-honed political instincts into reflective channels, picking up work on his autobiography that he had begun earlier, part of which turned into his *Inquiry Into the Origins and Course of Political Parties in the United States*. His previous stints on this project, aided by Martin as his research assistant and secretary, had been casual and intermittent and, in the later words of his sons, "exposed to frequent interruption, even by unimportant accidents." There must have been a great many of the latter.

But, now, first in Italy, and then, after returning home in the summer of 1855, he worked harder than he had before at completing what he had started. Smith did some of the necessary research and a great deal of the clerical work connected with the project. Old friends, Francis P. Blair, Benjamin Butler, and George Bancroft among them, contributed information and reminiscences and sent documents for him to use. Ultimately, Van Buren managed to compose an incomplete draft of the project. As his energies flagged, it remained unfinished and not in publishable shape. Later, his surviving sons edited the long section on political parties and brought it out as a separate volume, in 1867, after their father's death.

Much of the political parties section is a detailed description of the evolution of popular politics in the United States, beginning with the English background, and the early constitutional years, concentrating heavily on, and not getting beyond, except intermittently, the battle between the Hamilton Federalists and the Jeffersonian Republicans. Not unsurprisingly, Van Buren found the existence of parties to be a necessary condition for the proper workings and health of a democratic republic. His celebration of Jefferson and his Republican allies, and his contempt for those who opposed political parties, such as James Monroe, was palpable. And, of course, the Federalists remained, throughout, the villains of the American political story. Van Buren did not develop, however, the connections between them and the anti-Democratic forces that followed after 1815, the connection that had been the basic defining motif of his outlook throughout his political career. The brief references to events after the Federalist-Republican era in the volume were few and far between, and only intermittently illuminating.

The rest of the project, his incomplete autobiography, which had only reached the 1830s when Van Buren put it aside, was not published for more than fifty years after his death. It remained in the family and was still in manuscript form when Smith Van Buren's second wife donated it to the Library of Congress early in the twentieth century. In 1920, the American Historical Association issued it as part of its annual report. It is as straightforward as one can imagine, revealing very little about what lay behind the public face of its main subject. But it does cover the events of Van Buren's life into the Jacksonian era and has interesting things to say about many of the battles that he had engaged in to that point and, especially, about the people with whom he had spent so much of his time: Jefferson, DeWitt Clinton, Calhoun, Clay, Webster and the always overwhelming Jackson himself.

The two volumes are clearly without many surprises for anyone who had followed Van Buren's life throughout his active political career. The Federalist-Republican dichotomy, rooted in sharp, unyielding differences over economic policies, forms the backbone of the political parties inquiry, with some exploration of issues of liberty and coercion as well. The autobiography adds, as noted, useful descriptions of events and much material for others to draw from for their own studies of Van Buren's times, including many sprightly and useful quotations. But the author offers few lessons or provides much evaluation, or insight, beyond the surface events comprising his life.

TWILIGHT

In the late 1850s, Van Buren often had to face the death of those who had been close to him. Many of his old friends, Benton, Butler, William Marcy, as well as other members of the original Albany Regency, passed from the scene. The Jacksonian generation was fading into memory. Few remained of the significant figures engaged in the furious battles of the 1820s and 1830s that had shaped American politics for a quarter of a century thereafter, and, to Van Buren, still did, and always would. James Buchanan remained active, to be sure. But in Van Buren's view, his administration was a disaster, both for the country and for the Democratic Party.

Family matters remained, as always, near the surface of his life. His son, John, was once more becoming something of a problem due to his reportedly renewed dissolute living in New York City. There was little that the elder Van Buren could do for him except to chide and warn, and worry from a distance. John, after all, was approaching fifty years of age. Van Buren's other sons remained solid citizens. Both were devoted family men. Smith had remarried and then moved out of Lindenwald to set up with his new wife near her family, fortunately not too far away from his father's house. Visits from all of them, and their children, remained a centerpiece of the elder Van Buren's life as they always had.

Politics continued to intrude into his retirement even as he approached his eightieth year. He still readily shared his opinions of what was going on around them with his trusted friends, but could do, or wanted to do, little else. As the Union collapsed into its final sectional confrontation in 1860–1861, he was, however, called on to engage in one last public effort. From New Hampshire, ex-President Franklin Pierce, also in retirement, wrote to him in April 1861, right after the firing on Fort Sumter, suggesting that the New Yorker, as the senior of the five surviving ex-presidents, call on the other former chief executives: Tyler, Buchanan, Fillmore, and himself, to come together to try to mediate the desperate dispute that had now ripped the country apart. Van Buren replied that he was too old to be able to take the lead in this endeavor, or be effective in seeing it through. He would leave the initiative to others, attend such a meeting if it took place, but doubted that it could do anything to solve the nation's current problems. Events quickly outran Pierce's effort, and nothing came of this particular initiative.

As the crisis deepened, he remained a strong Unionist in his thinking, denouncing secession as unconstitutional, and supporting Abraham Lincoln's call for volunteer troops to put down the slave states' rebellion. His head and his heart were still in the same place that they had always been and, like many Democrats at the outset of the war, he placed the survival of the Union ahead of all other concerns. He believed that Andrew Jackson would have been with them. But dealing with national events now remained in other hands. Van Buren's few responses to queries about his view of secession were the end of his political presence on the American scene.

In the year after the firing on Fort Sumter and the outbreak of the Civil War, the aged ex-president tried to maintain his retirement style as he had enjoyed it for almost a decade despite the ever present tumult, both around him in Kinderhook, as its citizens mobilized for war, and in the nation at large. He continued to dabble at his manuscript. But he was no longer able to persevere at it for very long at a stretch, or do much of anything else. He was falling into rapid physical decline. He became ill several times with the recurrence of the asthma that had often plagued him in the past, and other, increasingly serious, complaints.

He made one last trip to New York City, in early 1862, to consult a doctor there. But little could be done for him. Back home at Lindenwald, he grew increasingly feeble and spent more and more of his time in his second floor bedroom with its many mementos of Andrew Jackson and portrait of Silas Wright hanging on the wall. In the summer the end came. On July 24, 1862, with his three surviving sons at his bedside, Van Buren died, a few months short of his eightieth birthday.

Chapter Eleven

—————————————○—————————————

"The Honors
of Their Statesman"

VAN BUREN WAS BURIED at Lindenwald after funeral services held at
the old Dutch Reformed Church in Kinderhook. A large crowd attended his last appearence in his home village. It included his immediate family and such old political friends as Samuel J. Tilden
and Benjamin Butler's son, William, a lawyer in New York City. The
younger Butler later wrote a charming description of the scene.
"The church was more thronged, I presume," he remembered,

> than it had ever been before. . . . At the close,
> the vast concourse of people passed silently
> by the bier and took their last look at
> the face of the dead. . . . All seemed moved with a
> common and sincere grief. This was the best
> tribute that could be paid. They felt that
> they had shared in the honors of their statesman.
> His fame had made all the neighborhood famous.
> He had been the link by which the quiet inland
> center had been bound so long to the great world
> beyond, and now it was broken. Our sorrow is
> never so sincere as when it is part of ourselves
> that we have lost.

Martin Van Buren brought more to the people of his home village,
and to many other Americans, than the enlargement of their iden-
tities. As suggested at the outset, he deserves to be remembered as

217

one of America's most talented political leaders. James Madison had raised, and addressed, the problem of adversarial factions in *Federalist* 10, seeking, as he wrote, some effective means of coping with them. In the next generation, Van Buren did as well, in the greatly expanded sphere that now comprised the political world. He sought to tame the unsettled chaos of American politics, rooting his efforts in organizing certain groups—his beloved plain republicans—into a disciplined force to oppose those that he considered to be dangerous assailants against American liberty.

To be sure, his public life was mired, throughout, in bitter controversy. Among his contemporaries he never lived down his reputation as a person of overresilient policy views and altogether too dextrous political skills. Certainly, most of his enemies (Henry Clay excepted) neither liked nor respected, him, and made their feelings clear as often as they could. "His principles," John Quincy Adams wrote, summing up the contemporary case against him, "are all subordinate to his ambitions."

At the same time, while often a strong vote getter among the Democratic faithful, he was no exciting popular hero among the large number of Americans more generally. He never could draw upon a sense of acclaim that other of his contemporaries did, acclaim that might have overshadowed the negatives that the partisan press so assiduously articulated against him. Van Buren certainly lacked charisma, the elements of self that provoke intense popular admiration for, and deep felt loyalty to, a leader. A sympathetic friend wrote that "he never inspired enthusiasm, as Jackson did, or Henry Clay. The masses accepted him as a leader, but they never worshipped him as a hero." Therefore, the writer continued, "the day of his birth will not be commemorated in distant cities or in remote periods of time. His name will never be a watchword." And neither has been. "In the end," Michael Schudson has written, he "was forgotten. Father of the American political party he may be, but it is Washington, Jefferson, and Jackson, who have survived as models for emulation. The ambivalence with which Americans honor their great invention, the political party, is perhaps in no better way indicated than by the obscurity into which Van Buren fell."

But, if the American party system served useful purposes from the 1830s onward, as it did, then its founder deserves more consideration than he has usually received. He helped frame politics into different channels that made political understanding cohere, held off the Federalist threat that he so feared, and brought into this new architecture a powerful current of popular involvement in the formerly exclusive, and arcane, political arena of pre-party America. In doing so, while he was not the progenitor of American popular politics, he made significant contributions to its expression and performance.

His opportunism, as he did these things, supposedly trumped any ideology or policy purpose present in his makeup. Yet when his political life is explored, that, too, seems to be an overly harsh assessment. Van Buren was not as cynical as many descriptions of party politics suggest about partisan leaders. Of course, one unfriendly person's notion of an intriguer is another's concept of a careful, moderate, and prudent manager, always sensitive to the consequences of pushing too forcefully in one direction or another. And, to be sure, some of Van Buren's ideas evolved from what they had originally been as circumstances changed and unexpected difficulties had to be confronted. But whatever that evolution might have been, the basic impulse underlying what he was trying to accomplish in policy terms always remained steady in his mind and in what followed when he entered the Senate and served as president.

It is also true that Van Buren's vision and political orbit had serious limitations to them, both in their own time and in ours. Whatever its larger achievements, there were omissions, missteps, ambiguities, hesitations, and, yes, evasions, as his democracy dealt with public policy, all of which was necessary, he would have argued, in order to fulfill his larger ideological purposes. At the same time, he was neither a progressive thinker about economic policies nor a social reformer. His attitudes about the darker side of American life, its substantial racial and gender inequities were, at best, undeveloped, always approached through the lens of political caution, and the existing, powerful prejudices of the majority of those he sought to lead.

Van Buren drew his sense of policy and commitment from the past, from the glories of the Revolution of 1800 that had overthrown the Federalists and brought the Jeffersonians to power. He never wavered, thereafter, from his view that that event was the critical moment in American history under the Constitution. Perhaps, in so doing, he clung too long to an obsolete ideology as well as inadequate social values. His rigidity on the former, and his instinct to turn away from the most divisive issues outside of the old Jeffersonian-Federalist core, are not to be celebrated, even if that was, in his view, necessary in order to maintain the public peace, and ensure the triumph of the democracy and its ideals. In short, however flawed it was, his point of view did have some substance to it.

HE REMAINS, IN FINAL SUMMATION, something more than a useful citizen, a polarizing contestant in a permanent political battle over the direction of the United States, or a failed president, out of his depth in a major national crisis. While he was all of that, he should earn some recognition as well for grappling with a problem that American politics still finds difficult to deal with in an effective manner—controlling the violence of faction and turning it in a positive direction. For that effort he deserves to be acknowledged by those who remain involved in the politics of a complex and fractious nation, one that with the decline of the party system in the late twentieth century lost much of its ability to deal with its normal political chores, let alone its national crises. A panel of scholars once agreed that Van Buren should be remembered as the last of the Founding Fathers for his contribution of a highly organized and ideologically directed partisan vision to the American constitutional order. That suggestion seemed reasonable when it was offered, and remains so. It serves as an excellent epitath for this most interesting political figure.

Suggested Reading

THE BASIC STARTING POINTS to learn about Van Buren are the two fine, richly detailed, critical biographies of him by Donald B. Cole, *Martin Van Buren and the American Political System* (Princeton, 1984); and John Niven, *Martin Van Buren: The Romantic Age of American Politics* (New York, 1983). A number of monographs on specific topics add a great deal to the biographical record. These include Robert V. Remini, *Martin Van Buren and the Making of the Democratic Party* (New York, 1959); Jerome Mushkat and Robert Rayback, *Martin Van Buren: Law, Politics, and the Shaping of Republican Ideology* (DeKalb, Ill., 1997); James Curtis, *The Fox at Bay: Martin Van Buren and the Presidency, 1837–1841* (Lexington, Ky., 1970); and Major L. Wilson, *The Presidency of Martin Van Buren* (Lawrence, Kans., 1984).

In addition, several useful biographies of Van Buren's colleagues and enemies fill out the story of his life, and are critically important in understanding the man. Among the best of them are Robert Remini's very laudatory three-volume life of *Andrew Jackson* (New York, 1977–1984); and the same author's less celebratory, *Henry Clay: Statesman for the Union* (New York, 1991); and *Daniel Webster: The Man and His Time* (New York, 1997). Irving Bartlett, *John C. Calhoun: A Biography* (New York, 1993) is the most recent study of the South Carolinian. It should be supplemented by the older, more extensive, and overwhelmingly sympathetic, Charles Wiltse, *John C. Calhoun* (Indianapolis, 3 vols.,

1944–1951). John Garraty, *Silas Wright* (New York, 1949) and Lynn Parsons, *John Quincy Adams* (Madison, Wis., 1998) are examples of useful scholarship about other figures who were important in Van Buren's life.

The social and political atmosphere in New York, and in the Hudson valley as Van Buren was growing up, has been extensively investigated. I found particularly helpful David Maldwyn Ellis, *Landlords and Farmers in the Hudson-Mohawk Region, 1790–1850* (Ithaca, N.Y., 1946); and Alan Taylor, *William Cooper's Town: Power and Persuasion on the Frontier of the Early Republic* (New York, 1995). Lee Benson, *The Concept of Jacksonian Democracy: New York as a Test Case* (Princeton, N.J., 1961) is a marvelous and revisionist study of the New York political scene from 1815 to the mid-1840s, although I think that his treatment of Van Buren is harsher than it might be. On DeWitt Clinton, see Craig Hanyan with Mary L. Hanyan, *DeWitt Clinton and the Rise of the People's Men* (Montreal, 1996).

For very useful background about the political dynamics of the era, a number of books are unsurpassed: Richard Hofstadter, *The Idea of a Party System: The Rise of Legitimate Opposition in the United States, 1780–1840* (Berkeley, Calif., 1969); Richard P. McCormick, *The Second American Party System: Party Formation in the Jacksonian Era* (Chapel Hill, 1966); Ronald P. Formisano, *The Transformation of Political Culture: Massachuetts Parties, 1790s–1840s* (New York, 1983); and Harry Watson, *Liberty and Power: The Politics of Jacksonian America* (New York, 1990). In addition, Leonard Richards, *The Slave Power: The Free North and Southern Domination, 1780–1860* (Baton Rouge, 2000) makes a strong argument illuminating the relationships between the Democrats' Northern and Southern wings before, during, and after Van Buren's time.

Van Buren's political enemies are well covered in Michael Holt's magisterial *The Rise and Fall of the American Whig Party: Jacksonian Politics and the Coming of the Civil War* (New York, 1999). See also, Daniel Walker Howe, *The Political Culture of the American Whigs* (Chicago, 1979). The best introduction to the Southern political mind in its many vagaries is William Freehling's superb *The Road to Disunion, 1776–1854* (New York, 1990). I also learned much from William Shade, *Democratizing the Old Dominion: Virginia and the Second Party System, 1824–1861* (Charlottesville, Va., 1996).

Richard B. Latner, *The Presidency of Andrew Jackson: White House Politics, 1829–1837* (Athens, Ga., 1979) and Donald B. Cole, *The Presidency of Andrew Jackson* (Lawrence, Kans., 1993) provide much information and insight about politics in the nation's capital in the late 1820s and early 1830s. Jacksonian economic policy, and the Panic of 1837 is nicely investigated in Peter Temin, *The Jacksonian Economy* (New York, 1969). Jacksonian (and Van Buren) foreign policy is the subject of John M. Belolavek, *Let the Eagle Soar!: The Foreign Policy of Andrew Jackson* (Lincoln, Nebr., 1985). On the Polk and Free Soil period, one should begin with Charles Sellers, *James K. Polk, Jacksonian, 1795–1843* (Princeton, 1957); followed by his, *James K. Polk, Continentalist, 1843–1846* (Princeton, 1966); Richard Sewell, *Ballots for Freedom: Antislavery Politics in the United States, 1837–1860* (New York, 1976); and Joseph G. Rayback, *Free Soil: The Election of 1848* (Lexington, Ky., 1971). On the presidential elections from 1824 to 1852, see the appropriate essays in Arthur M. Schlesinger Jr., *The History of American Presidential Elections* (New York, 4 vols., 1971).

See also Martin Van Buren's two posthumously published books, *Inquiry into the Origin and Course of Political Parties in the United States* (New York, 1867) and *The Autobiography of Martin Van Buren*, edited by John C. Fitzpatrick (Washington, 1920). Although frustratingly incomplete, they provide the basic foundation for understanding the man and following his career. I have quoted much from them. In addition, his correspondence, primarily in the Library of Congress, and available on microfilm, is indispensable. Much of the correspondence of his important contemporaries—Jackson, Clay, Calhoun, Webster, and Polk—all of which contain a great deal about Van Buren, have been edited and published in multivolume letterpress editions by university presses.

Finally, the biographies, memoirs, and reminiscences of his contemporaries add a great deal to the record. See, in particular, William A. Butler, *Martin Van Buren: Lawyer, Statesman & Man* (New York,

1862); the same author's, *A Retrospect of Forty Years, 1825–1865* (New York, 1911); George Bancroft, *Martin Van Buren to the End of His Public Career* (New York, 1889); and Thomas Hart Benton, *Thirty Years' View* (New York, 2 vols., 1854–1856). William Lyon MacKenzie, *The Life and Times of Martin Van Buren* (Boston, 1846) is a most unflattering portrait written by a disgruntled leader of the Canadian rebellion turned Whig propagandist.

Michael Schudson, *The Good Citizen: A History of American Civic Life* (New York, 1998) says useful things about American attitudes toward politics and politicians. The most recent evaluation of American presidents by professional historians is reported in Arthur M. Schlesinger Jr., "Rating the Presidents: Washington to Clinton," *Political Science Quarterly* 112 (summer 1997), 179–190.

Index

About the Author

JOEL H. SILBEY is President White Professor of History at Cornell University where he has taught since 1966. He has written and edited a dozen books about the history of American politics in the nineteeth century, including *The Partisan Imperative: The Dynamics of American Politics Before the Civil War* (1985); *The American Political Nation, 1838–1893* (1991); and, most recently, *The American Party Battle, 1828–1876* (1999). Professor Silbey has held fellowships from the National Endowment for the Humanities, the Social Science Research Council, the Center for Advanced Study in the Behavioral Sciences, the Russell Sage Foundation, and the John Simon Guggenheim Memorial Foundation.

237